Torcello

D1201508

JOSÉ MANSER

Hugh Casson

a Biography

VIKING

VIKING

Published by the Penguin Group
Penguin Books Ltd, 27 Wrights Lane, London W8 5TZ, England
Penguin Putnam Inc., 375 Hudson Street, New York, New York 10014, USA
Penguin Books Australia Ltd, Ringwood, Victoria, Australia
Penguin Books Canada Ltd, 10 Alcorn Avenue, Toronto, Ontario, Canada M4V 3B2
Penguin Books India (P) Ltd, 11, Community Centre,
Panchsheel Park, New Delhi – 110 017, India
Penguin Books (NZ) Ltd, Private Bag 102902, NSMC, Auckland, New Zealand
Penguin Books (South Africa) (Pty) Ltd, 5 Watkins Street,
Denver Ext 4, Johannesburg 2094, South Africa

Penguin Books Ltd, Registered Offices: Harmondsworth, Middlesex, England

First published 2000
1 3 5 7 9 10 8 6 4 2

Copyright © José Manser, 2000

The moral right of the author has been asserted

The endpapers are taken from Hugh Casson's Venice sketchbooks

Set in 11/15.5 pt Monotype Trump Medieval
Typeset by Rowland Phototypesetting Ltd,
Bury St Edmunds, Suffolk
Printed in Great Britain by Clays Ltd, St Ives plc

A CIP catalogue record for this book is available from the British Library

ISBN 0-670-87115-X

CONTENTS

LIST OF ILLUSTRATIONS

Colour Illustrations

1. Early Casson drawings.
2. Wartime drawing of crashed aeroplanes, 1940.
3. Design for a stand at the Ideal Home exhibition, 1948.
4. Chalk drawing of the Dome, Festival of Britain, 1952.
5. Street decorations for the Queen's Coronation, 1953.
6. Decorative emblem for the Coronation, Whitehall, 1953.
7. Prince Philip's study and library at Buckingham Palace.
8. Scheme for the Royal College of Art, London.
9. P&O liner *Canberra*'s first-class Meridian lounge.
10. Guest suite at Windsor Castle.
11. 'Birthday ball' – fantasy drawing for Rosie d'Avigdor Goldsmid.
12. Sketch of Venice.
13. St John's, Smith Square, London.
14. The Royal Academy of Arts, London.

Black-and-White Illustrations

1. Reta's parents in South Africa.
2. Hugh's mother May Man in Burma.
3. Hugh with his sister Rosemary in Burma.
4. Hugh's birthday greeting for an aunt and *right*, as a boy scout.
5. Rowing team at Cambridge.

Illustration Acknowledgements

All the illustrations come from the Casson family with the following exceptions:

Colour: 3, 5, 6 and 9: British Architectural Library, RIBA, London; 4 and 11: Chloë Teacher; 14: Royal Academy of Arts, London.

Black and white: 2, 3: David Leather; 8 right: Tim Nicholson; 12, 13, 14, 15 and 17: Leslie Gooday; 17 right: Philip Powell; 18, 25 and 26: British Architectural Library, RIBA, London; 24: P&O/Orient; 27: Casson, Conder and Partners; 28: photograph by Paul Caffell.

Line drawings in the text: pp. 113, 127, 133, 144, 148: Leslie Gooday; pp. 154, 206: British Architectural Library, RIBA, London; pp. 164, 224: Casson, Conder & Partners; p. 187: Lord Montagu; p. 190: Joyce Conwy Evans; pp. 206, 333: Pamela Robinson; pp. 272, 299, 367: Chloë Teacher; p. 280: American lady!; p. 352: Joanna Benton; p. 144: Abram Games.

ACKNOWLEDGEMENTS

When listing the people who were kind enough to help by telling me of their own encounters with Hugh Casson – some of them sparing an inordinate amount of time to do so – I am very conscious of those I did *not* ever get round to speaking to. Hugh knew so many people. And though I waded steadily through lists of his friends and colleagues and acquaintances, time just ran out. I would like to thank those I did meet, for they were unfailingly eager to talk about a man they had liked. I hope they will feel the book has done him justice.

There are two people I should pick out for special mention. This book could not really have been written without them.

Cathy Courtney, a devoted friend of Hugh's, runs the National Life Story Collection at the British Library National Sound Archives. Both Hugh and Reta were interviewed for the Collection (Hugh by Cathy herself), and the transcripts provided me with a wealth of interesting material.

Carola Zogolovich, Hugh's eldest daughter, looks after his archives. She also looked after me during the long months of this book's gestation, striving to answer every tedious question, foraging through records, suggesting sources. She was very much her parents' daughter, remaining witty, helpful and encouraging when some might have become impatient. I cannot thank her too much.

My thanks go to other members of the family: Hugh and

Reta Casson themselves, Roger Zogolovich, Nicola and Ian Hessenberg, Dinah Casson, John Casson, Andrew Man, David Leather and Freda Levson. And to The Duke of Edinburgh, Rosie d'Avigdor Goldsmid, Ines Burrows, Patience Bayne Powell, Jim Cadbury Brown, Julian Bicknell, Joanna Brendon, C. M. P. Bush, Michael Cain, Sherban Cantacuzino, Peter Carolin, Meg Carpenter, Neville Conder, Terence Conran, Joyce Conwy Evans, Flavia de Grey, Martin Drury, Eileen Duveen, Susan Einzig, Mary Fedden, Selina Fellows, Norman Foster, Leslie Gooday, Stella Gowers, Ronald Green, Richard Guyatt, David Heycock, Simon Hornby, Sydney Hutchison, Jean Jackson-Stops, Anne James, Griseld Kerr, David Lyall, Leonard Manasseh, George R. Millar, Edward Montagu, John and Su Miller, Commodore A. J. C. Morrow, Tim Nicholson, Kitty Ockenden, Jo Pattrick, Philip Powell, Alan Powers, Tim Rendle, Pamela Robinson, Piers Rodgers, Norman Rosenthal, Thomas Russell, John Sainsbury, Peter Shepheard, Stuart Taylor, Chloë Teacher, Dan Topolski, Mariel Toynbee, Dosia Verney, Carel Weight and Paul Wright.

My husband, an architectural student at the time of the Festival of Britain, had always admired Casson's achievements, and he was informative and characteristically encouraging, as was my editor, Eleo Gordon.

A Child of the
Indian Civil Service

Judging by early photographs, Hugh Casson was an exceptionally appealing child. Small and slight, with wide-set blue eyes
and golden hair, he was a beautiful little boy, and it is sad, even
shocking, to reflect that his own mother never saw him during
the years when he must have been at his most attractive,
between the ages of four and nine. At that time, his father was
in the Indian Civil Service, working in Rangoon, capital of
what was then the Indian province of Burma. But Hugh and his
sister Rosemary, who was one year older, had been sent back
to England. This was the common lot of children whose parents
were colonial civil servants, but with the outbreak of war the
Cassons were dispatched in August 1914, at an earlier age than
they might have been. The British government of the day
instructed that all children, regardless of whether they had
reached the preparatory-school age of seven or not, must return
home, with mothers leaving or staying as they pleased. Hugh's
mother chose to stay with her husband, and the children travelled with a nurse. Their destination was Sandgate in Kent, the
home of their maternal grandparents, Edward Garnet Man and
his wife Catherine.

Were they refugees washed up by the tyranny of war, or
simply middle-class children of professional parents leading a
life which was shared by their peers and perfectly acceptable
to all involved? With attitudes to family life and the upbringing

of children now so vastly different, it is difficult to decide, and the temptation to view Hugh Casson's parents as an extraordinarily unimaginative couple who remained together but sent their children away to a country which had just entered a major world war must be tempered by the proviso that at the time everyone was certain the war would be over within six months.

However it is viewed, Hugh Casson, product of this seemingly puzzling act which resulted in his seeing neither of his parents for over four years, became the most sunny-natured and uninhibited man imaginable. People have described the difficulty in penetrating his surface warmth, and queried if there was anything within to discover. But who can be sure that this reserve, which seems to conflict quite sharply with an otherwise outgoing demeanour, was not the result of his childhood, the one adverse effect of being temporarily orphaned during his formative years? Depth – of the sort referred to rather menacingly in the phrase 'he's a deep one' – is not always an enviable characteristic. Some of those to whom it is attributed might also be described as warped by less sympathetic observers. Hugh Casson could never have been described in that way. He managed a public and successful life, well supported by a happy marriage and three daughters, without any such indication of murky depths. What we saw was what we got, and it was engaging. Both Hugh and Rosemary, it must be said, resisted any attempt in later years to have their parents' actions questioned. Both insisted that, as children of a colonial civil servant, they took it for granted that they should have been sent back to England.

Hugh Maxwell Casson was born at a small private nursing home in north London on 23 May 1910, a delicate baby about whose survival there was considerable anxiety. At some point in the early weeks, he was given into the care of his mother's sister Josslyn, always known as Jo, because she was convinced she could rescue him from the brink of premature death, which she did.

His mother had made the three-week boat journey back from Rangoon for the birth, bringing Rosemary, who had been born the year before, but leaving her husband behind. For May Man, as she had been before her marriage, such long-distance travel and periods of separation were perfectly normal. Her own parents had lived in both India and Burma, where her barrister father, Edward Garnet Man, had been posted as a member of the Indian Civil Service; and many members of her extensive wider family also spent a large part of their lives overseas in the service of the old Empire.

In the traditional manner, May Man had met Randal Casson on one of the P&O liners which at the time plied between Southampton or Liverpool and Rangoon and were witness to innumerable shipboard romances. Young men set to spend their working lives in the East, many of them well educated (as Randal was) and with a good future ahead of them in the Civil Service, were a reasonable catch. The catching process was not likely to be a difficult one. The prospect of a bachelor existence far from home meant they were susceptible to the attractions of pretty girls on board.

May was pretty. Randal, a lively and amusing man, liked women, and the romance developed satisfactorily during the time she was with her family in Rangoon. Only one letter home from Randal to his mother during his early years in Burma seems to have survived, but it is a long one. Written on 21 January 1904, he bemoans (not very seriously) the rumours which were apparently rife about his amatory activities and his pursuit by various young ladies amongst the English community. One gave him particular trouble, and he described her as 'the kind of girl that deprives one of the power of speech altogether. Fortunately she has turned her attention to somebody else and is running after him for all she is worth.' But

Randal was not immune, and May had been the one to whom he was drawn on board ship.

Goodness knows what rumours are rushing round about May Man and me as we ride out nearly every morning. I enjoy these rides very much but Mrs Heald informs me that May Man is in a most perturbed state as she imagines that I am doing it out of duty as her brother-in-law's personal assistant. I hasten to remind you of my statement in my last letter dated January 14 1904 that May Man is the one with the already attached affections. I had always regarded myself as a rather retiring untalked-about sort of person, and it was rather astounding to hear news of oneself that had been spread out here, sent home, sorted out, sent out again and almost confirmed. I am much inclined to chuck up ladies altogether.

Despite this very Edwardian disclaimer, he clearly had no intention of doing so, and whoever had first engaged May's affections failed to hold them. By the time she went back to England later that year, she and Randal had become engaged. But with the sensitivity his son Hugh was to inherit, the ticket Randal sent which would bring her from England to Burma for their wedding was a return one. He wrote, Hugh recounted later, that if when she arrived in Burma she looked down from the promenade deck of the liner and thought, 'It will be absolutely terrible,' she was to stay on board and return to England, and no offence would be taken. Perhaps he simply felt confident that this would not happen. Anyway, it didn't. They were married in Rangoon less than two years later on 13 November 1906, an event duly noted in a local newspaper, its description of the wedding gifts as 'numerous and costly' abhorred by the unassuming Randal. They eventually bore two children, Rosemary and Hugh, and led a quietly happy married life, but one which was marked by none of the recognition and sophisticated social success their son Hugh was to enjoy.

It might have been different for them. May came from a family which was successful in its middle-class way. This, and the fact that his career in India was reasonably distinguished, allowed her father Edward to set up in some style at Sandgate when he retired, despite having brought up nine children. He was first Assistant Commissioner and a JP in Bengal, where he served with the 3rd Sikh Irregular Cavalry during the Indian Mutiny, before becoming Government Advocate in Burma (and acting as special correspondent to *The Times* during the Perak War). Her husband Randal, on the other hand, intellectual ability notwithstanding, somehow missed the route which would have led him to make his mark on the world. Genial, and with what a nephew later described as 'a wicked wit', he seemed content to forego the pressures which surround a public and socially ambitious life. After retiring from Burma at the early age of forty-four, he and May went to live at Southampton, where he became a part-time lecturer in Mathematics at the University, a job which can have made few demands on him.

The Cassons, originally from the Lake District, had lived in Wales since about 1800. Randal Casson, born in 1879, was a clever child. Like his wife, he came from a large family; he was the fourth son and fifth child of Thomas and Laura Casson, who went on to produce two more daughters. Laura, a religious woman and daughter of a Liverpool sea captain, had also been born in Wales. She was the more literary of Randal's parents, encouraging all the children to read widely throughout their childhood, and Randal was not the only one of demonstrable ability. His brother Will, who was killed in the First World War at the Battle of Loos, had a keen intelligence; Lewis became a celebrated actor and director, and of course married Sybil Thorndike, whilst his sister Elizabeth (Elsie) was the first woman to graduate in medicine at the University of Bristol. But Randal seems to have been the most cerebral. Their father,

Thomas, worked in the small family Casson Bank as a young man, staying on to manage the Denbigh branch when it was taken over by the North and South Wales Bank, and it was here his children spent the earlier part of their childhood. However, Thomas's long-time passion for organ building, which he had been practising in an amateur way with some success in Wales, eventually took the family to London when he abandoned the bank to join an organ-building firm there. Randal stayed in Wales to finish his schooling and was clever enough to win a scholarship to St John's College, Cambridge, where he read Mathematics. Such was his ability that he became a wrangler.

A fine career must have seemed in prospect, and he yearned to be an astronomer. But by the time he graduated, his father had set up a new business to manufacture the Positive Organ of his own design. And despite the Positive Organ's recognized merits – it was installed in churches throughout Britain and in many missionary churches across the Empire – Thomas was no businessman, and money was always very short. It was imperative that Randal should establish himself in a profession. As his son Hugh commented many years later, there was no great demand for astronomers either, so Randal, with his first-class degree, took and passed the examination for entry to the Indian Civil Service. This was an élite body of men, open to a limited number of entrants, and respected for the efficiency and rectitude of its administration. Boys leaving public school were the main candidates and many of them attended crammers specifically directed to getting them through what was recognized to be a tough examination. Randal had no need of such extra tuition, and was soon dispatched to Burma, where he set about learning the language and, eventually, embarking on marriage and fatherhood.

Having survived the early sickly months of his infancy, Hugh – or Chappie as he was always called as a small boy –

went with his mother and sister to join his father in Burma. He retained only a few, scrappy memories of the three years he spent there, and even those were likely to have been the result of stories he heard related by his parents years later. Some eventually found a place in his own repertoire, because from earliest childhood Hugh Casson recognized the appeal of a good tale, particularly if it was expertly embroidered, changed in minor detail to suit the mood or credulity of his audience, and then delivered with dramatic flourish. Genuine memories of the big house and garden in Golden Valley in Rangoon included standing at the top of the staircase and throwing his toy wheelbarrow to the bottom with a satisfying clatter. But, sequestered with Rosemary and their nurse in the house and large garden where they lived, he probably only got fleeting glimpses of Rangoon. He retained no images of the beauty with which he was surrounded during the few infant years he spent in this most exotic of cities. He was, in any case, too young to have memories of the great golden Shwedagon Pagoda, encrusted with jewels and dating from 585 BC, which towered over Rangoon, of the graceful, good-looking people in their traditional longyi, the yellow-robed Buddhist monks, the tropical flowers and the many gilded pagodas and pavilions which were such dominant architectural features.

Life in Rangoon, with its wide, tree-lined streets built on a grid-plan by the Victorians after the country became completely absorbed into the British Empire in 1886, was agreeable. Or it was for those compliant servants of the Crown who were not concerned about being in something of a backwater, away from the mainstream of events, in this least prestigious of the Indian provinces. There were sufficient servants, and there were ponies for Hugh's mother and father to ride, all typical of the lifestyle enjoyed by Colonial Civil Servants in Edwardian times. A photograph taken outside the house, when Hugh and Rosemary were about three and four years old, shows the

family complete with its full complement of servants, including an English nurse.

Entertaining at Government House was both lavish and
formal, and was marked by intermittent visits from such minor
members of the Royal Family as the Duke of Connaught, none
of which the young Casson could have possibly remembered.
Even then his life was fairly detached from that of his parents
on a daily basis. His father, at first an Assistant Commissioner
and finally a Divisional Judge, travelled the country adminis-
tering British justice and spending nights under canvas *en
route*. His mother, who liked the cosseted existence of a Colonial wife, was also extremely fond of this other aspect of
Randal's work and usually travelled with him, attended by
enough servants to ensure her complete comfort. Back in Rangoon they were busy with visits to the Club, which constituted
such a major factor in the life of British Colonial Civil Servants,
along with parties, polo matches, amateur dramatics and formal receptions, so that Hugh and Rosemary spent most of their
time in the care and company of nurses. Like many wives of
her generation who had little purpose to their lives apart from
being adjuncts to their husbands, May Casson, small, pretty
and reputedly flirtatious, was prone to fall in love with young
men other than her husband, and was herself the recipient of
long ardent glances from subalterns amongst their group, who
were probably finding more appropriate targets for their affections thin on the ground. None of this nugatory activity affected the solidity of Randal and May Casson's marriage. It was
more a case of them both being amusing, well liked and entirely
acceptable in a small social milieu far from home.

Randal's older sister Frances came out to visit them not
long before the First World War. Now in her late thirties and
unmarried, Fanny, as she was known, was a schoolteacher in
Derby, and she may have hoped, as did so many other young
women, that she would acquire a husband in this land where

bachelors abounded. She kept a diary, some of which has survived, of this adventurous journey, and it includes an account of a shipboard romance which sadly ended when her swain, whom she christened Prospero, left the ship at Port Said. Her good spirits and unflagging enthusiasm were revived when she reached Rangoon and Randal and May arrived to meet her. Fanny was an enthusiast, and she quickly succumbed to the pleasures of Rangoon, finding the Golden Valley where the Cassons lived 'charmingly pretty and close to real jungle. They say a tiger was killed in a compound near here only the other day. The house is on the side of a hill, near a little lake and is very pretty with its verandahs and balconies.' Arriving with Randal and May in a tum tum, she met the children, Hugh aged three, Rosemary four, 'who are looking bright and happy and well, and are very friendly and sweet'. After that, they figure little in her account of her stay, though she did peep into the nursery where 'there was a huge mosquito curtain over the bed and the cots'. Walks in the jungle with Randal, tennis parties, a fancy-dress dance, sketching, punting on the lakes, a visit to a horse show and to the Wingabar Monastery, reached through lovely rose gardens 'where there is a colossal Buddha of brick', all filled her days. One afternoon she and May took the children, wearing topis as protection against the intense sunlight, to Dalhousie Park, but this was unusual, and there is no mention that Hugh and Rosemary went with them to the open-air swimming tank. 'It is a lovely spot in the jungle, and is a big one, very jolly . . . It is all protected from snakes by big sheets of iron at the side.' A garden party at the home of a very rich Burmese was held to meet members of the Commission on the ICS. 'I was not struck with any except Ramsay Macdonald, who has a beautiful face: he looks very, very sad . . . The Burmese, Parsi and Hindu visitors were most beautifully dressed and looked far more graceful than the English: the dresses were of exquisite colours in silk, but the most graceful were the Parsi women's: black or white embroidered in silver and falling in lovely folds. The garden seemed full of human flowers.'

Fanny enthuses frequently about the Burmese children whom she encountered in the streets, but saw little more of her niece and nephew, because by the time she returned from a trip to Mandalay which Randal had organized for her, it was mid March and 'the dear little children and May' were just about to depart for the cooler climes of Maymyo, the hill station to the north of Rangoon, some forty miles from Mandalay, where they would avoid the excesses of the hot season. Here in the summer capital of British Burma, 4,000 feet above sea level, and on a gentle plateau unlike the precipitous terrain of most of the hill stations, they could enjoy fresh, comparatively cool air, and spend their days in a milieu reminiscent of Surrey or Sussex, with Victorian mock-Tudor houses, gardens full of flowers and pine trees, a clock tower with a chiming clock, and quiet, tree-shaded roads. 'We went down to the station with the children and Nanny. The trains to Mandalay are splendidly arranged and as comfortable as they can possibly be made. Rosemary and Hugh both were quite worried about the luggage. Just fancy that baby, Chappie, almost as soon as he was in the carriage saying "Mummie, is the luggage coming?" with a distraught and burdened air. We do miss them so.'

She didn't see them again, although they too returned to England in the following year, and she died in 1915 at the age of forty-two.

Several of May's letters to her sister Jo have survived from these Burmese years, and though none is properly dated, the contents reveal all of them to have been written after the war, during the last years of her stay in Burma. Rosemary and Hugh never returned to the East, though, after the end of the war, their parents made the occasional visit home.

Some of these letters to Jo were written in late 1922 and early 1923, when the Prince of Wales visited India in an effort to revive flagging Anglo-Indian relations, and when the Cassons encountered him in both Rangoon and Delhi. Randal had been sent to Delhi for several months early in 1923 in what appears to have been a move to a less demanding post than he had held in Burma, prior to his retirement. 'How the papers do lie about the Prince's visit,' wrote May. 'It's done no earthly good. He says so himself.' There were riots in the streets by groups of disaffected Burmese, but there were also innumerable social occasions, some of which the Cassons attended, and which May found overwhelmingly exciting. There is a graphic description in one letter of the ball at Viceregal Lodge in Delhi to wind up the Prince's stay, which apparently ended in a riot of laughter.

The Prince is of course the Prince Charming of every fairy tale with his sunshiney hair and blue eyes, with that half-shy manner which is so captivating and always makes me cry. He looked really happy and jolly last night ... He danced with Lady Reading and all the stodgy members of council and their wives. Lord and Lady Rawlinson, Lord Montagu of Beaulieu and his second wife and Lady Falmouth were all in there, and the rest of us climbed on chairs or went into the gallery to see it. I had a strong position standing on a sofa and saw everything. The Prince hadn't an idea how to dance them and Lady R is stone deaf which made it difficult for him to ask her. He suddenly began to laugh hopelessly, he caught the Viceroy's eye and it set the Viceroy off too and then Lady R began. I've never seen such a jolly scene. He wandered off absolutely at sea, Lady R hauled him back, he got mixed up with the ladies in one figure and in another stood quite by himself looking wildly round for Lady R whom he'd lost – he clung to her like a life buoy. He was

laughing so much he couldn't stop and so was the Viceroy –
the whole room shouted with laughter too. One lady near
me laughed so heartily she stepped over the edge of the sofa
and crashed heavily to the ground, which made me laugh
more heartily than ever. At the end the whole room shouted
'Hooray'. Wasn't it dreadful!! Fancy, at Viceregal Lodge too.

There is much more in a similar vein. May was then, and
remained to the end of her life, an ardent royalist, who derived
immense excitement and satisfaction from her own glancing
encounter with the man who was to become Duke of Windsor,
and eventually from the working relationship and friendship
which her son enjoyed with members of the Royal Family from
a later generation.

When Randal retired later in 1923 at the age of forty-four,
his career, which had been marked by no striving ambition,
was over. During the war he had enlisted as an officer of the
Volunteer Mobile Battery in Rangoon, where his lectures on
ballistics and other technical subjects would, according to a
fellow officer, 'have done credit to a proficient artillery man'.
He used to say in later years that he had become deaf because
of this service. It is not clear why, but maybe it was owing to
his involvement with ballistics. Back home and installed in a
modest post as part-time lecturer in Mathematics at Southampton University, he would explain that he had left Burma a
little earlier than he needed to because 'Justice is often blind
but I don't think it should also be deaf'. It is uncertain, though,
whether this was the precise cause of his retirement. The
deaths in 1919 and 1920 of first May's mother and then her
father, who had both been unstinting in caring for Rosemary
and Hugh, may also have had something to do with bringing
them home. Or maybe the punishing climate had finally
become insupportable. There is nothing to indicate that Randal
was suffering from the distaste for his job or the disillusion-

ment with his imperial role that prompted George Orwell to resign from the Indian Imperial Police in Burma only a few years later. Although, since the war, pockets of unrest and hostility had begun to foment amongst the hitherto quiescent Burmese, Randal had always loved the place and its people. The return to England deprived him and May of many things: of status, primarily, which May almost certainly mourned more than the equable Randal; of money, for their pension was reduced by his early retirement; and of the full social life and companionship which they had enjoyed in Rangoon.

Meanwhile, Hugh and Rosemary had spent the war years in England, staying for much of the time at Sandgate. Their wartime experiences had been largely undramatic. They sometimes heard the guns across the Channel, and there were occasional air raids on Folkestone, during which they were made to take shelter under the grand piano. They were once disconcerted to see spots of blood on the pathway leading up to the church porch at Hythe, where many tombstones had been blown awry and a verger killed in the previous night's raid. Two coastguards blew themselves to pieces trying to secure a stranded mine quite close to the Man house. But this was over a period of several years and, apart from such rare incidents, life was tranquil.

Edward Garnet Man and his wife Catherine lived at Halstead, a spacious house of great comfort though no architectural distinction. There was ample room to accommodate the children, together with their newly acquired governess, Miss Frampton. Their cousin Andrew, whose father was at that time the Vicar of Lydden, which is between Canterbury and Dover, said in later years that he remembered them as being spoilt. 'We lived at Lydden between 1912 and 1918, so we used to visit Halstead quite often. I know we resented these two in our grandfather's house which they seemingly regarded as their own. Rosemary used to greet us on arrival as though she was the daughter of the house. We didn't like that or the way our elderly relatives, particularly the aunts, fussed over them.' They seemed specially to dote on Hugh, who then and for the remainder of his long life was regarded as frail. Rosemary, only a year older, perhaps enjoined by her parents, also felt protective towards him.

Halstead was full of memorabilia brought back from India, including two figures in traditional Burmese costume which stood at the top of the staircase. Their wooden hands, which were removable, sometimes fell off, and the small Cassons found them unnervingly realistic, especially on dark evenings when they were on their way to bed.

With its white-wood balconies, hung tiles and elaborate chimneys, Halstead was a typical Edwardian seaside house – of a fairly substantial order. Hugh found it quite imposing enough to boast about later on when he was at boarding school, and he was impressed by the painting of his grandmother in her court dress which hung in the drawing room. Surrounded by lawns, it faced directly on to the sea and it was possible to scramble over a low stone wall where there were tamarisks bent double by the wind, down steps and on to the beach for a swim. There was a large, heated conservatory with hot-house plants and an encaustic tiled floor where, according to his cousin Andrew, Hugh was often sent to play, protected from the dangers of the cold sea air. Mr Prior the gardener spent a great deal of his time pushing a lawnmower over the hard, salty turf, on which a tent was set up in summer to shelter the family whilst they took afternoon tea.

The Casson children were happy here, but, despite the absence of parents and the affection with which they were regarded by their grandparents, this was an Edwardian household in which they certainly were not allowed to run wild. Rosemary remembered that even as a child she realized that civilized behaviour was imperative. Good manners became a way of life. There were prayers every morning, led by their grandmother and attended by all the staff from the cook to the scullery maid. Cousins came to the house too, either to stay for a while because their parents were also abroad or, as Andrew did, on family occasions. Edward Garnet Man was of an expansive disposition, with leanings towards eccentricity which became increasingly evident during his retirement. He would invite any likely person – man or woman – whom he met when he was out walking, or on one of his morning rides along the Lees at nearby Folkestone, back for lunch. Some accepted. These spontaneous bursts of hospitality were not very popular with his wife – nor were her husband's jokes, which verged on the risqué – but their recipients were greeted with ostensible courtesy in the household. Like any gentleman of his generation, Hugh's grandfather wore a flat-topped bowler or a truncated topper when he went out; unlike most others, though, one of these hats was already on his head, atop a thick thatch of white hair, ready for the next engagement as he dozed in one of the tall dining-room chairs after lunch.

Edward was just the sort of character to appeal to children, and the crowds of cousins who came and went – Hugh Casson claimed there were thirty-two in all – had the happiest memories of him. Huge family Christmas parties took place where all the children were roped in to put on a play by their Aunt Dollie, the Mans' youngest daughter, who still lived at home. Dollie was as eccentric as her father, but since her mother suffered from painful and debilitating arthritis, which worsened as she got older, she cheerfully shouldered many household responsibilities.

Andrew Man may have thought the Casson children regarded Halstead as their own home, but they did not live there all the time. There were periods in lodgings where they were supervised by Miss Frampton or subsequent governesses. (Twin cousins, nicknamed Pink and Blue, were the focus of much envy because for a long time they lodged with the milk-man in Sandgate High Street and were allowed to handle his great zinc cans with their brass hinges.) Such random visits increased after their grandparents' deaths, although by this time both children had been sent to boarding school, Hugh aged seven, Rosemary eight. There were even periods at holiday schools, of which there were many along this part of the south coast. But generally, more agreeably, and certainly remembered by Hugh with more precision and enthusiasm in his old age, they were able to spend the school holidays with aunts and uncles – all on the Man side of the family – in various comfortable and well-staffed homes.

Hugh's mother's sister, Josslyn – Aunt Jo, who was credited with rescuing Hugh from death as a tiny frail baby – went on to become his favourite aunt, and some of the best holidays were spent at Ellesmere, the house where she lived with her husband, Cecil Lewis (recently retired from the Indian Civil Service), at Farncombe near Godalming. Jo, a tiny, good-looking woman with a great sense of humour, firm religious beliefs, and a swath of necklaces and chains around her neck, took in all the cousins at various times. Whilst Cecil wrote books about Burma in his study, she played hymns on the upright piano which they would join her in singing, rubbed Vick's into their chests at bedtime, and generally provided the stability, firmness and affection which was so lacking in many of their lives. Ellesmere, a rambling late-Victorian house with a large garden, billiard room, tennis court and complement of servants, accommodated them with no apparent strain. Meals, to which they were summoned by a gong, were wholesome though unimaginative, and one of Jo's granddaughters remem-bers the pervasive smell of cabbage and carbolic soap which prevailed even during her own childhood in the thirties. But Hugh and Rosemary loved the schoolroom, with its large table hidden under a green chenille cover, and toast made on a steel

A page of caricatures, including one of Hugh's uncle.

toasting fork over the fire, and they instinctively felt at home in this house with its liberal complement of artefacts brought home from Burma by Jo and Cecil.

The unmistakable streak of eccentricity which ran through the Man family was manifested here by the eldest daughter of the household, cousin Elaine, whose craving for fresh air was such that she removed her bedroom window to allow the wind and rain access at all times. Next came Stella, and then there was cousin Angela, a lively and tomboyish girl of roughly Hugh's own age, to whom he was particularly close. All appeared to enjoy the invasion of their home territory by this group of itinerant cousins.

Miss Rope, the governess who generally accompanied the

Casson children when they stayed at Ellesmere, took them for endless walks along the winding lanes around Charterhouse. One of May's letters to Jo, written from Burma just before they departed for Delhi in January 1923, starts, 'What a lovely Xmas you gave the children – thanks *awfully* for having them – I would have loved to see the play. They certainly have had much jollier holidays without us than they do with us!' She goes on to talk of the move to Delhi and the fall in pay it would incur, and then, 'Is Rosemary rough in manner?', blaming her school for not being particular enough. There are effusive descriptions of the Prince of Wales, 'who so reminds us of Chappie. I don't know why, his smile or his sunshiney hair, I think. You always said Chappie was just like the King when he was born!' Chappie, now thirteen, was certainly of a similar physical type to his future sovereign, and it is easy to comprehend the satisfaction this afforded his royalist mother.

It was when staying in Godalming with Aunt Jo that Hugh, as a small boy, helped by an older cousin, spent hours illustrating his own story of a one-legged submarine commander. It was here too, as he liked to recount later, that he joined in what the *Evening News* of the time described as 'The Great Sunday Hunt for Mrs Christie'. This followed the disappearance of crime writer Agatha Christie after her husband demanded a divorce because of his love for another woman. Christie had driven from her home in Sunningdale late one December night, and her car was then found abandoned off the road at the well-known beauty spot, Newlands Corner. Because she was so well known, and because of intensive press coverage, Christie's disappearance captured the public imagination to the extent that hundreds of civilians joined the police in searching the local downs for the missing woman. Hugh was a Boy Scout at the time and, because all Boy Scouts had been asked to join the search, beat the undergrowth with enthusiasm, slashing the gorse bushes and watching whilst police dragged local pools and rivers for possible drowned bodies. In vain. Christie, in an appropriately mysterious manner, turned up in Bolton seven days later apparently suffering from amnesia. This whole bizarre episode took place in 1926, when Hugh was sixteen. By this time his parents were back and living in Southampton, so he was probably only staying with Aunt Jo for a short visit.

Back in those early days, the children sometimes went to London and stayed with their Great Aunt Tory (Victoria), who was their Man grandmother's sister, and who lived in a tall terraced house in Montagu Street, Marylebone. Here they spent most of their time in the kitchen with three elderly maids, sending a china pig up and down in the service lift and making occasional trips to nearby Madame Tussaud's. Hugh especially liked going to Selfridges, where he spent as many hours as were allowed, roaming through the various departments and riding the handsome bronze lifts. There were visits to aunts at Chatham or Aldershot or Putney; and an annual summer fortnight with a widower uncle – one of their grandmother's brothers – who lived at Sunbury-on-Thames and, as chairman of Grindlay's Bank, was amongst the most prosperous members of the family.

These holidays in Sunbury, Hugh was to write later, 'were prized beyond measure because life here was sybaritic. We went shopping in a plum-coloured Vauxhall driven by Guerney the chauffeur who wore a long dust-coat, and we had lemon squash with our lunch. In the afternoon we played tennis or went for a picnic in the punt. For hours Rosemary and I would paddle and punt up the backwaters, exploring creeks, and banging on the green canvas covers of boats which were moored along the banks to enquire in the friendliest possible fashion of couples locked in embrace within whether they were married. They never seemed to mind. On Fridays we used to drive to Bentalls at Kingston on Thames and a shop assistant would come out with a notebook in hand to take the order. We were always at Sunbury for Regatta Week and one year the prizes were presented by Jeffrey Farnol – who was at the time my favourite author. At the fair afterwards we watched entranced as he whirled past overhead on a Chair-o-plane in his brown knickerbockers.'

If, viewed all these years later, Hugh's childhood seems lacking in the close parental ties which are usual now, it gives every appearance of having been a happy one. He always insisted there were no traumatic memories, such as the one endured by writer Raleigh Trevelyan who, in similar circumstances, once flinched on hearing a relation tell her sister, 'It's your turn to have Raleigh for Christmas.'

Preparatory-school days, when they arrived, were comparatively painless. Wootton Court, just west of the road which ran between Canterbury and Dover, took no more than thirty or thirty-five pupils. It was a happy, homely place, despite its share of young male teachers who had returned neurotic and sometimes shell-shocked from the war. At the age of seven, games were already anathema to Hugh and so they remained all his life. His cousin Andrew, who had already been at Wootton Court for several years when Hugh arrived, remembered that he often disappeared into the rhododendron bushes to avoid games of cricket or football. 'In those days such behaviour was strange indeed. We were all expected to play games and to try to excel. I do not think, though, that Hugh was to suffer in any way for this abnormality.' That was because already his ability to mimic others, tell a good story and make people laugh was well developed. The years spent in various houses with a constantly changing group of relations were now to prove his salvation, and he never endured the abuse and contempt which were the lot of so many games-haters in boys' preparatory schools, especially those who were academically bright, as he was. Instead, the charm which he had consciously exercised when he was very small, in the well-founded belief that it would make him a welcome and loved visitor, now came into full play. He extended his repertoire of skills to include a facility for irritating masters, and found his popularity was ensured.

Rosemary, a tall slim girl who did not share Hugh's hatred of games (she was later to become a teacher of physical training), was shy and socially more awkward than her brother. She and Hugh always got on perfectly well together, but she never quite managed his easy relationship with the various aunts and cousins, and suffered as a consequence. He looked back on this childhood period with some remorse in his later years. 'She had more trouble with the constantly changing venues. I don't think I was as nice as I should have been. I didn't betray her, say "don't let's have her with us" or anything like that, but I don't suppose I was as helpful as I could have been, because if you have made yourself the sort of person who is good with others, you forget how uncomfortable it is if you aren't very good.' In her old age, Rosemary told one of Hugh's daughters that she had always found it tough being relegated to the fringes of every group whilst her brother was the focus of attention. This was said without rancour, because she adored Hugh and was proud of his subsequent high-profile career. But, consciously or not, he dented her confidence to the end, making it clear, even when they were very old, that he was irritated by her attempts to talk about their childhood, and abruptly dragging their conversation back to the present – and future. Life was too busy for him to dwell on the past.

Wootton Court, small and felicitously bereft of bullies, became for Hugh a place where he could play the piano, sing (he had a fine voice and to the subsequent ribaldry of his family earned the Entertainment Badge in the Boy Scouts), draw – though not with any particular intent at this stage – and read voraciously: the usual schoolboy diet of P. F. Westerman, Ian

Hay, and books about the Navy. Not so usual was his weakness for Angela Brazil, who wrote school stories for girls. Some boys made wireless sets and Hugh vividly remembered the silver wound coil, the cat's whisker and crystal, and the varnished bases with inexpertly champfered edges, though he never made one himself, being then, as he was to remain, 'bad with his hands'. There were weekly letters to the parents in Rangoon, and an annual photograph 'to show them how you'd grown, which in my case was not very much'. He was bad at Mathematics, which must have been a disappointment to Randal, who tried to coach him on one holiday from Burma, and found him quick in understanding and able to work out problems well, but careless because he wasn't interested. Otherwise, he did well, being above average at Classics, and eventually he became Head Boy. In that capacity, provided he polished the brass headlamps of the headmaster's car (an early Minerva limousine), he was allowed to go shopping in Canterbury every Friday with the headmaster's wife. More exciting were trips in a curious boat-shaped sports car (alleged to contain the engine of a Bentley) which belonged to the Latin master, who, despite his postwar neurosis, was an excellent teacher. It all sounds comfortingly homely, and in the holidays, the aunts (and Man grandparents during their lifetime) continued in their surrogate roles, providing the parental support which was lacking.

Hugh never knew his Welsh grandparents, who died before he was born, and there was little connection with the Casson branch of his family during those early years, except with Lewis Casson. Lewis and his wife Sybil Thorndike, who were already well advanced in their distinguished theatrical careers (as well as having four children), had a cottage at Dymchurch, which was quite close to Wootton. They were passionately fond of their own children, who were casually drawn into their parents' circle of thespian friends, and they occasionally made the time to drive down and take either Hugh or Rosemary out to lunch. Even at such a young age, Hugh appreciated the cachet which went with these visits. They certainly encouraged his incipient passion for the theatre.

Eastbourne College, the public school to which Hugh was sent in 1924, was quite naturally a different proposition. The war had been over for some years. The eight-year-old Hugh had marked the Armistice on a bus going from Folkestone back to Wootton Court, alone except for the driver, with whom he had stood on the road in embarrassed silence as the peace sirens sounded. Relations had been renewed with his parents on one or two home leaves, and without any apparent difficulty or disruption to the children's quiet lives. Now their parents were back, living permanently in Southampton. Again, Randal's aspirations – this time for his son – were modest. Hugh was not entered for one of the great schools. Winchester had been considered. In fact, in one of her letters home to Aunt Jo, May, more ambitious than her husband, wrote:

> Chappie is being rather lazy this term I think. Mr Yates says he won't get a Winchester scholarship but ought to get a £50 one at some other school – but I'm going to make C try for Winchester. I believe he'll get one and so does Miss Nesbit, the mistress who teaches him English. His French is good and Classics above average. It's Maths he is bad in.

Despite Randal's coaching in this subject, Hugh did not sit the Winchester scholarship, and was sent to Eastbourne College. Eastbourne was chosen partly because it was near the sea, in deference to his supposedly frail health. His father, newly retired, took him there for his first term, and it was a place Hugh was to remember without pleasure. However, it was fairly gentle by the standards of the times, not renowned for flogging and bullying, and in no way the stuff of which horrendous schooldays are made, although E. C. Arnold, the

Headmaster (always known as Og), like others of his ilk indulged in a fondness for beatings with a slipper. These were administered to boys' bare bottoms as they lay flat across a table, but were not renowned for being of an excessively vicious variety.

In School House, boys were allowed individual cubicles in the dormitories, so there was a measure of privacy. It was at Eastbourne that Hugh Casson – the only boy in the art department, he afterwards claimed – started to acquire the techniques of drawing which were to become something of an obsession. It was about now that he experimented with caricature, focusing mainly on his teachers, his friends, and the relations with whom he'd spent pleasant holidays. He didn't go on to develop this style of drawing, despite the fact that his efforts were reasonably successful, but he filed away the drawings he had made of a favourite aunt and uncle. Though never an intellectual, he was a clever, thoughtful boy who did well in most subjects, particularly Classics. The major problem, as at his prep school, was the emphasis on games, and the glory that went with athletic prowess. If Eastbourne won a match against another school, everyone gathered to bellow out a special, triumphant song to mark the victory. Casson found such demonstrations distasteful and practised non-cooperation – for one of the few times in his life. The housemaster of School House, Stephen Foot, was imaginative in his methods. He dealt with Casson and one or two others of an anti-games persuasion by allowing them to miss organized games and giving them a boat to row on the River Cuckmere, some five miles from the school. This turned out to be the beginning of rowing as a regular sport at Eastbourne, but predictably Hugh Casson's interest flagged once it got to that stage.

The art department comprised one room. Og was an ornithologist of some repute and this room was shared with his collection of stuffed birds, which the incumbent was supposed to draw. The part-time art master, Mr Aldom, who wore a black hat and a long blue mackintosh with the belt tied behind, liked to talk about the single picture of his own which had been accepted for the Royal Academy Summer Exhibition, but he left Hugh to work in his own way. His only contributions to the budding water-colourist's advancement were to point out the use of blue as a recessive colour, and to teach him how to draw feathers. With his dormitory cubicle decked in pictures he had cut out from magazines, including some sugary Russell Flint prints depicting voluptuous Spanish dancers, Hugh was always described to visitors as 'our artistic boy', followed by the chortled rider, 'but you have to keep an eye on the sort of pictures he puts up!'.

A history master called D. E. Paton – whose grandfather was the Victorian artist Noel Paton – took a fancy to the young Casson. Remembered by Hugh as a plain man with pebble glasses and a moustache, he would encourage visits to his own house to listen to his stories. His interest may or may not have been a healthy one, but Casson himself never registered it as anything other than normal, and the friendship could have generated his early and abiding interest in Victorian art.

Hugh found it difficult to explain exactly why he left Eastbourne in 1927, after only three years at the school, though boys did drop in and out of public school more easily then than they do now. A photograph still hanging in School House at Eastbourne shows him to have been very small and pretty, with a centre parting. He was – and this would have been suspect in that place at that time – arty, and his parents took him to see a psychologist, because they feared he might become a homosexual. Hugh himself had no memories in later life of these visits. Nor was his sexuality in any way equivocal. He was not happy at Eastbourne, it was not academically renowned, and in retrospect his leaving seems to have been a sensible curtailment of one of the few unsuccessful periods in his life.

It is ironic that the first full-time art master was appointed at Eastbourne College two years after Hugh left. It is also indicative of his insouciant character that, despite insisting he loathed the place, Casson on several occasions had quite happy engagements with Eastbourne College, which obviously in due course became keen to claim such a notable old boy as one of its own. In 1956, he designed a lych-gate entrance to the playing fields in memory of old boys who had died during the Second World War: a pleasant, four-square structure which in its way was typical of his gently Modernist approach to architecture. Many years later, when he was President of the Royal Academy, he opened a splendid, custom-built art department at the school, and accepted the gift of an old Eastbournian tie – the first he'd had – which he instantly substituted for the bright red and purple one in which he'd arrived. Quite apart from the art department, there is now a small through route in the school which is used as a gallery for changing exhibitions; it is called the Casson Gallery.

Just after the First World War, probably when Hugh was already a pupil, E. C. Arnold had set up a group of old Eastbournians whose aim was to improve and embellish the school buildings. Hugh Casson almost certainly knew or cared nothing of this group until years later, but gifts and legacies from the Arnold Embellishers, as they came to be known, were responsible amongst much else for such artefacts as silver candlesticks on the Chapel altar, stone pillars with lamps, a rose garden, the Chapel centenary improvements and, in 1983, for commissioning a water-colour by Sir Hugh Casson depicting the wedding of Prince Charles and Lady Diana Spencer in St Paul's Cathedral. It cost them only £230, which must have come as a pleasant surprise, and it hangs in the Headmaster's study. The *rapprochement* was complete.

II

A Student Architect

Boys who quit public school early – whatever the reason – present a problem to a conventional family. In Hugh's case there must have been a large measure of disappointment, particularly as he was bent on entry to his father's old Cambridge College, St John's. Randal decided to fill the first part of the gap in his son's educational trajectory by enrolling him as a rather immature student in the Classics department at Southampton University, a curious route for a boy of seventeen but one presumably facilitated by Randal's own position on that University's staff.

By now Hugh was experiencing the common teenage disillusionment with his parents, and most particularly with their station in life. The car in which his father collected him from his final summer term at Eastbourne was a small Rover with a dicky seat, inoffensive enough but cruelly unprepossessing for a youth who was already conscious of his image. He became moody, prone to falling silent and treating his parents with contempt, or retiring to his room at the unremarkable house they had built at East Bassett near Southampton, Viewed over fifty years later, this looks a rather pleasant building. Double-fronted and with a confident lack of unnecessary embellishment, it had a certain architectural presence which plenty of larger houses in the area completely lacked. The older Cassons had been attracted by its site on the edge of heathland, and never cultivated the garden which, with its indigenous pine trees, heathers and bracken, was redolent of the outdoor life they had grown used to in Burma and which they still enjoyed. But it was not nearly so grandly bourgeois as the houses where Hugh had stayed with his grandparents and his various aunts. Its name, Little Heath, bothered him too. 'It sounded coy and unassuming and a little common. By now I was encased in snobberies of every kind. I told my school friends the house was near Romsey because that sounded more gentlemanly than Southampton. I never mentioned the car.' He may, though he never acknowledged this, have been irritated by Randal's booming voice with its faint Welsh lilt. His own was low, quiet and beautifully modulated. And in some ways, these two nice but ordinary people with whom he now lived were like strangers. Most of his earlier life had been spent with relations or at a succession of schools, not with them, so it is quite understandable that they had difficulty finding a common meeting ground.

Hugh would make occasional solitary trips to London, travelling on one of the buses that ran from Southampton to the capital for a fare of five shillings return. Years later, he described these visits as resulting from a need to be alone rather than a desire for metropolitan adventure, and far from visiting famous sights, he would do little more than tramp the streets savouring the pleasure of being anonymous amongst the crowds of a great city. Then, nothing accomplished, but with a sense of having explored the romantic potential of solitude, he'd return to the security and support of home, where he had painted his own room a deep *café au lait* colour, with a lacquered orange skirting, and hung papier mâché masks around the walls, 'like some macabre tea-room'.

What he has never admitted, but what must have contributed to his *malaise* during the adolescent years, was his now very marked lack of height. He never grew beyond five feet

four inches, but whether consciously or not (perhaps it was
something he determined on those lone trips to London), he
rejected the arrogance behind which some small men shelter,
and continued to develop the famous charm which successfully
distracted people's attention from his physical limitations.

Hugh would have entered St John's quite easily to read
Classics, because he was good at Latin and Greek, which had
been well taught at Eastbourne, but for once his parents had
aspirations: he was to try for a scholarship. Meanwhile, he
studied Classics, not very zealously, at Southampton, hung
around the docks drawing ships and sheds and cranes, and
learnt to sail in his father's sixteen-foot, half-decked boat
which figured much – in an enlarged form – in conversation
with friends. Rosemary was by now at teacher-training college
in Chelsea (her son David later put this career choice down to
a desire to escape the literary and artistic aura which surrounded her family), but came home at weekends. Untroubled
by Hugh's yearning for something grander, she was a keen
participant in these sailing trips. She adored both her parents,
most particularly her father, and unlike Hugh was always
perfectly happy with life at Little Heath. There were tennis
parties, picnics, subscriptions to Boots' Library (Hugh often
read two books a day), and, for him, solitary walks in the woods.
He led the life of a typical teenage youth, without aim or
ambition, and with a faint and largely unjustified grudge
against those around him.

The end to this idyll when it came was not particularly
surprising, nor did it cause Hugh to despair, since no door was
thereby closed for him. But it was to change the course of his
life. In 1928, he took his Classics scholarship, and failed. The
story of how he then enrolled in the Cambridge School of
Architecture at Scroope Terrace changed in detail over the
years. But it always had the same ending. During his oral
examination at St John's, Casson was told he would not be

recommended for a scholarship, but that his written answer to a question on the Acropolis had been outstandingly good. Why didn't he abandon Classics, 'in which you are plainly not remotely interested' and which would only lead to a job in the Civil Service, and develop his obviously latent interest in architecture? Why not see if they'd take him at the School of Architecture? This does not exactly accord with written records. On Casson's form of application for admission to the Joint Entrance Scholarship Examination at St John's, he stated quite clearly that he wished to be examined in Classics, but that the subject he intended to study was Architecture. Not perhaps an important variation between fact and legend, this is a clear example of Casson's propensity for changing a story in the interests of dramatic impact to the point where the new version becomes fact in his own memory.

The Cambridge School of Architecture, which had only been established in 1912, was at that time of a markedly academic bent with much emphasis on the history of both art and architecture, as indeed it has remained. Whether his mentor – if he existed – envisaged the young Casson becoming a practising architect, an architectural historian or even something less specific, is not known. Whatever the chronology of events, the idea of studying architecture must certainly have entered his consciousness by the end of 1928 when he filled in the form for the scholarship examination, and it appealed to him. He applied, and was accepted. And from the moment Hugh started his studies in the autumn of 1929, his moroseness and lethargy dropped away. His abiding keen interest in everything he did was ensured from that point forward.

In the months before he went up to St John's College, Hugh spent more time drawing, an activity which, along with sailing, helped him to form a loose bond with his father. Randal was a competent Sunday painter (although his son barely accorded him even that fairly lukewarm acknowledgement), and exhibited his oils at the local art-society exhibitions. More demandingly, Hugh worked in the office of T. D. Atkinson, the Winchester diocesan architect, a tall, mild but remote figure, and this constituted a gentle introduction to his chosen profession; he learnt how to measure up, to use a T-square, a scale and a set-square, and to do simple architectural drawings. These were abilities not shared by many of the other students newly arrived at Cambridge, and they gave him a headstart. Meanwhile, he travelled to Winchester each day on an elderly motorbike lent to him by a neighbour, a beast which controlled him, rather than he it. 'I've never been mechanically minded and I was frightened by this weapon which was difficult to control, inclined to overbalance when I wheeled it about, dragging me with it.'

When he arrived at Cambridge in the autumn, life at the university opened up for Hugh Casson, as it has for so many others, a rich new seam of activity; one with many layers of interest and experience. He embraced it all. The ferocious energy which was to drive him through so many different fields of play now became evident. His father, who had been a good oarsman himself and had rowed for St John's, suggested Hugh joined the College Boat Club. At eight-and-a-half stone, Hugh was destined to become a cox

The main Gateway.

and spent his mornings at the Architectural School, his afternoons on the river. This was Hugh Casson, for the first time in his life, involved in sport, and he was vocal in describing its

" Take Her Home now "

*Casson's sketches of life at Cambridge were drawn some
years after his own time there.*

limitations. The oarsmen were not always those he would have
chosen as soul companions. 'I mean, they would sit on their
window-sills with their legs hanging out, rather than lying on
a couch, twisting hair round their fingers . . . But I had one or
two aesthetic friends from school, one in King's who used
to spice oranges by sticking cloves into them. He'd mount
them on a great tripod he'd made and hold them out of the
window to make the courtyard smell nice.' Despite his alleged
reservations, Hugh entered into the oarsmen's world with
gusto, attending dinners, being photographed in rowing
gear, and even, to his pleasure, being tried out as cox to the
University boat. He also made lifelong friends amongst the
rowers.

One such was George Millar, who had entered the School
of Architecture with Hugh, 'both of us shy young men in

the then standard dress
of tweed jacket, grey-
flannel trousers, collar
and tie'. Prosperous
himself, he remembered
Hugh as being very poor,
at least by the standards
of students at the time,
and living in digs near

the College whilst he himself had rooms in the heavily Gothic precincts of New Court. Assigned contiguous places in the large shabby room at Scroope Terrace where they were to work, they became friends and shared a supervisor, Harold Tomlinson. Tomlinson, who had just scraped into the First World War as a pilot, still suffered from wounds he had received, which, said Millar, 'gave him extra authority'. Hugh obviously indulged in a little exhibitionist ploy on his first day in the school. George Millar describes the thirty-strong class being given sketchbooks and then arrayed before 'a rather revoltingly stylized plaster effigy of a seated lion. See-ing that Hugh was looking at my efforts and that his page was blank, I remarked on the hideousness of the wretched lion. Hugh smiled and agreed but added, "I don't  know how to begin." He didn't appear to be joking so I advised him to imagine he was Picasso and boldly draw and outline as you imagine he might do. Bung in a couples of eyes, nostrils and a fang here and there. Pick out a detail, say of a foot, concentrating on the claws, then sign it HMC with apologies to Picasso. His drawing was the only one to receive a favourable mention.'

From then on Hugh's draughting abilities were in no doubt. He rarely worked in silence at his drawing board, his transparent happiness in what he was doing made manifest by a constant outpouring of both popular songs and hymns. George Millar said, 'It was a powerful voice and the acoustics were excellent in that big bare room. Several of us would join in from time to time depending on how our work was going, but Hugh's was always the strongest voice and, I think, the gladdest.'

At the end of a successful first year, Millar was given a black Chrysler roadster, which was, he remembered, 'silent,

powerful and fast. I was concerned about Hugh working, always
working, in his mouldy digs, so I drove him about a lot. In the

early summer of 1930 we
drove to Chelsea and
stayed with Sybil and
Lewis Casson in Carlyle
Square.' Hugh relished
beautiful cars (he had
some of his own in later
years) and the exotic out-
ings which went with them. George Millar provided other
excursions, including one with a group of Cambridge rowing
friends to a bothy in the heart of the Cairngorm mountains.
Red deer walked past their door in the early mornings, Cairngorm was climbed, and grouse were shot for dinner. Already,
Hugh was getting a heady view of a wider world than his own,
and the modest, self-contained existence to which Randal and
May had been reduced since leaving Burma was receding in
importance.

By his second year, Hugh's activities had expanded further.
He became Secretary of the University Architectural Society
(his year master and future business partner, Christopher
Nicholson, was the Vice-President), and he was responsible
for the organization of speakers at Society events. He did a
creditable job: one programme included Eric Gill, whose outstanding draughtsmanship Hugh must have revered (though
he described him later, long before Fiona McCarthy's revealing
biography was published, as a vain and somehow disturbing
man), on Architecture and Industrialism, E. Maxwell Fry on
Town Building, Geoffrey Jellicoe on Gardens, and Clough Williams Ellis on Soviet Architecture. Another had Grey Wornum
(designer of the Royal Institute of British Architects' headquarters building in Portland Place) on Flats as Housing at
Home and Abroad, Robert Byron on the Aesthetic Tradition of

Architecture, and Robert Lutyens (son of Sir Edwin) on the Fulfilment in Art of Western Style. The acquisition of such eminent speakers took con-
siderable effort and a streak of audacity. Evelyn Waugh was one who refused. But Casson enjoyed this task. 'You met most distinguished characters because people like talking to Oxbridge undergraduates. It's more interesting than going to give an important lecture in

Sheffield.' He exploited the contacts made on these occasions to further his own interests at later dates.

It was probably the Casson/Thorndike connection which drew him to the theatre. He had certainly relished Sybil and Lewis's fame, went to see them perform during the holidays, and kept photographs of them in celebrated dramatic pro-
ductions, including Sybil Thorndike's memorable St Joan, which Lewis directed and which had had its first night in 1924. Every week while he was at Cambridge Hugh went to the Festival Theatre, which was run for a time by Terence Gray and his mistress Doria Paston, who had a penchant for cubist stage designs, most of them silver and grey. Eventually Hugh wrote to ask them if he could help paint the scenery, as he wanted to learn about designing for the stage. Attracted perhaps by his lustrous name, they agreed. Every Saturday night thereafter, with the scenery struck at ten-thirty at the close of the week's performances, he'd start painting for the following week, generally working all night. The scene painter under whose instruction he worked, an army chaplain's daughter named Stella Pelly, lent an additional frisson to the proceedings, which could otherwise be tiring, dull and rather spooky in the darkened theatre. 'There weren't many girls in Cambridge

then, just people's sisters who came for the day on a Sunday.'
Stella, an attractive blonde who was a little older than Hugh,

-Back to Trumham

was a delightful
companion in this
deficient milieu
and they became
friends, with Hugh
exercising her Dal-
matian dog Lordy
when she was too
busy. 'It was a
close friendship. We'd hold hands in the cinema. But nothing
more,' she remembered.

It was in a vacation during this period that Hugh and Rosemary went on a cruise around the Norwegian fjords, an
unexplained voyage which might have been intended to give
Rosemary a sociable interlude with suitable people, and was
presumably funded by their parents. Eileen Duveen (then
Eileen Gowers), who was on board with her parents and brother
Dick, remembered that cruise years later. 'Hugh was the life
and soul of the ship, thinking up things to do and organizing a
big fancy-dress party. Rosemary was very much in the background.' Hugh took to the whole Gowers family. He immediately spotted the distinction of Eileen's father, Ernest Gowers,
a high-ranking civil servant (who would go on to write that
seminal book, *Plain English: A Guide to the Use of English*),
becoming friendly with Dick, who was also a Cambridge undergraduate, and paying extravagant court to Eileen. 'I was flattered because I was only sixteen and unsure of myself, but was
actually more attracted to another rather handsome boy on
board.' Eileen and Hugh remained friends for some time
though, with Hugh writing her long, loving letters while she
was at finishing school in Switzerland. Back in Cambridge, he
introduced Dick to Stella, his scene-painting friend, and the

two subsequently married. Casson's own romantic attach-ments did not prosper, though he was obviously casting around for someone on whom to lavish his fund of warm affection.

He continued to be interested in the theatre. A new manager, Amner Hall, brought actors like Robert Donat and Jessica Tandy into the company, and a designer called Hedley Briggs, whose taste ran to Victorian gothic rather than grey-and-silver abstraction. The drawings were rudimentary but Hugh learnt something about scale during his scene-painting duties which was to come in useful. He even gave serious consideration to the idea of designing for films, which struck him as being more interesting than designing office buildings. With introductions from Sybil Thorndike, he managed during his last term at the University to visit a filmset at Denham, where Marlene Dietrich sat blowing cigar-ette smoke through her eye-lashes during a rest period, and the Gaumont Studios at Shepherd's Bush, where they were making a film about the French Revolution. But this was a chancy world, one which Hugh found less appealing than he had ex-pected. In any case, he'd done

... Resting ...

so well in his final exams it would have been foolish to veer off in another direction. A career in films stopped there.

Notwithstanding his manifold spare-time activities, Hugh had packed in a formidable amount of work. His year consisted of twenty undergraduates, nineteen men and one woman, Aline Gale, who eventually married a man called John Stafford, both of whom remained Hugh's friends. As well as George Millar, he made another good rowing friend in Tommy Russell.

Russell, son of a successful Manchester-based building contractor, liked Casson, describing him as 'kind and modest,
often giving me a hand in a friendly way. But I think he kept a
lot to himself. He was not a frivolous party man and sensibly

— Cinema Queue —

concentrated his mind on the main objective, and developed
more intimate friendships with those likely to help in his
career'. Hugh successfully juggled the hours spent on the Cam
with the hours spent on more cerebral pursuits, to the apparent
benefit of both. Though he coxed the first eight of Lady Margaret Boat Club, as St John's boat club is known, at Henley, he
failed to achieve that rare distinction of coxing the Cambridge
eight in the University Boat Race.

None of his friends, curiously enough, went on to become
architects of any particular renown and some, like George
Millar, who became a journalist, drifted off into entirely different professions. Tommy Russell, who joined his father's contracting firm, was able in the summer of 1935 to take his
friend Hugh, a notably keen sailor, on a cruise in his father's
magnificent 56-foot sailing cutter around the Isle of Arran. 'But
he never invited me to visit his home or boat,' remarked Russell
later. They drifted apart thereafter, until Russell turned up
again in the late 1960s as contractor to one of Casson's major
architectural jobs, the regional headquarters building of the
National Westminster Bank in Manchester.

The ethos of the Cambridge School of Architecture was set by its Director, Theodore Fyfe, a small, dapper man, who had worked on the Knossos excavations in Crete with Arthur Evans during those years in the earlier part of the twentieth century when the most thrilling discoveries were made there. Fyfe was devoted to classicism rather than modern architecture. Despite this, Hugh always said that, like his fellow students, he went through the classical stage during his first year, and – helped by excellent tutors – emerged on to the sunlit uplands of early modernism for the remainder of his time at Cambridge. 'We went around visiting the various Modernist shrines in the Home Counties and London – I think there were only about twelve in the whole country – because this was before the distinguished refugees from Nazism like Walter Gropius, Eric Mendelsohn and Marcel Breuer had started to arrive. Harold Tomlinson, remote, wary, but a wonderful draughtsman and demanding of high standards, insisted we drew with fountain pens so we couldn't rub out.'

Other tutors included Christopher Nicholson, usually known as Kit, a staunch Modernist some six years older than his students, who had not too long before obtained a good degree at Cambridge himself, and George Checkley, who built two houses at Cambridge in 1930. Flat-roofed and white, with horizontal fenestration, 'They were impressive examples of the new architecture, and they made him a recipient of great respect though he was a hopeless teacher, poor man. We were set a design project every two or three weeks, anything from a set of gates to a railway station. That's where we abandoned classicism; it didn't seem appropriate to cover railway stations with columns.'

Beresford Pite, exponent of neo-classical architecture and an architect whose reputation was to enjoy an enthusiastic revival in the 1980s, was also a lecturer at the school for a time. He had taught at the Royal College of Art and had only recently

*In the thirties, Hugh's drawings of London buildings were
often commissioned by the lay press.*

retired from being architecture director at the Brixton School
of Building. But he was now over seventy and finishing one of
his last projects – the opening out of the Piccadilly entrance to
the Burlington Arcade – before his death in 1934. His approach
was remote and he rarely walked round looking at the student
work on the drawing boards. He was one of the few tutors who
made little impact on Hugh.

Until he entered the School of Architecture, Hugh Casson
had taken no interest in the new Modern architecture. 'But I
was fascinated by ships because I'd spent several years apprais-
ing them. Good training really, because you get a sense of
structure from ships, and they don't dress themselves up as
something else. I was probably a good subject for conversion
to this new architecture. We were all rather solemn, of course,

a bit stylistically priggish and convinced about Modern architecture, but my theatre work did give me a frivolous side too.'

A broader knowledge came from the architectural press; it was particularly seductive at that period in its coverage of what was happening in Europe, notably in Scandinavia. Britain trailed – architecturally speaking – pathetically in its wake.

Tomlinson taught Casson to make good architectural drawings: not just plan, elevation and section, but perspectives too, so that he was informed and aware of his design in totality, with no hidden solecisms or clumsiness. 'I've always been grateful to him, because that's been a godsend to me, though in a way I suppose I've been hypnotized by drawing rather than designing. But it's been marvellous with clients, being able to draw very quickly and simply in three dimensions. If you go to a meeting with a client and want to explain on the spot, so that he can understand what you're going to do, that's the best way. It's invaluable.' What Hugh did not say was that Cambridge demanded a high standard of essay writing, and that his fast-developing talent for assembling his ideas in attractive written form was becoming a huge asset.

A few months after Hugh Casson came down from Cambridge, Theodore Fyfe wrote a reference for him, in which he said, 'He was one of the best students I have ever had in the School of Architecture at Cambridge, where he obtained the BA Degree in 1932 with a first class in each of the three examinations of the architecture course.' In later life Casson never mentioned this academic distinction, nor is it recorded in the faded copies of early curriculum vitae which were still to be found amongst his papers for many years, despite the fact that it might have made a useful contribution to the beginnings of his career. Fyfe's glowing accolade languished in the files, unremarked and unused. But because of this triple first, he was awarded the College Prize: three guineas' worth of books. His capacity for hard and sustained work was proven even if the route along which he would direct his energies was as yet unclear.

Cambridge – although he remembered the University as 'a pretty non-visual place' and admitted to having rarely made use of its facilities – had been a successful and happy period in Hugh's life in ways other than the purely academic. He had been able to tinker on the edge of the theatrical world with which he was to become more seriously involved in later years. And he'd developed his social ease to a remarkable degree, making many friends. Some were women. Hugh was never the type of man for whom women are playthings and not to be taken seriously. He accorded them exactly the same liking and respect as he did to men. But he was now fully awakened to the sexual possibilities of these friendships. He was clearly remembered by Stella Gowers and Eileen Duveen, talking about him when they were both in their eighties, as being flirtatious and affectionate in his approach.

However, Randal was hurt during these University years by Hugh's careless approach to his own feelings. Randal would go up to see him, perhaps to watch the rowing, and Hugh wouldn't have time to meet him afterwards, or he would forget he was coming. It's easy to put too much emphasis on the callous behaviour of an undergraduate with a large number of activities and demands on his time. But it does seem as though he rated the self-effacing Randal quite low as a father. The fact that he virtually never saw him between the ages of four and thirteen – the years when a close rapport between father and son is most likely to develop – probably accounts for this perceptible rift. Nor had Hugh entirely grown out of his teenage discontent with what he saw as his modest background, and for a period he continued to carry his obligations to Randal – who was probably finding his son's time at Cambridge a financial burden – rather more lightly than is seemly.

Though he had enrolled to take his second degree at the

Bartlett School of Architecture in London, Hugh Casson had been awarded a grant from the Craven Fund for Travel and Study in Greece, which he was going to take up first during the winter of 1932–3. His award was made, according to Fyfe, 'when the competition was particularly keen, as there was an impressive lot of classical entrants against him'.

It was an exciting interlude, with his chosen subject, Byzantine brickwork, interesting despite its comparative obscurity. Before setting off on his three-month trip, Hugh, with tremendous aplomb, wrote to that famed Byzantine specialist Robert Byron, with whom he had last had contact apropos the Cambridge Architectural Society. He had read his books, most particularly *The Byzantine Achievement*, and articles Byron had written for the *Architectural Review* about his stay on Mount Athos. Now, he wanted personal advice and information. He was invited to tea at Savernake Lodge, the Byron family home in Wiltshire, a generous gesture on the part of this already acclaimed (and distinctly snobbish) writer. 'Byron was a great podgy unhealthy-looking fellow with grand tastes,' Hugh was to recall later. All the same he was a fruitful source of information on the Peloponnese and was even forthcoming with introductions which were duly put to good use.

Hugh Casson travelled to the British School in Athens, where he was to be based, via Ravenna and Brindisi, and since his scholarship was worth only fifty pounds – not a luxurious amount even in the early 1930s – it was hard class all the way, sitting up throughout the night on wooden seats and spending as little as possible on food. There were twelve scholars at the school, about four of them from Cambridge, each with a particular area of study, and lecturers to assist them. The archaeologist Humfry Payne, himself an ex-student of the School, had been its Director since 1929, and his distinction and archaeological successes were now lifting the place from the slough of lethargy and obscurity into which it had fallen during the early 1920s, so that Casson was there at a good time. A few years earlier, Payne had married Dilys Powell, who after her husband's early death became well known as a writer and film critic. In her memoir, *The Villa Ariadne*, she describes the arrival there of another graduate a year or so before Hugh:

He was a little overcome, as well he might have been, by the company in the British School Students' Hostel, where a year earlier I had made my first acquaintance with archaeological society. I was newly married at the time. Humfry was still a postgraduate student; and for three months we dined at a table where nobody, to the best of my recollection, ever spoke of any subject outside the range of the antiquarian. The phrase 'Students' Hostel' may mislead. The house was intended to afford board and lodging not only to young men and women just down from the University but to established scholars doing a stretch of work in Greece. [He] found himself mixing with some pretty formidable characters.

'I only wish,' this same student wrote home to his father, 'everybody wouldn't be so obviously learned to the eyebrows. It makes me feel such an impostor being here at all.'

Hugh, who always viewed his own achievements with amused surprise if not disbelief, felt the same as he sat in that small, cold dining room, with its lumpy, dun-coloured linoleum and photographs of former Directors lining the walls. He and his fellows formed a serious group, pursuing their chosen interests but little else, and drinking only small amounts of the local retsina. At weekends they walked in the mountains, and gradually acquired a smattering of conversational Greek. Some of them played tennis or hockey and there was even fencing, none of which sporting activities appealed to Hugh. He liked Athens though, a city which Dilys Powell described later as being of ramshackle smartness, with a view of the Acropolis at the end of every turning. The two buildings which comprised the school, the Director's house and the hostel, were set in a shady garden on the slopes of the conical hill of Lykabettos, which was at that time almost on the outskirts of the city. It all seemed quieter, 'more peasanty' than London, Hugh thought, but there were plenty of dingy green trams to take him rocketing down to the centre where the streets were busy and the cafés full. His exploration of Byzantine brickwork (which was to form the subject of his degree thesis) was undertaken with zeal, and he amassed copious pencil drawings and fuzzy photographs of the best examples, most particularly of Mistra, the only Byzantine town in existence. Robert Byron, who had been there a few years previously, described it as the weirdest place, perched on a precipitous hill with houses and a huge palace still three-quarters standing and nearly uninhabited: 'Wonderful frescos open to wind and rain – cisterns, fireplaces, ovens, all the domestic life is apparent. We spent the most entrancing and tiring two days there, our shoes being cut to ribbons on the rock.'

Casson was equally entranced. Unlike Byron, who had a car, he travelled mainly on foot or on local buses. The regular letters he sent to his parents contained vivid evocations of vehicles crammed with peasant women who, more used to the motion of donkeys, screamed and wailed as they bounced along winding roads which, as Dilys Powell commented, were spine wrenchers with the buses lurching from rut to rut; and of visits to monasteries, where the monks fed them, for there were few lodging-houses or inns. All the time Casson was measuring and recording the elaborately patterned coils and zigzags of the brickwork he had come to see. In this way he spent three months travelling the country, from Sparta in the south to Salonika in the north, while the weather became increasingly cold and unpleasant.

Casson's journey back to England by train was slow. He went first to see the Byzantine churches of Istanbul, where he enjoyed some luxury provided by one of Byron's introductions, an American Cultural Attaché. This man's loan of his car and Turkish driver eased Casson's appraisal of Istanbul's great edifices immeasurably, and made the hard-seated train he then caught and which chugged its way slowly northwards to Venice seem even more painful. The solitary gesture towards passenger comfort, he remembered afterwards, was being able to listen to music which issued from the ear-phones attached to each seat.

Venice was lonely because he knew no one. But there were compensations, like arriving as a snowy dawn broke over the Grand Canal which, its water black as ink, coiled like a serpent out of sight down to the sea, while the houses opposite began to turn apricot coloured. He stood there for several hours, trying to draw what he saw. His first instinct, as ever, had been to reach for pen and paper at the sight of something notable. 'I was still drawing with a fountain pen. But no colour. I didn't even take a paintbox with me.' And there was the obvious delight of six days with nothing to do on this, his first visit, except explore and record the buildings of Venice.

Casson's completed study of Byzantine brickwork described the history of the style, the bricks, the mortar, building techniques and decorative usage, all illustrated by drawings and photographs. Submitted as his thesis for RIBA Final ('Owing to its recondite nature it was accepted without question,' he commented drily), it was published in full in the RIBA Journal, for these were expansive times when editors were able to be profligate with the number of pages they could allow for a feature. It was Hugh's first important piece of writing. From then on he recognized the benefits of an expressive pen, and before long the pecuniary benefits became apparent too.

Casson had been away from September 1932 until February 1933, missing all of the first and most of the second term at the Bartlett School of Architecture. He would not have chosen the Bartlett as the best place to do his second degree. Like many ambitious architectural students – before and since – he hankered after the Architectural Association School in Bedford Square, the AA – 'a sort of experimental madhouse'. But the AA demanded that graduates from other schools took a three-year course, whereas at the Bartlett you could finish in two. Hugh, as ever, was in a hurry, and settled on the Bartlett.

Bartlett students in the thirties tended to be disconcertingly contemptuous of the place, perhaps driven into a weakly disloyal stance by the overshadowing presence of the AA. Hugh described its methods as being old-fashioned and still enmeshed in the Beaux-Arts traditions, although having done his first degree at Cambridge he escaped the first year, which was devoted to a study of the architectural Orders. Some realized in retrospect how much there was for which the Bartlett could be commended. The History of Architecture lectures by the Head of the school, Professor Albert Richardson (designer of the dark red-brick Financial Times building in Greystone Place, EC4), were remarkable for their graphic, histrionic quality and the depth of knowledge which Richardson was able to

impart. They were always packed. Many Bartlett students also
attended open lectures at the AA, including Hugh, who had
friends there.

His life, in these student years, was conventional and
unadventurous for a young man in his twenties, particularly
one who'd hankered after the anarchic experiences he envisaged taking place at the AA. He shared rooms with another
architectural student, Frank Adie, on the Chelsea Embankment. Then, because they couldn't stand the roar of traffic
which was already making that road untenable, they became
lodgers in a damp, faded villa in Little Venice.

The smell of the canal was pervasive, and there were none
of the floating art galleries and waterbuses which turned Little
Venice into such a lively area after the Second World War. At
the end of their stay here they got to know the Polish artist
Feliks Topolski, who had been dispatched to England by a
Polish magazine in 1935 to write about and draw the Royal
Jubilee celebrations of that year, and had stayed on. A passionate romantic, Topolski was entranced by what he described as
'the exotic otherness' of the English, and abandoned both Paris
and his native Warsaw to settle amongst them. He eventually
acquired a huge, shabby studio balanced above the sloping
banks of Paddington Basin in Warwick Avenue, where he established himself as a burgeoning success both artistically and
socially. There he held court, voluble, extravagant and avid for
all that life had to offer.

Hugh reminisced, 'You couldn't see across the room for
cigarette smoke. People talked and nobody ever seemed to go
home. How Feliks got any work done I don't know. It was like
a cross between a filmset version of an artist's studio, and my
vision of a Prague café.' At first the crowd consisted mainly
of Polish aristocrats and intellectuals (Topolski spoke little
English in these early days), but quite quickly it expanded to
include the close bohemian coterie which was still a cogent

force in London during the thirties. 'The first time I ever set eyes on Prince Philip was in that studio, but this was years later after the war. Feliks had met him when he was serving as a war artist.'

This encounter with the newly arrived Topolski was Casson's one venture into bohemia as a student and young architect, and he enjoyed it (although Topolski's more celebrity-packed parties would have taken place after the war). A sometime cavalry officer in the Polish army, Topolski was a gregarious and well-connected man, a type Hugh relished. The friendship flourished, and Topolski became someone with whom Hugh would work on several significant occasions.

His student life was otherwise prosaic, even philistine. They never, he remembered with some embarrassment, visited any of London's architectural set-pieces, such as Westminster Cathedral, Greenwich, or the Wren churches, but plodded off to the school in Gower Street every morning, ate supper at the same restaurant in Charlotte Street, Bertorelli's – usually the same dishes served by the same waitress, Lily – and then went home. Once a week they went to the cinema. They wore long, striped college scarves and plus-fours which made them feel more dashing than they were, and moved about in groups. 'We might have been bookies' clerks or accountants. Nobody went off to Kathmandu or to sit at the feet of a swami in the holidays, partly because it was too expensive, partly because it was too far away, and anyway it was too frightening. We were young for our age. We went home to our parents.'

III

Reta and the
Insouciant Years

The group which constituted Hugh Casson's intimates during his years at the Bartlett increasingly began to include another architectural student, Margaret Troup, who would later become his wife. He'd spotted her on his first day, the minute he entered the large studio where all the architectural students worked. She was wearing a beautiful white blouse with blue embroidery, and a blue skirt. 'There were only about three women students in a room of sixty, and one working just inside the door was, I thought, of surpassing beauty. She had long, thick, fair hair which she wore in a plaited coil on the nape of the neck. She was very demure, but she gave a quick look to see who was coming through the door, and I decided that this was it.'

Margaret, who was three years behind Hugh in her studies, remembers him, tiny and slimly built, coming in with two Cambridge friends, both of them over six feet tall. 'It was a bizarre sight.'

As his first term progressed, Hugh realized she was surrounded by admirers. With a dramatic style of dress which was very personal and reflected her own visual tastes rather than what was currently fashionable (she sometimes wore a long black cloak), she was extremely attractive physically although, as she admitted herself, she was shy and spoke little. She came from Pretoria in South Africa, where her father, now a distinguished doctor, had gone as a young man to escape the Scottish climate which was bad for his weak chest. Like Hugh, Margaret, along with her older sister Freda, had spent a large part of her childhood away from her parents, either at Wychwood, a boarding-school in north Oxford (which her mother had selected after reading a feature article about it in *The Lady*), or, during the school holidays, staying with their father's older brother, Uncle Edward, and his wife Winifred at their house in first Grosvenor Place, then Addison Road, Kensington. Sir Edward Troup was a senior civil servant, and the houses were substantial, but life there with only the childless and elderly couple for company was staid and restrictive for the two young girls.

Margaret and Freda had arrived in England in 1924 when the First World War was long since over, and they were sent away to school because their parents wanted them to grow up as young English women, rather than South Africans. For the whole of their six years at Wychwood, their mother visited England only once, their father never.

In old age Margaret described the trauma of being left in a strange place, far from home, at the age of eleven, and its devastating effects. 'I remember very clearly the total paralysis which set in at that point. It was the most traumatic thing that ever happened to me . . . Freda and I did not get on very well at that time, so that although we shared a room at first, we were soon separated. I just shut up like a clam. It was very difficult to get any words out of me at all . . . I was very unhappy for the first two years.' The letters she wrote home, preserved by her mother, reveal little of the misery she suffered and, for the first years at least, give the impression that she was a dutiful child trying to spare her parents any worry on her behalf. 'Please don't be worried because Freda says she wants you to take her away by Christmas,' she wrote in October 1925. 'I think she will settle down by then and will be quite happy. I read my Bible every day you will be pleased to hear, though sometimes I wish you were here to explain things to me.' On 24 October

1929 though, four years after arriving in England, she wrote, 'Only seven more months now to seeing you.' She and Freda were to make their first visit home to South Africa in the summer of 1930.

Fortunately, Wychwood was a good school with enlightened methods of teaching and caring for children, and eventually both Troup girls were very happy there. It was well situated, too. As Margaret wrote home when she was about sixteen, 'The best of being in a university town is that we can get to lectures for undergraduates that we wouldn't get elsewhere, and they are always first rate.' She also led a far more cultured life than her future husband did during his school days, being taken to concerts and plays along with other pupils (including a production of *Macbeth* by OUDS), as well as by the generous friends and relations of her father who frequently asked the two Troup girls to stay. Visits to family in Scotland, where life was more relaxed and lively than in London, were special treats. In Oxford, Margaret attended performances by the London Symphony Orchestra, with Thomas Beecham conducting, and this was when her love of music began to develop; she continued going to concerts and occasionally the opera when she was a student. There were visits to London for the Royal Academy Summer Exhibition, and to see both the Italian Artists and the Persian Exhibitions. By the time she was sixteen she had begun to demonstrate an obvious aptitude for art, and was going to life classes every week at the Ruskin School of Art in Oxford where Gilbert Spencer, brother of Stanley, was one of her teachers.

Shy or not, Margaret also began to enjoy a varied social life. After a lovely half-term with some school friends in the winter term of 1930, during which she bought two new pairs of shoes for £1, listened to records, watched a rugger match, went to a film and also a dance, she wrote wrily about returning to her 'pensive citadel. I think I've had enough of school'. Wychwood was, in fact, far more liberal in handling its pupils than many other girls' boarding-schools at the time. In the summer term of 1931, when Margaret was seventeen, she described a Saturday spent in London when she 'knocked about Kensington' and then went to Oxford Street for lunch at Lyons Corner House before going to the Albert Hall to hear *Hiawatha*. Her appearance of shyness may have been partly deceptive. As she wrote to her mother in response to a negative school report, 'It's a pity I always look languid. Actually I look more so than I am, which is unfortunate.'

The sisters' life at school was extremely contented in the later years, and they were successful students, Freda leaving first to read geography at Oxford, Margaret to become an architectural student at London University's Bartlett School in 1931, her interest in the subject influenced by her favourite uncle Frank Troup, an established Arts and Crafts architect. At her entry interview a black picture had been painted of prospects in the profession she now wanted to enter, with few jobs available, especially for women. The Registrar suggested she would do better to study interior design. 'But I sat looking determined, and as I seemed so keen they said they'd have me.' Her father thought she was enrolling at the Architectural Association School – whose reputation must have reached as far as South Africa even in those days of slow communications – and only discovered his mistake when he came to write the cheque for her first term. Margaret wrote:

> Sorry you are living under the disillusionment I was going to the AA. I thought I made it clear it was London University. I only heard of the AA a little while ago after everything was arranged. But I see no reason why this shouldn't be as good. Anyway, we meet students doing all sorts of other things besides architecture here, which is a very good thing in a way.

To Hugh's dismay, Margaret disappeared to Pretoria for eight weeks of every summer she was at the Bartlett, taking advantage of Union Castle's half-price fares for students. And she went back there for a whole year after finally completing her course. Hugh proposed by letter during her year away, and she returned to marry him in the autumn of 1938.

Lady Burrows, who as Ines Walter had been at Wychwood with Margaret and remained a close friend throughout her life, described Margaret as being quite mature for her age during her student years and of a spiritual and philosophical bent. She was also tall and slender, and there was an undeniable incongruity about the small figure of Hugh – 'my little friend Hugh' as she was wont to describe him – buzzing around this dignified and reserved young woman like a persistent insect, which bothered some of her friends. But he had a beautiful voice and was good-looking, with wide-set blue eyes and a steady gaze.

If it was Margaret's fine looks which immediately drew and kept Hugh's attention, it is not quite so easy to determine the reasons for her own gradual rejection of a plethora of other suitors in his favour. She was closely involved with a medical student called Jim Green for a lot of the time she was seeing Hugh, going to dances with him at St Thomas's Hospital, frequently spending the weekend with his parents near Oxford and taking him to Sunday lunch with her aunt and uncle, dining at his flat once he was qualified, and sometimes accompanying him on professional visits to patients in the East End. She also had a close friendship with another architectural student, Gontran Goulden (later to become Director of the Building Centre in London), who was in the year above her and who shared her love of music. Hugh often vied with him for Margaret's company at college events, but Gonnie Goulden remained a good friend to them both until the end of his life.

Margaret said later that Hugh had everything she lacked in

the way of confidence and social aplomb, and he immediately provided a front for her own self-proclaimed inadequacies, breaking down barriers for her, opening doors and generally encouraging her to follow him along the path through life which she was finding difficult, something he was to go on doing for a very long time. They were both, moreover, amongst the Bartlett's most able and committed students, and although attraction is not generally dependent on such prosaic attributes, the persistence Hugh demonstrated (perhaps the most potent element of this courtship), accompanied by wit and genuine kindness, proved to be irresistible. By the time he left the Bartlett in 1934, three years ahead of her, they were spending much of their free time together.

After qualifying, Hugh's first serious job was with a flamboyant young Australian architect called Wylton Todd, whose source of work was the clubs where he played jazz music on the piano at night. 'Most of our work came from these clubs and restaurants, putting in new lavatories, enlarging the kitchen, redecorating the bar.'

The experience Hugh gained with Wylton Todd was useful and, like other fledgling architects, he made his early mistakes. Most memorable was when he designed a typist's desk for the receptionist at a chic hairdressing salon. It was a smart affair in white painted wood, with the hairdresser's signature scrawled in black across the front. Unfortunately, he had completely forgotten when he worked out dimensions that the movement of the typewriter's carriage as the receptionist typed would send it crashing into the wall; almost worse, when designing showcases for chocolates at the Hungaria restaurant, he omitted to ventilate them, so that the heat of the display lighting reduced the chocolates to a melted heap over the course of an evening.

However, he had managed to secure a job, and now that Hugh was earning money, he and Margaret would go to Promenade concerts at the Albert Hall, or to the cinema, or they would queue for tickets to theatre performances such as *Private Lives*, with Gertrude Lawrence and its author Noel Coward in the main parts. They often spent evenings at the Café Royal, which they afforded by eating cheaply at Bertorelli's (in those days frequented by a motley gathering of impecunious intellectuals), then repairing to the grand old establishment in Regent Street – still a haunt of artists and would-be bohemians – for coffee. Described by Feliks Topolski in his memoirs as a huge, ungainly, balconied room, painted ochre and with red plush banquettes so that it seemed like a close relation of the Paris Coupole, the area of the Café which they frequented had one half devoted to meals, where the tables were covered in white linen cloths, the other to coffee and drinks served on marble-topped tables. Topolski saw Augustus John at those marble tables, Jacob Epstein, John Rothenstein, Claude Cockburn and Michael Redgrave – 'an array of the amiable best in young arts . . .'.

Hugh and Margaret would be there too, but in rather different company. Ines Walter, whose family had founded *The Times* in 1785 and whose own father, John Walter IV, was still a co-proprietor with John Astor, had drawn them into her circle of wealthy and mainly carefree young things, and she recalled that Hugh would enthral a table of friends with his drawings and dramatic imitations. 'He was a performer and we egged him on. Margaret used to treat him in a mock motherly way, and he was extremely endearing. Everyone liked him.' Ines Walter in fact talked about Margaret as 'Reta'. All her life she was known to some as Reta, to others as Margaret. Hugh christened her Moggie, and this was a name picked up by several close friends. In this book she will be Reta, because that is what I have always called her.

The thirties were insouciant years for them both, and neither showed the slightest interest in politics or appeared to realize that their peaceful life was in any way threatened by what was happening in Europe. Reta spent several holidays in Germany and wrote home to her mother in April 1933, 'Saw simply hundreds of Nazis in Frankfurt. Everything seemed very peaceful and happy. None of the Nazis was even armed.'

One day in November 1934 she went to see Sir Edwin Lutyens. King George V was opening the new RIBA building in Portland Place that day, so she was late because of the heavy traffic. Otherwise it proved to be an uneventful visit, with Lutyens offering no words of architectural wisdom but telling her she was charming and just like her architect uncle, Frank Troup, and that the best thing for her to do was to marry an architect, not to try to be one herself. She was left unmoved by her encounter with this eminent man – whose reputation was, in any case, on the decline amongst younger architects – and more intrigued by the Belisha beacons which looked like lollipops and which she noticed were now appearing at pedestrian crossings all over London, though she reckoned that after the next big rugger match they would all be smashed.

As their friendship deepened, she and Hugh paid occasional visits to his parents, sometimes with other friends, and sailed on the Solent, though Hugh devoted part of one such visit to Southampton to coaching Reta for her approaching exams. Once she and Hugh drove to Bron-y-Garth, the fine house above Portmadoc in North Wales that belonged to Hugh's uncle, Lewis Casson, and to which he was making some alterations. They spent luxurious weekends at Ines Walter's home, The Ham at Wantage, and Ines, by now 'doing the Season', would occasionally pass on to them invitations for smart events which she didn't want to attend herself but which appealed to Hugh, or would include them in her own parties. She was on the junior committee for a ball at the Hurlingham Club in aid of the Victoria Hospital for Children, and at this Reta was persuaded to wear a crinoline and dance in a cabaret, which seems to accord ill with her much-vaunted shyness. But she had a wonderful time, writing home that

> it was just marvellous. I took Hugh Casson as partner. We went out for dinner first. Hugh was terribly amusing and enjoyed it very much and altogether it was a jolly good show. Hugh's frightfully small, and was Cambridge reserve cox, so you can imagine how funny we must look together. It was a glorious night in a lovely room, with a floor laid so you could dance outside where there were Chinese lanterns in an enormous garden.

Sometimes, Hugh took Reta to visit Sybil Thorndike in her dressing room, a treat he liked to bestow on those he held most dear. They also went away with friends on holidays abroad. Jean Jackson-Stops, one of that rarefied group of women students at the Bartlett, was Reta's closest friend – a friendship which continued when their student days were over and their lives broadened. Jean owned a Riley car, and she, her future husband, Tony, who was a lawyer, Reta and Hugh took several holiday trips, once driving to the Paris Exhibition, and then on to Le Lavandou in the South of France. 'I realized Reta was in love with Hugh when I found her washing his clothing after a stomach upset,' Jean recalled later. Nor was this the only unwelcome event on that particular trip. 'Driving along the road looking at Mont Blanc, my husband drove up a bank and ripped off the undercarriage. Hugh subsequently drove over a rock in the road.'

Speaking of those times, Reta admitted, 'We had great licence before the war,' and though they never shared a flat, Hugh was often at the one in Gower Street where she lived during the latter part of her time at the Bartlett. She had become tired of living in hall, which she found depressing. 'I'm not made the right way to live with a crowd of people. I can't stand it. It just swamps me.' From the windows of her flat, she and

Hugh would watch her neighbour, the famously theatrical Lady Ottoline Morrell, parading along the street below. There was no question of home cooking, though. When she became tired of eating in restaurants in early May 1937, Reta decided to employ a cook. She was also at this time complaining that because of the imminent Coronation of George VI, London was crowded and uncomfortable for its inhabitants. 'London is becoming a most fearful place. Crowds increase every day and are stiff with foreigners. The parks have been ruined – they're covered in tents and awful corrugated-iron lavatories. It's an awfully sordid sight. And everything takes twice as long because there's a bus strike.' She stayed the night before the Coronation at Jean Jackson-Stops's flat in Curzon Street, near to the processional route. The rain held off until it was all over at four p.m. and the two young women had seats overlooking Park Lane, where they could watch the newly crowned King and Queen, who 'seemed tiny and weighed down by their crowns'. They also managed to look in on two sherry parties.

The minute it was all over, Reta and Jean fled with Hugh and Tony for a bank-holiday weekend at Bron-y-Garth. The weather was fine, they climbed mountains, sailed and got sunburnt, with – or so Reta wrote to her mother – Uncle Lewis as chaperon.

Hugh had, of course, been an outstandingly good architectural student, and so in a less dramatic but perhaps more measured way had Reta. Pushed towards the domestic and interior-design work which tended to be the lot of women architects in those days – and even, if they are not sufficiently steely, up to the present – one of her first jobs was designing Ines Walter's bedroom at her parents' London house in Lowndes Street, a job that was, as such small jobs generally are, worrying and demanding, with initial estimates for the construction work coming in far higher than she had expected. 'If it wasn't for Hugh I should probably be in a law court by now,' she wrote to her parents. 'My ideas on business are distinctly vague.'

They were married in St Margaret's, Westminster, on 19 November 1938, Reta in an elegantly simple dress of white satin brocade made by her dressmaker, who lived in Hamilton Terrace. (She had, at Hugh's behest, been shopping for flat-heeled shoes in the morning.) Frank Adie was best man, Freda was matron of honour, and they had a reception for 200 guests in the nearby house of Canon Storr, the Dean of Westminster. Such a stylish wedding resulted from Reta's father not only having treated Canon Storr's son when he was seriously ill in South Africa, virtually saving his life, but having taken him to live in his own home until his convalescence was complete. This was the Dean's thank-you. Reta's mother had come from South Africa for the wedding. Her father, medical adviser to the country's President, General Smuts, who was ill at the time, was detained by his work, but telephoned his daughter and her new husband during the wedding reception, an exciting and unusual occurrence in those days.

Hugh and Reta spent their honeymoon at Bron-y-Garth, which had splendid views across the bay to Harlech. This was the house where Lewis Casson had spent part of his own honeymoon with Sybil Thorndike. When Lewis inherited Bron-y-Garth from his Aunt Lucy in 1933 he had employed Hugh to improve it for him. In her book *A Speaking Part: A Biography of Lewis*, Diana Devlin, Lewis's granddaughter, recorded, 'The most striking change Hugh made was to open up the ground floor so that you could look right across the Traeth [the bay] as soon as you entered.' And Jean Jackson-Stops remembered it as 'a low white Victorian building, with wonderful staff. There were polished floors and a huge dining room, and the whole place seemed filled with sunlight.' It rained all the time during Hugh and Reta's honeymoon, but Aunt Lucy's old maid, Sarah, was still in residence as housekeeper to look after them in what Diana Devlin called 'a beautiful old house designed for a life of genteel elegance'.

A photograph of the Casson wedding featured in *The Architect and Building News*. This was not because either of them was a well-known architect. They were not, yet. It was because John Summerson (later to be a distinguished architectural historian and Director of the Soane Museum) was on the editorial staff and had become a friend. They had met through Hugh's work for what is now known as the media, which he had been intent on infiltrating from the time he completed his studies as an architectural student, and which he had done with apparent ease. He was by now a frequent contributor of both articles and drawings to a variety of lay and architectural publications. As early as 1934, the year he left the Bartlett, Hugh had made a most appealing set of drawings, supported by captions, showing his ideas for street decorations during King George V's Jubilee celebrations. They were published in *The Sphere* magazine, and although the decorations depicted were never realized, they made the printed page not just because they were good ideas, but because they were good ideas expressed in delightful, fresh drawings, albeit by a young, unknown and newly qualified architect.

Hugh Casson grew up in a time when much emphasis was placed on the written word, and children were educated to use it clearly and accurately. Communication, whether of facts or ideas, was almost invariably by letter, and in the absence of telephone cards or frequent weekends at home, the weekly letter to their parents was an obligation which children at boarding-school took for granted. Hugh found none of this a chore. Writing was easy, and if his early letters were typical schoolboy screeds in one sense, conventional in content and not particularly adventurous in their use of words, they were well constructed and had a relaxed style which he was to develop and refine as he got older. Cambridge essays were not ground out with the laborious intensity which marks the prose efforts of some architectural students, because, unlike them, Hugh was blessed with a literary as well as a visual mind. This would be an invaluable asset to him in the future, and its importance had already been demonstrated in the excellent examination results to which his fluent prose must have contributed. Already, he was making his mark as an able contributor to the general press as well as to architectural magazines.

Young architects setting out in private practice have prescriptively boosted their incomes by teaching. Hugh had been a temporary studio supervisor at the Cambridge School for a couple of terms from January 1935, when he was very newly qualified. And then years later came his long stint running the Interior Design department (on what may be loosely described as a full-time basis) at the Royal College of Art. But it was with writing and drawing that he most successfully augmented his income, and during all the years ahead when he was making an outstanding name in the fields of architecture, teaching and public service to the arts, he would successfully manage this complementary career.

Writing for his co-professionals naturally provided the easiest and most obvious outlet. But he also gave a much wider readership the benefit of his views (always illustrated) in women's magazines and in that now extinct newspaper, the *News Chronicle*. The women's magazine articles, on such subjects as how to turn the attic into a nursery or utilize the cupboard under the stairs as a study, were not in the highest echelons of journalism, but they helped boost his earnings, and Hugh – still in his twenties and not earning enough as an architect – was not proud.

In 1937, right at the beginning of his career, Hugh wrote a short architectural guide to London at the behest of London Transport, which was doing a series, with the ubiquitous Robert Byron writing another. Entitled *New Sights of London*,

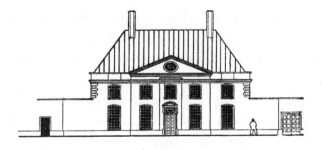

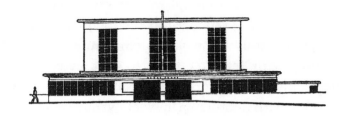

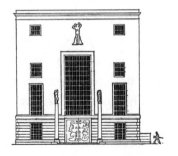

Vernon House, Chelsea Square; Arnos Grove Underground Station; Royal Institute of British Architects, Portland Place and Martello Airport, Gatwick from New Sights *of London.*

it was little more than a list, illuminated by introductory essays to each section and excellent small drawings. But it was commendably comprehensive and, at sixpence, it was good value for architecture buffs. In a letter home to her mother in April of that year, Reta, not yet married, complained that she was required to produce sixty drawings of buildings for this booklet and so far had only managed two. When the book came out, the drawings were credited to Hugh Casson 'with the assistance of Margaret Troup'. Even this early on Casson, under pressure of work, was obliged to seek help in setting up some drawings, certainly those of an architectural nature. Many of his outings with Reta, to Oxford, to Paris, even to his parents in Southampton, were primarily spent gathering material for his articles, with Reta drawn inexorably into the web of unceasing activity. In May, she was apologizing to her mother for missing the mail because she had to meet a deadline for drawings in some architectural paper.

Hugh had also by this time, with the increasing aversion to saying no for which he would become renowned, agreed to become the architectural correspondent of a magazine called *Night and Day*, which was launched by Chatto and Windus in the spring of 1937, with Graham Greene as literary editor. Boasting an impressive group of contributors – Elizabeth Bowen, Herbert Read, William Empson, Cyril Connolly, Stevie Smith – it had the highest of intellectual aspirations, but a lighthearted approach which belied its cutting edge. Casson, despite the fact that his new friend Feliks Topolski had been commissioned to provide the first cover, felt daunted at the prospect of keeping such editorial company. However, he valiantly produced several articles, illustrated with his own thumbnail sketches of the buildings he was discussing. 'Roadhouse Tudor', for instance, in the August issue took a mocking look at the current fashion for roadhouses in their different, and largely inappropriate, styles. His own style was cautious,

'The Barn' and 'Laughing Water' from Night and Day magazine

that of the new boy in company he considered a cut above him, with drawings which were neat and conservatively detailed.

Casson need not have worried about his critical weight, for the *Night and Day* venture was to be short lived. In the fourth issue, Greene's review of a film called *Wee Willie Winkie*, which starred the nine-year-old Shirley Temple, described her as 'a fancy little piece, a complete totsy', and talked about middle-aged men and clergymen responding 'to her dubious coquetry, to the sight of her well-shaped and desirable little body, packed with enormous vitality, only because the safety curtain of story and dialogue drops between their intelligence and their desire.' There was more. Graham Greene's biographer, Norman Sherry, recorded these and other facts: Temple sued, with Sir Patrick Hastings appearing for the plaintiff, whom he described as a child of nine with a worldwide reputation as an artist in films. There was effrontery implicit in his every word. The company, Twentieth Century Fox, was awarded £3,500 damages, plus costs. It was curtains for *Night and Day*, and the end of at least one job for Hugh Casson, who didn't much care, but cheerfully embroidered and exaggerated this odd story for the amusement of his friends.

A writer who can support his or her text with passable illustrations is likely to be a favourite with editors. Hugh's drawings were much more than passable. He had already become adept at wooing clients with his spare, romantic images. Now he employed them to add zest and individuality to his writing. The Architectural Press – publishers of the *Architect's Journal* and the rather more magisterial *Architectural Review* – provided some of his first outlets and would continue to employ him for years to come. Other young writers with whom he rubbed shoulders at the Architectural Press in the thirties included Osbert Lancaster and John Betjeman, and it is not difficult to imagine the levity with which these three faced their editorial tasks, although the resultant publications were professional and well compiled. The eccentric but clever H. de Cronin Hastings, who owned the company – and frequently operated from a club porter's hooded chair near the entrance door to the building in Queen Anne's Gate where they all worked – was an exacting man. He would have stood for nothing less.

Casson had, by modern standards, set himself up in a certain amount of style now that he was a fully fledged architect. In the months before his marriage, he and Frank Adie – abandoning Little Venice – had been sharing a small Georgian house, complete with sash windows and panelled rooms, in Holland Street, close to Holland Park in Kensington. Architects in the 1930s, along with other young professionals, led an infinitely grander and more formal existence than do their modern counterparts, and a daily manservant would come in to cook them breakfast and supper. Now that Hugh was married, Frank left this comfortable abode to make way for Reta, and the couple settled down to a full and interesting married life. They already had many friends garnered from the various worlds they inhabited. Feliks Topolski, by now designing sets for Bernard Shaw plays and with commissions from both private patrons and a variety of publications, painted Reta's portrait. They were reasonably untrammelled by money worries, since Reta had a small allowance from her father in South Africa, and Hugh's writing was providing a generous supplement to his earnings as an architect. For a few weeks they gave shelter to a refugee from Spain's civil war, a young man who had lost everything in the conflict against the Franco regime.

During this period, Randal Casson had a small inheritance which he generously made over to Hugh to use as he thought best. The £1,200 was sufficient to design and build a small house which he was able to sell at a profit. As he was never one to take much interest in money, and lacked a strong entrepreneurial instinct, this may have been Hugh Casson's single commercial enterprise. Fortunately it was successful. He was wily enough not to jeopardize its chance of a quick sale by risking anything too progressive, despite his professed allegiance, albeit a fairly lukewarm one, to the new Modern Movement style, and he arranged for the house, which had a pitched roof, to be illustrated in that genteel publication *The Lady*. He knew that having your work published in publications only read by other architects, as so many of his peers chose to do, was not likely to broadcast your talents to potential clients. His ploy worked: more commissions for houses followed.

Casson was much concerned in the thirties with the cavalier way in which fine old buildings, unprotected by any listing process at that period, were fast disappearing from the London streets. In a Review of the Year 1938 for the *Architect's Journal*, he reeled off their names: Adelphi, Norfolk House (acquired for demolition by Roland Palumbo, whose son Peter was then a schoolboy), and the east side of Berkeley Square, with Wellington Barracks and Euston Arch both threatened. On the other hand, he bemoaned the delays, restrictions and form-filling with which architects were beset even at this period, and though he posited the need for town-planning control, as would most intelligent and reasonable members of his profession, he believed it should apply to siting only. He deplored the idea of aesthetic control, though he certainly lived to see the time when it would grip the planning profession with fervour.

He shared with almost every other architect an interest in fine old buildings, but it did not preclude him from celebrating the new and avant-garde along with his colleagues. As another Architectural Press journalist of the time, J. M. Richards, is quoted as saying about their proprietor, H. de Cronin Hastings, in Bevis Hillier's biography of John Betjeman:

[Hastings's] comments were incisive and he had a keen journalistic sense, insisting, for example, that the news value of a story must never be lost in the recital of facts. It was news sense rather than any profound philosophical convictions about architecture which caused Hastings to espouse the Modern Movement.

But espouse it he did, and Casson, not perhaps the most fervent of disciples, would have been expected, even required, to follow the same line.

IV

The Beginnings of
an Architectural Career

Apart from his marriage, the most significant event in Hugh's life during this relatively short interlude between qualifying and the start of the Second World War was the move, in 1935, to work in the newly established office of his ex-Cambridge tutor, Kit Nicholson. Nicholson, a wiry, energetic man with close-cropped dark, curly hair, needed an assistant because he had just landed the job of designing a building for the London Gliding Club at Dunstable, of which he was an active member, and Hugh with his brilliant academic record must have immediately come to mind as an obvious choice. By now, too, Hugh's writings had begun to give him a usefully high profile in his profession. He was hard to forget.

Sharing a quick wit and a wonderful facility on the drawing-board, the two men had always got on well since their first encounters at Cambridge. This was despite Kit's other life as a passionate and accomplished sportsman, in which Hugh certainly had no interest.

Hugh settled effortlessly into the Nicholson office, where both the work and the atmosphere of cheerful intensity suited him perfectly. This was his entrée into another world: the beguilingly atavistic world of artists and writers, the last remains of a bohemian and artistic London which had flourished from Edwardian times, one which he had also glimpsed in Topolski's studio and during his evenings at the

Café Royal, and which would be finally expunged by the war.
Now he met Kit's father, the painter Sir William Nicholson, a
dandy in spotted shirts, white duck-trousers, patent-leather
buttoned boots, and a little green pork-pie hat. A gregarious
and popular man, he had made a notable silhouette portrait of
Queen Victoria, and his later work as a portrait painter had
gained him entrance to fashionable and influential circles.
Kit's older brother Ben was already a powerful force amongst
younger painters, particularly admired for his pure, geometric
reliefs, and he was a clear influence on Kit's own designs, with
– by the time Hugh joined the office – the brothers sharing the
same sparse aesthetic. Hugh found Ben frightening: 'So much
conviction and concentration packed tight into that frail-
looking frame,' he wrote in 1988. But he was pleased to know
him. And artists from the old guard such as Augustus John, as
well as the Nicholson family's wealthy relations and acquaintances, were proving to be useful sources of work. Unlike Reta,
Hugh never met Edwin Lutyens, though Lutyens was one of
William Nicholson's closest friends and for some years had an
office close to his studio in Apple Tree Yard, St James's, and
Kit – a staunch but undogmatic Modernist – regarded him with
huge respect, employing a system of geometry and proportion
in his designs in emulation of the older man.

Based in one room over a chemist's shop in the Fulham Road,
with Kit's wife E. Q. Myers consigned to the role of part-time
secretary (she was actually a talented textile designer), and the
occasional student, including both Reta and Jean Jackson-
Stops, employed during rush periods, the small practice began
to succeed. Reta, who would have liked a permanent job in this
lively office, loved her intermittent periods of working there
and was flattered that she was paid; her friend Jean apparently
did the work for nothing other than experience.

Apart from the Gliding Club there were other challenging
commissions. Kit's Close (the name was coincidental), an

expansive, white-walled house in Fawley Green, Oxfordshire, is described by Dr Neil Bingham in his monograph *Christopher Nicholson* as 'one of Britain's major Modern Movement houses of the 1930s'. There was also the more traditional Dalingridge Farm at West Hoathly, Sussex, alterations to Monkton House in Sussex for Edward James, the wealthy patron of Surrealism, designs for the Garden Landscape section at the MARS Group Exhibition in 1938, and a porch and entrance lobby for the much-publicized studio which in 1933 Nicholson had designed for Augustus John at Fordingbridge in Hampshire.

Hugh went down to the John house, Friern Court, to take instructions for this small project from Dorelia John, 'a tall, grave and beautiful lady, very dignified and contained. I measured up the site, took the measurements back to Kit who designed the porch, and then I did the drawings.' Thirty years later, finding himself in the area, Casson drew up outside the studio and sat looking at the porch he'd worked on so long before. Accosted by the present owner, he revealed his own part in the design of the porch, to be pounced on with the cry, 'I'm glad you're here. It's leaking badly.' Casson told him that after thirty years it was probably time to renew the felt on the porch roof, and drove away.

All these projects were built but there were others which, though full designs were worked out, never came to fruition. Hugh Casson had already developed a most attractive style of perspective drawing, and his drawings featured large in the work of the practice. Neil Bingham said, 'Casson was a major force in Nicholson's office, perhaps not always in the early design stages of a project, but certainly in the finished drawings. Casson's perspectives are especially lively and seductive, the perfect bait for capturing clients and clinching commissions.' Some of Hugh's early professional drawings were reproduced in this monograph. Both men drew exceptionally well, with Nicholson sharing in large measure the artistic talents which ran so strongly in his family. But once Casson joined his office, Nicholson concentrated on the primary role of designer, his work including furniture as well as buildings. Casson, his graphic abilities by now highly developed, was encouraged to exploit them for the purpose of selling Nicholson's schemes. Kit, despite an early Beaux Arts training and his admiration for Lutyens with his dependence on geometry, had formed a wholehearted commitment to functionalism and to the Modern Movement, which was just beginning its feeble struggle for survival in Britain. Casson's ambivalence about this new style of architecture was to grow, but at this period it was barely manifest and certainly did not inhibit him from portraying it in a most flattering way, imbuing Kit's Modernist designs with an informality which served to blur if not mask their more rigorous and uncompromising intentions. Often, he employed a soft-pencil technique to moderate a harsh outline.

As Neil Bingham says, 'the excitement of Nicholson's design for the Gliding Club inspired Casson to create some of his finest architectural drawings'. Now in his mid-twenties, Hugh thrived in the milieu of well-known creative people into which his talents were leading him. He was at first very much in Kit's shadow, though. He did not design furniture and, famously unsporty, did nothing so glamorous as flying. Nor, despite the cherished Lewis Casson connection, was his family anything like as gifted as Kit's. He was gradually to attain a position of force in the office, however, not least because of the potency of his drawings. By now he had, as he recalled, begun 'cautiously to colour in my drawings like children do. It was infantile stuff really because I was frightened of it.' His axionometric of the bar at the Gliding Club, which he made using pen, gouache and Chinese white, was a masterly evocation of Nicholson's design and of the strong, unusual blue, black and rust colour scheme which had been devised by EQ, Nicholson's wife. Only a few architects, now as then, have developed such a confident and vivid style of drawing by their mid-twenties. Meanwhile, Kit asked Reta if she could help out with some of the secretarial work. Not a bit put out at this apparent attempt to divert her from the work for which she was qualified, Reta determined to learn to type, though she never did.

A commission Hugh and Kit both enjoyed was designing the Garden Landscape section of the 1938 Modern Architectural Research Group Exhibition. This MARS Group was at the heart of the Modern Movement in architecture during the thirties. Comprising many gifted foreigners who had escaped from the totalitarianism which was sweeping across Europe – Gropius and Mendelsohn *en route* for the USA, Lubetkin, the Hungarian Maholy-Nagy – the group, many of them communists, most intellectuals, would meet for evening discussions. Casson said, 'I always hated that sort of evening, partly because of the pretentiousness, the thick cigarette smoke and the thick spectacles, and the broken accents. The whole evening was to me a nightmare, so I'd never go. I was on the fringe of it anyway because I'm very thick about theory. I don't like talking about theory, and the MARS Group talked theory all the time. They hadn't had much opportunity to build. It seemed to me that unless you'd been brought up in the cafés of Prague and Vienna and Budapest and Paris ... it wasn't the sort of thing I was brought up to.'

There was more than a hint of xenophobia here, which Casson displayed on other occasions, and no apparent reference to the horror of the regimes from which so many of these foreign architects had escaped. And Casson forebore to mention that such English architects as Basil Spence, Wells Coates, Leslie Martin and his respected friend John Summerson were also part of the MARS Group. His loathing of their meetings was due primarily to the lack of humour with which they were conducted, rather than to any unease about their content.

Casson and Nicholson shared a strong sense of humour, and the office was often filled with laughter.

This was never more so than during the years from 1936 to 1938, when they were working for that rich and strange patron of the arts, Edward James. James, who was about the same age as Casson and Nicholson, was extravagant, though often mean, capricious as only the rich can be, though a most generous patron, nomadic but with a love of houses and architecture, surrounded by friends and sycophants, but nevertheless a tragic and lonely figure. Intrinsically homosexual, he had just endured a short and much-publicized marriage to the dancer Tilly Losch, a marriage which his biographer John Lowe wrote seemed devised in hell'. His father, Willie James, had died when Edward was a small boy, and at the age of twenty-five Edward inherited West Dean, the 12,000-acre Sussex estate on which, as well as the main house, there was a summer home, Monkton, which the elder James had commissioned Lutyens to build for him at the beginning of the century. Shortly after his divorce from Tilly in 1934, James decided to make considerable alterations to Monkton, which he judged to be too cottagey. He had by now become deeply interested in the Surrealist movement, indeed he was its main patron in Britain and a friend of one of its leading proponents, Salvador Dali. It was Dali, widely believed to be his lover at this time, whose ideas he intended to incorporate in his transformation of Monkton and, probably because of Kit Nicholson's family links with Lutyens, he appointed Nicholson executive architect.

The proposed alterations were strange indeed, and in reaction to James's eccentricities, the hilarity with which Kit and Hugh customarily faced their daily tasks now reached dangerous levels. Kit found the Surrealist duo so laughable he could barely remain in the room with them. Casson, whose stern self-control proved to be an abiding asset, was able to restrain himself and acted as go-between.

Monkton, set on the height of the West Sussex Downs with views across the Solent to the Isle of Wight, is, with its enveloping mansard roof and three tall chimneys, often regarded as the prototype of all the medium-sized houses that Lutyens built. James and Dali now briefed Nicholson and Casson to deck it in great sculpted sheets suspended from the first-floor windows. Chimneys were to be draped in dust-sheets which hung in formalized folds so they looked as though they'd been put away for winter, and the central chimney turned into a huge clock which told the days of the week. The fenestration was 'modernized', drainpipes were made to simulate bamboo, new glazed tiles covered the roof, brickwork was rendered and painted puce, a colour Dali mixed himself in the Nicholson office.

Casson baulked at producing exploding swans on the lake, telling Dali he'd have to consult theatre people about that diversion. His own major contribution was a new, curving staircase featuring a porthole window through which an adjacent bathroom and a tankful of fish could both be glimpsed – as well, presumably, as any occupant of the bath. This demonstration of risqué but fairly harmless humour was Edward James's idea, but it was one his architects found intriguing to effect. Casson judged James, who was small and elegant, with tiny feet and hands, to be an attractively creative and witty man. He wasn't so sure about Dali. 'He looked so bizarre with that terrible moustache and an exaggerated way of talking. I suppose I was slightly frightened of him. Kit and I were fairly orthodox architects. This was the first madhouse we'd tried and we weren't very practised at it.'

Monkton was not large but, as designed by Lutyens, it was quietly beautiful with a recessed main façade, symmetrical wings and a felicitous combination of bricks and tiles and white-painted windows. James chose to change all that, and his architects went along with him. Their attitude to meddling with a Lutyens house was that it was acceptable because none of the changes would be irrevocable. Hugh said later, 'I admit we were justifying ourselves because sometimes it's pretty difficult to put things back as they were in a building. The stairway, for instance . . . But I suppose we thought this was a sort of gentleman's folly, and that follies had a long tradition of eccentricity. Anyway, Monkton was small and charming, with a high tiled roof and huge chimneys, a typical Lutyens farmhouse, but not one of his masterpieces.' This was a matter of opinion, and the result of their work was pretty awful.

His position regarding the alterations at Monkton is an early example of the pragmatism which prevented Hugh Casson ever getting entangled in the savage arguments which were to surround architecture in the future. Not the committed Modernist that Nicholson was, he admitted to 'never having been tremendously adventurous as a designer'. Some of his writings at this time reveal his decidedly equivocal view of the Modern Movement. Reviewing F. R. S. Yorke's seminal book *The Modern House in England*, for instance, he expressed misgivings about the efficacy of the very modern house, and wondered whether it would not be better to return to traditional materials.

The irrepressible Casson wit bubbled forth in drawings of a second project for Edward James. The plan was to transport the façade of the Pantheon, which had been designed by James Wyatt, from Oxford Street to the James estate in Sussex, where it would form the façade of a new, modern house. In one Casson crayon-and-pencil drawing of what was to be the rebuilt Wyatt elevation, two small figures can be seen sunbathing in the grounds; in another, the rear elevation, unequivocally modern apart from its decorative screen of caryatids by John Piper, is shown complete with sun-blinds and loungers. There is an unmistakable hint of irreverence, of the playful confronting the classical. The project foundered, but Casson's drawings remain as an animated reminder.

Neither his extensive social life nor his job with Kit Nicholson had prevented Hugh from increasing the range and scope
of his architectural writing. By now he was writing most of the
Astragal column for the *Architect's Journal*. Astragal was and
still is a lighthearted feature which mixes hard facts about
architectural events with a liberal helping of gossip. Read by
all architects with a lively interest in their profession, it was a
perfect vehicle for Hugh's racy style of prose.

One of his most prestigious journalistic jobs was as an advisory editor on another Architectural Press publication, the
Architectural Review, which he undertook along with
Nikolaus Pevsner, who was already moving towards his position as a most distinguished architectural historian. Hugh
described Pevsner afterwards as a man of outstanding industry,
'the only man I ever knew who once fell asleep giving a lecture,
because he was so tired. When people asked him to lecture,
he'd enquire which one they wanted – modern architecture
in France, for instance, seventeenth-century baroque central
European architecture, or the Arts and Crafts Movement, and
whether they wanted it in French, German or English. Then
off he'd go. I was very fond of him and he was a remarkable
man. He was our resident scholar on the *Architectural Review*
because he would know who did what, any period, any time,
any country. I was hired as a sort of common reader, I think.'

There has always been a weight of ponderous verbiage written about architecture, some of it so obscure as to be almost
impenetrable for the average architect, let alone interested lay
people. Hugh's pieces, neither pompous nor philosophical as
he was always quick to point out, but elegantly written and
demonstrating a weight of background knowledge, were
accessible to all. Because he saw everything in visual terms,
the book reviews he wrote for both the *Architect's Journal* and
the *Architectural Review* often contained a vivid word-picture
of how, on the evidence of their writings, he envisaged the

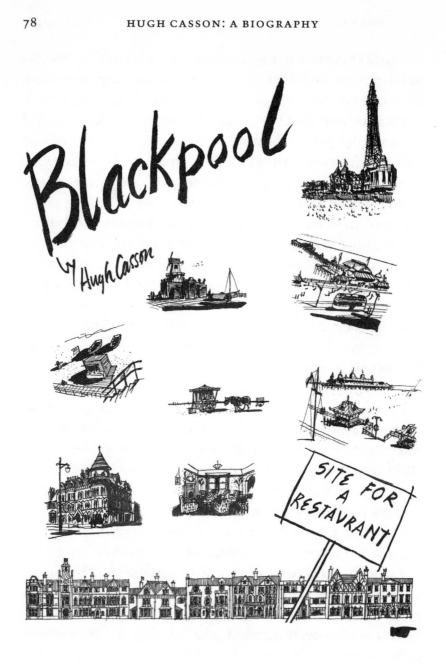

A page from the Architectural Review, *1939.*

authors. This must have been a startling experience for some of them, because his imagination was apt to step outside the boundaries of the probable and enter the realms of the surreal.

Whenever he could give publicity to a friend's efforts and accomplishments in his writing, Casson did so. Or perhaps this was just the last resort of a hard-pressed journalist struggling to fill the space allocated to Astragal? Whatever the reason, architects in the thirties were told about Kit Nicholson's gliding, there was a eulogy of John Betjeman's latest book of poetry, *Old Lights for New Chancels*, and several years later, when Hugh noted an exhibition of war artists at the National Gallery – they included John Piper, Eric Kennington, architect Raymond McGrath, and Edward Bawden with his most moving depictions of Dunkirk – he took care to express regrets that his friend Feliks Topolski was not amongst them, despite his having endured a long and perilous convoy to Archangel in Russia with the Royal Navy.

Casson met John Betjeman first not when they were both working at the Architectural Press, but through another money-earning activity with which he had become involved thanks to the good offices of Robert Harling. Harling – later to become a novelist and long-serving editor of *House and Garden* magazine – was the art director of an advertising agency in Park Street during the thirties. A dapper, urbane figure with a stake in a number of diverse projects, he was keenly interested in modern architecture and Hugh wrote some articles on the subject for a typographical monthly he ran, called *Image*. More interestingly, Harling commissioned Hugh to produce the artwork for a series of advertisements, including drawings to publicize the furniture shop Heals, and a number for Boots the Chemist, depicting the interesting old buildings in which many of their shops were housed. This proved to be a far more lucrative source of earnings than Hugh's work for the architectural magazines, and other young architects and writers, including

Boots the Chemist in Kingston-upon-Thames occupied a
particularly fine old building in the market square.

Hugh's future partner Neville Conder, who had already become known for his fine draughtsmanship and who did some work for Harling when he was still at the Architectural Association School, were also to benefit from his patronage.

When Harling started yet another magazine, called *Decoration*, he appointed John Betjeman as editor and Hugh as assistant editor, with editorial meetings commonly held at the Café Royal, that gathering place for creative people which suited the aspirations and social habits of his new employees perfectly. Hugh wrote a series on architects' homes for *Decoration*, featuring Kit Nicholson's house, including drawings of his furniture designs, Clough Williams Ellis's home in Romney's old house in Hampstead, and number 2 Keats Grove, which belonged to the architect Edward Carter. They were all his friends, but their fastidiously assembled homes made excellent features none the less, so his nepotism seems excusable.

Casson thought Betjeman, with his discoloured teeth, untidy hair and bulbous nose, was 'a strange-looking man', but that he had an engaging sense of the absurd and 'as a person to spend an evening with he was wonderful. One of the most engaging things was that he'd laugh hysterically and naturally at almost everything you said, which is always welcome.' This friendship brought Casson to the very edge of that circle of aesthetes – Robert Byron, Harold Acton, Evelyn Waugh, Lord Birkenhead – who swanned their histrionic way through the thirties, but unlike Betjeman, who clung to their coat-tails, he never quite joined the circle. Perhaps this was because he was of a slightly younger generation, perhaps he was not sufficiently flamboyant, or perhaps, given his evident attachment to establishment values, he didn't really want to. It certainly was not company Reta would have enjoyed, and her preferences were now an important consideration. Looking back in one of his regular moods of introspection many years later, Casson saw a likeness between himself and Betjeman, though: 'He was very amusing, which shows, as a rule, that you're not confident, I think. You're hiding your shyness or unease under a constant lighting of sparklers and hoping people won't notice you aren't as interesting as you think you are. I think John was unconfident and not entirely happy all the time, until his last years when he enjoyed being a telly star. Rather like me. He was a professional jester, the sort who gets asked to parties because he'll liven them up.'

Despite his dalliance on the outer edge of their group, rather than at its centre, Casson shared many interests with Betjeman and his friends, most particularly with Robert Byron, who had helped him with letters of introduction during his stay at the British School in Athens, and who, years later, Casson described as one of the best travel writers of this century. In the mid-thirties, Casson rallied to his support when Byron mounted a furious campaign against a proposal to pull down Carlton House Terrace and replace it with an office block. Byron flew into one of his ungovernable rages at the very idea of such destruction, produced pamplets decrying what he rightly considered a disgraceful proposal, and generally stirred up opposition. His campaign succeeded (though not before one of the houses in the terrace had been destroyed) and was one of the factors which led to the birth of the Georgian Group in 1937, which Casson joined and of which he was later to be Vice President for many years.

From the time that Reta became part of his life, she had given willing if sometimes weary support to Hugh's journalistic and artistic activities, writing home to her parents in 1937, the year before her marriage:

> Next weekend I may be going to Paris with Hugh and Kit. Hugh has got to do some drawings . . . for the AR so I suppose I shall spend my time holding the extra pens and india rubbers. Maybe I'll be allowed to do some of the drawings.

By the time the Second World War started, James and Dali had both decamped to the United States (James not returning to Europe until the war was over), leaving their instructions unrealized for a sitting room with rubber walls that breathed in and out. 'Dali had wanted it to resemble the innards of a not very healthy dog,' Casson recalled later. 'When I said, "What's that like? I've never been inside a dog, healthy or unhealthy," he told us it would be a dog which panted unevenly. We worked out a system of rubber sheeting just clear of the walls, with compressed-air jets behind which were controlled by a machine'. This extravaganza was never to be.

All inessential construction work was now halted. Kit Nicholson shut the office and enlisted in the Royal Naval Volunteer Reserve, where he was commissioned as an officer in the Fleet Air Arm and spent the war flying a wide range of aircraft from Spitfires to Wellington bombers. Hugh was by now on a three-month trip to South Africa with Reta, meeting her father for the first time (her mother was still in England, having stayed on after their wedding), because it had become obvious that if they did not go now there was little likelihood of their doing so for a long while.

Hugh found, to his obvious gratification, that Reta's parents' house in Pretoria, complete with stable block and tennis court and built around a central atrium to ensure cross-breezes, was enormous. Set amongst jacaranda trees in two acres of land, it was far more impressive than his own parents' modest home with its small uncultivated garden. 'It has a lovely garden,' he wrote home to them, 'and is jammed with amazing furniture and pictures.' He didn't tell them about its wonderful view across a valley to the government buildings designed by Herbert Baker, South Africa's most prominent architect, who had worked on the government buildings at Delhi with Lutyens. A spinster cousin, Aimee, ran the household as she had throughout Reta's childhood, helping to care for Reta's younger sister, Isobel, who had been born with Down's Syndrome. Aimee, helped by five or six black servants, including a male cook, gave Mrs Troup the freedom to participate in Pretoria's active social life and was regarded affectionately by them all.

On this visit to her home, Reta was able to show Hugh some of the building projects on which she'd worked during her long summers at home in Pretoria, and particularly in the year after

she had left the Bartlett. These included a small block of flats
in a field owned by her father, which Hugh thought was a
terrific success, and a studio house for an old friend, designed
especially to accommodate her slight disablement. Like so
many women architects, Reta never developed her obvious
talents to become a prolific architect. Teacher, interior
designer, photographer and splendid consort, she was to
become all of those things, but despite her early successful
efforts she did not go on to design many more buildings.

The weather was sometimes bad but they travelled widely,
driving down through Natal to the sea and to Durban. Early on
they visited a game reserve where Dr Troup, one of those
involved in its establishment, was helping with a census of the
animals. All this was recorded in Hugh's weekly letters to
Randal and May in Southampton, some of which were rather

A drawing Hugh made in Pretoria, Reta's home town,
accompanied one of his articles about South African
architecture which was published in Britain.

Left: Reta's mother, Alberta Davis, was born in Demerara and met James MacDonald Troup when she went to South Africa to work as a nurse.

Below: Her father, a Scot, who had come to South Africa because of his weak lungs, became a distinguished physician, one of whose patients was General Smuts.

Below: Hugh's mother May Man came from a family which had a long history of service in the Indian Civil Service. On her marriage to Randal Casson they lived in Burma.

Hugh with his older sister Rosemary in Burma. They were sent home when Hugh was four, and the 1914–18 war was imminent.

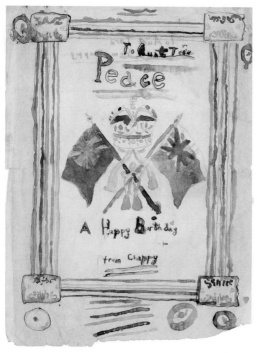

Aged eight, Hugh made this greeting for an aunt's birthday which coincided with the end of the war.

Not normally a member of clubs and societies, he enjoyed the Boy Scouts.

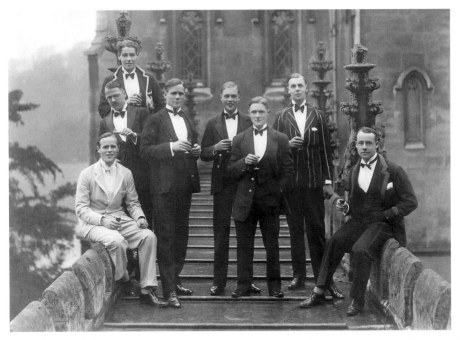

Hugh, like his father, took part in the rowing at Cambridge and he coxed the Lady Margaret first eight, seen here on St John's College's Bridge of Sighs.

Hugh as a young man with his parents, May and Randal.

Hugh and Reta after their marriage at St Margaret's, Westminster.

Top left: Reta just before the war.
Bottom left: Casson in Feliks Topolski's studio.

Top right: Reta painted by Feliks Topolski in 1938.
Bottom right: Kit Nicolson.

Hugh with his daughters
Carola and Nicola.

Hugh and Reta with Carola.

Mrs Aldridge, the Cassons'
housekeeper, with Dinah.

Drawings of contemporary life which Hugh made
on a visit to Italy in 1946.

An artist's bird's-eye view of the Festival of Britain
site on the South Bank.

The Sea and Ships Pavilion designed by Basil Spence, who
later designed Coventry Cathedral.

Leonard Manasseh's winning design for the 51 Restaurant and Bar.
It was later altered to save on cost.

Misha Black was responsible for the decorative treatment of the Bailey Bridge which
was built especially for the Festival.

in the nature of travelogues and displayed nothing of the vivid style he was to develop in the future. Or perhaps he just didn't bother.

One incident on this trip provoked in both Reta and Hugh an abiding antipathy to the apartheid regime in South Africa. They were driven by James, a black African who had worked with the Troup family for years, and was liked by them all. Staying at an hotel in Durban, they found that James was forbidden a room by the management and would be sleeping in the car. Reta said later, rather ingenuously considering her South African upbringing, 'We made a row with the hotel and got him a proper room. It was this which first alerted us to the state of affairs. From then on we wrote letters of protest to South African papers during our stay there, and of course many more over the years to come. The signs of change were barely beginning then, and there was nothing on the surface, it was all underneath.' Having left South Africa at the age of eleven, she knew little of apartheid. With a European education – and husband – she now began to see things differently.

Hugh made few references to the war in his letters home, apart from such brief comments as on 13 August: 'News from home seems as bad as ever, but far less worrying at this distance. I expected it to be worse away from the centre of events, but it isn't.' Nor, at the age of twenty-nine, does there seem to have been any question of his enlisting in one of the fighting services as Kit, six years his senior, had done. He certainly at this point felt no compulsion to do so. But he was due to report for duty as a member of the Auxiliary River Fire Brigade in which he had enrolled before leaving London.

Despite his many other activities, including travel, Hugh continued writing the Astragal column for the *Architect's Journal*. He would go on doing so all through the war and until the Festival of Britain engulfed him. Many of his Astragal columns during 1939, before he set off on his South African trip, had been concerned with problems regarding ARP (Air Raid Precautions), though in that year Frank Lloyd Wright gave four lectures at the RIBA and 'brought for a few weeks romance into our lives so for a time the ARP was forgotten'. By September he was talking of 'statues and monuments disappearing behind casings and sandbags, taking on the appearance of Florentine palaces, complete with rusticated bases'.

He also noted the election of architect Edwin Lutyens as President of the Royal Academy, only the third architect to receive this honour. Casson was to be the fourth, and though Lutyens' reputation as an architect is by far the greater – in 1921 he received the RIBA Gold Medal for Architecture, which Casson never did – there are notable similarities between the two men which became evident as Casson grew older, not least their addiction to abundant social lives. Comparisons may tend to dissemble, but I think that in this case they are often to Casson's advantage. Both men were funny, but whereas Casson was witty, Lutyens was facetious to the point of being embarrassing. Lutyens drew, but Casson drew better. Lutyens decorated his letterheads with his own drawings. So did Casson, and in this he may well have been emulating his predecessor. Lutyens was often regarded as a butterfly, and so was Casson. But Lutyens was apt to commit social solecisms of a high order, witness the scene described in Christopher Hussey's *The Life of Sir Edwin Lutyens*:

On a visit . . . to Castle Acre in Norfolk, where there is an almshouse of which the inmates wear red cloaks and sugar-loaf hats, he upset the decorum of these grave signors being entertained at tea, by capering round the table draped in an old red curtain with a tea cosy on his head and waving a warming pan.

Casson would have been incapable of such gaucherie. When it came to the Royal Academy, Casson was by far the more effective and well-regarded President, though inevitably

Lutyens was handicapped by serving much of his term during wartime.

At the end of 1939, despite his three months in South Africa, Hugh managed to assemble an interesting Review of the Year for the Astragal column, in which he listed some of the best buildings of the year, which he had asked sixty 'more or less famous persons' to select. The first three buildings chosen were the Peter Jones department store in Sloane Square, Battersea Power Station, and the St James's Park headquarters of London Transport. The reputations of all three (despite the Power Station being in a state of dereliction) have survived to this day.

Hugh never regarded any journey, whether in this country or abroad, purely as a holiday. Astragal at that time contained several contributions from 'our South African correspondent', and he also wrote for such publications as the *South African Architectural Record* – forthright, sensible pieces, illustrated by his own drawings or with photographs by Reta, which were generous in praise of what he saw. But his voice was that of the sophisticated European. After being driven round Cape Town on their arrival off the boat, he had written to his parents: 'It's smaller than I expected, with few old buildings, and looks very makeshift and temporary.' Nevertheless, he had become interested in the country during his stay there, and profited from his visit, so he was quite sad to leave when, in late October 1939, he and Reta embarked for England and a precarious future.

V

Camouflage and
Extra-Mural Activities

Despite understandable pressure from Reta's father, Hugh had refused to consider remaining in South Africa. In October 1939, their journey home was in a Union Castle ship which had arrived from Europe packed to the gunwales, and was returning on a zigzag course to avoid submarines. It was blacked out and virtually empty save for the ship's band, which thumped away each night for about fifty doughty passengers, but, this apart, the journey was entirely uneventful.

The Cassons returned to a London which was also blacked out, and had windows covered in criss-cross tape against antici-pated bomb blast. Most people carried gas masks, trenches had been dug in the parks to provide shelter during air raids, the policemen wore tin hats, and there were barrage balloons above the roof-tops, looking curiously festive in what was still a time of phoney war. Hugh approached a number of publications with illustrated articles he had written about South Africa and several were accepted, whilst Reta sold a set of photographs to *Country Life*.

In the next few months Hugh's war effort was limited to duties with the Auxiliary River Fire Brigade, learning to work the switchboard at the Battersea Bridge fire station (one of his few practical accomplishments) and manning a fire-pump barge. He particularly disliked the night watches, which took place on a fireboat moored midstream. This, he declaimed, was a brute – there were no bunks and the only heating in this exceptionally cold winter came from a filthy oil stove which stank. Even worse were the watches which involved sitting in a dinghy midstream between shore and fireboat to keep communications going. The men in his crew were nice, he decided, tough and kind-hearted. But none of them were 'varsity men', as he delicately put it, and he abhorred their language, their coughing and spitting and the loud noise of their radio. 'I've had a soft life till now,' he wrote to Reta's father, 'so I can't really complain – though I never cease to.' After a short period of this spartan regime he developed a persistent sore throat and cough, which by February 1940 temporarily absolved him from Fire Brigade duty.

Casson and his friend Frank Adie both went to French classes, in the hope of improving their knowledge of the language sufficiently to be accepted by the Intelligence Service, to which they had applied. In the event, they were both rejected. Reta started training as a VAD. Meanwhile, Hugh and Reta's existence was peripatetic, since they had let the house in Holland Street before going to South Africa, and were living for the time being with their friends Aline and John Stafford at 2 Ladbroke Terrace. By the spring, Hugh was back on duty with the Fire Brigade, where he decided that the worst aspect was the mental stagnation which afflicted its employees, or at least one of them. Letters to South Africa were now full of news about the Dunkirk evacuation, and Reta told her mother that, according to an acquaintance who was there, the discipline amongst the British troops had been remarkable, contrasting sharply with its lack amongst the French and Belgians.

The fear and talk throughout the country was of invasion. Rumours abounded and the Staffords were advised by a friend in the War Office not to go away on one particular weekend, as there was every expectation that this was when the Germans would make their first landings, and all road traffic would be stopped. At the end of June London had its first air raid. Hugh, meanwhile, was depressed, because he discovered by seeing an advertisement for the Canterbury branch of Boots that the advertising work on which he had been engaged for that company before the war started had now been passed to someone else. But the film *Dark Victory* was on at the local cinema, so he and Reta decided to go and cheer themselves up 'for a shilling each'.

Reta, whose letters to her mother were generally restricted to family news, wrote at the beginning of July:

> Things seem to be going on in much the same manner and one would really never think the country was on the verge of possible annihilation. This is a good thing perhaps, as it shows we are not in a panic, but may be because we don't altogether appreciate what's coming to us. People back from Dunkirk get terribly worked up about the apparent apathy of the country. Whether they are right or not is diffcult to tell. In fact we shan't know till it is put to the test. Quite a large number of people think we can't win . . . An influential friend has put Hugh's name down for the camouflage department. In the meantime, he is writing short stories to keep himself occupied . . .

Hugh's sister Rosemary, who had enlisted in the WAAF (Women's Auxiliary Air Force), came up for the day to see them from her Bomber Command Station on the east coast, and reported that according to the word amongst the pilots, Hamburg no longer existed.

By the end of July, Hugh had been accepted into the Camouflage Service of the Air Ministry, which had promised to deal with the problem, should it arise, of him being, at the age of thirty-one, still eligible for call-up into the armed service. He started training immediately in what he soon came to realize was an inexact science, writing excited letters to his in-laws in South Africa about trips in Anson light bombers to inspect camouflaged aerodromes from the air. The trainees were given parachutes without being told how to use them, but although it was noisy and very hot under the glass roof of the bomber, Hugh enjoyed the whole procedure, particularly since he was able to identify such architectural gems as Stowe, Woburn and Lincoln Cathedral from the air.

The bombing of London had now begun in earnest, and the Staffords had decided to leave London for the country, so on 16 August Hugh and Reta moved to a small flat at 129 Old Church Street in Chelsea, from where, for a few weeks, Hugh commuted to his office at the Ministry while Reta occupied herself with domestic activities like bottling plums. It was an agreeable place in a charming part of London, and on lovely summer mornings they would sit with the big French windows opening out on to the street, eating their porridge and maple syrup for breakfast. Their morale was high, as was that of most Londoners, and when they saw Freda off to Liverpool, from where she was escorting fifteen children who were being evacuated to South Africa, Reta had no desire to go too. She described Freda's task as one she thought unimaginably awful.

A few days later, she wrote telling her parents that she was pregnant with her first child, and though she sounded happy about this impending event, it was clear that their idyllic summer was coming to an end. The bombing was now very much worse. The London Blitz had started and 'Wimbledon got it last night,' she told them in South Africa, with fifteen people killed and fifty-nine injured. If she was out during the daytime, she was always prepared to dive for a shelter when the air-raid warning sounded, as it increasingly did. Buses would generally stop – though this depended on the whim of individual drivers – and passengers would pile off and into the nearest air-raid shelter. At night, Reta and Hugh slept in the basement of the house in Old Church Street along with their landlady, Miss Rose, who snored, so that there was a race to get to sleep before she started. During the long working day at the Ministry, Hugh and his colleagues were adequately provided with air-raid shelters. His friend Frank Adie remained in the Fire Service where, as autumn came, he endured the worst horrors of the Blitz, generally getting to bed only one night in three for weeks on end.

After a bomb fell further down their road in Chelsea, demolishing a terrace of small houses, blowing out the windows in the local dairy and covering them all in dust, Miss Rose decided on 10 September to shut up house. Eventually she fled to the country, but for several days she and the Cassons stayed at the Regent Palace Hotel, sleeping on the floor in the corridor. Here, where there was no danger of flying glass, they lay down with their pillows and rugs alongside many other guests and the shoes which had been put out for cleaning. Reta now found life so queer and disjointed that it seemed unreal. 'Like every person in London, I dread the nights and one just lives for the morning and the blessed all clear.'

The Regent Palace – which rocked when a large bomb fell in Regent Street – had nevertheless become a haven to them and to many other people. Reta remembered: 'Downstairs, there was an extraordinary sight: Jewish people from the East End which was being heavily bombed flooded in to find somewhere safe, and the Regent Palace, owned by Jews, gave them shelter in the basement.' She was now suffering badly from morning sickness, so she was forced to abandon her VAD work. They began looking for a big solid flat where they could stay in their beds during raids. Then all their plans changed because within a few days of arriving at the Regent Palace, Hugh was informed that he was being dispatched, temporarily he thought, to run No. 9 Works Area of the Air Ministry Camouflage Service, roughly from Oxford to Cardiff, and from Stratford-upon-Avon to Salisbury. It was a job for which he was well suited, and which he would enjoy, 'though if the invasion starts,' Reta wrote, 'it could all fall through'.

There was no invasion. She and Hugh ceased their search for another home and left London. They felt great relief at escaping the bombing. Meanwhile, Hugh's parents, whom they had not seen for over six months, were having a frightening time in Southampton, where the bombing was heavy and unremitting. 'They haven't slept in their beds since the middle of June.' They arranged to meet Hugh and Reta for a week's holiday at Cheltenham.

By most standards, the Cassons had an easy war. Hugh did not enlist in any of the fighting services, and the couple were never separated for more than short periods. At first they lodged in one room at 97 Montpellier Street, Cheltenham. Housing difficulties were acute as the town had filled up with civil servants and other evacuees, increasing its population by 30,000. Cooking, living and sleeping in the one large room, with use of the bathroom next door, the Cassons were allowed to bathe once a week on Friday, Saturday being their landlady's night. Occasionally, Reta made a trip to London, arranging to store furniture with their friends Anthony and Elizabeth Chitty, who had taken a large house in Barnet. But, staying with them for the night, she was terrified by the noise from anti-aircraft guns nearby. She braved London again in October to go to her doctor and to see her aunt and uncle, who were perfectly calm despite the cluster of incendiary bombs which had fallen in their garden at Addison Road and on the house next door.

The Cassons stayed in Montpellier Street until after Carola, their first daughter, was born. On 21 October 1940, Reta had written to her parents in South Africa, 'We've had our first bomb in Cheltenham,' and there were to be others, with 'the old familiar whistle of high explosives' disturbing their nights

from time to time; when Birmingham or Bristol was bombed
they could hear the planes going overhead, and often the noise
of anti-aircraft guns. On their second wedding anniversary in
November, an air raid prevented them from going to the cinema
to celebrate. But the bombing was only really serious on 15
December, when they sheltered under the stairs with their
landlords, clutching hot-water bottles and pretending not to
be frightened, while the house shook to loud explosions, plaster
fell from the ceilings, and the lights failed so that they had to
search for candles. The main attack was apparently on Birmingham, but several houses near them were destroyed, with most
damage around the railway station, the high street, the gas
works and a timber factory, and several people were killed.
Local people presumed that Cheltenham had been mis-
taken for Gloucester and had suffered this unwonted assault
accordingly.

Southampton meanwhile was, according to the newspapers,
'another Coventry', with the new Civic Centre destroyed apart
from the tower, which was now unsafe. Though May and
Randal Casson lived on the outskirts of the town, German
planes would swoop down over their house accompanied by
the deafening noise of machine guns. Reta wrote that her
mother-in-law was getting 'nerve shattered', especially as she
was often alone now that Randal was doing voluntary (but
full-time) work as a registrar at the local cottage hospital,
including a long period when he stayed all night, patrolling
the building and its roof-top because of the fear of incendiary
bombs setting it alight. As Reta wrote, 'There is no doubt being
alone is dreadfully demoralizing in a raid.' In the midst of all
this, though, the Southampton shopkeepers carried on
business, with the local grocer, whose shop had been bombed,
turning up the next day at May and Randal's house for their
order and subsequently delivering everything they required
except margarine and bacon. 'Refugees' were streaming out of

the centre of the city to escape the bombing, and with no proper accommodation apparently provided for them, May Casson took in a man, his wife and baby, who were pleasant enough but, as she told Reta, 'absolutely filthy', so that it took May a week to clean blankets, carpets and walls after they had gone.

Carola, Hugh and Reta's first baby, was born in the Imperial Nursing Home, Cheltenham, just across the road from their lodgings in March 1941. Shortly afterwards they moved to a rented house a few miles away on Cleeve Hill. Here they – or at least Reta – led the restricted and quiet life of country people obliged to forgo visits to major towns because of the bombing. She made marmalade, which was unobtainable in the shops, but it had to be grapefruit as there were no Seville oranges. There were no soap flakes either, and ordinary soap was rationed, so she warned her mother in South Africa not to send fancy clothing for the baby. Everything must be simple and easily washed.

Food rationing was eased by the regular food parcels from South Africa, and Reta would write letters of relief and gratitude when butter arrived after lengthy delays. 'I was worried that the delay meant another merchant ship has been lost. But the butter has now arrived safely and seems to be in perfect condition.' Rations were supplemented by vegetables grown in their large, ramshackle garden and from the few hens they kept. 'Could you send me some more crystallized fruit to give to the neighbours, who give us eggs, vegetables and fruit from their gardens? But no more cheese. The ration is large and we're always being told to eat more.' Tea was sent on to her mother-in-law so that it could be distributed to people in Southampton. 'None of our class use their tea ration, but the lower class drink more and I think those of Southampton need it more than those of Cheltenham.' A duck called Jemima laid nothing, but was an affectionate soul who, when they gave her away prior to their departure towards the end of the war, walked back to them from several miles away.

May and Randal Casson would occasionally come to stay at Cleeve Hill as a respite from the terrible bombing they were enduring at home in Southampton. In Cheltenham, they had difficulty sleeping because of the quiet, but enjoyed being able to shop in peace. Reta's life at Cleeve Hill was, by contrast, peaceful to the point of boredom.

For Hugh, who had been allocated a small car to travel around the area, it was different. The RAF had by now adopted a dispersal procedure, with small groups of aeroplanes hidden around the countryside in portable hangars which could be put up or taken down as required. The camouflage officer's job was to travel around his area, selecting sites for these structures and then disguising them to look like barns, roadside garages with petrol pumps and derelict cars, or cottages with gables, chimneys and a line of washing; anything rather than hangars. It was what the artist Julian Trevelyan described in his memoir *Indigo Days* as 'the formidable technique of deception' (as opposed to concealment). Architects and artists like Casson and Trevelyan were employed as camoufleurs in considerable numbers during the early years of the war, though in Trevelyan's case it was as an officer in the Royal Engineers. He writes in *Indigo Days* about working with Oliver Messel to disguise the pill boxes with which the country had been strewn.

We camouflage officers were given full rein to our wildest fancies. Oliver was here in his element, and he turned many of them into gothic lodges, and he even got special thatchers all the way from Norfolk to finish one of them. Others he ingeniously disguised as caravans, haystacks, ruins and wayside cafés, always with great attention to detail.

Hugh, not unlike Messel in his taste for theatrical illusion and his intrinsic ability to enhance almost everything on which

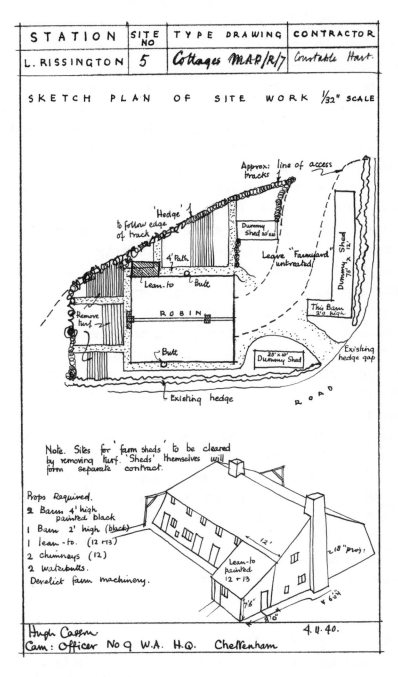

STATION	SITE NO	TYPE DRAWING	CONTRACTOR
L. RISSINGTON	5	Cottages MAR/R/7	Constable Hart.

SKETCH PLAN OF SITE WORK ⅟₃₂" SCALE

Approx: line of access tracks

'Hedge' to follow edge of track

Dummy Shed 20'x10'

Leave "Farmyard" untreated

Dummy Shed 7.5' x 12'

4' Path

Lean-to

Butt

ROBIN

This Barn 2'0 high

Remove turf

Butt

Existing hedge gap

25' x 10' Dummy Shed

Existing hedge

ROAD

Note. Sites for 'farm sheds' to be cleared by removing turf. 'Sheds' themselves will form separate contract.

Props Required.
2 Barns 4' high painted black
1 Barn 2' high (black)
1 lean-to. (12 r13)
2 chimneys (12)
2 Waterbutts.
Derelict farm machinery.

12'

18" proj!

Lean-to painted 12 + 13

7'6"

6'0"

8'0"

4.11.40.

Hugh Casson
Cam: Officer No 9 W.A. H.Q. Cheltenham

Wartime camouflage work required prosaic but meticulously informative drawings.

he worked, enjoyed his task of deception with its opportunity for the occasional flash of humour. And it was work which enabled him to polish his techniques as a water-colourist, using colour on his camouflage drawings in a bold and experimental way that he had never attempted before. He sounded quite startled years later when someone asked him if he'd actually been involved in constructing and painting his schemes for concealment. That was a task for others. Hugh was never a craftsman or even a handyman, never even attempted any of the useful do-it-yourself tasks around the home with which most men struggle, and probably – apart from the scene-painting weekends while he was at Cambridge – never held a paintbrush for anything less effete than to make a water-colour. Now though, 'because you had to give instructions for various standard camouflage colours', he really became a self-taught colourist, making his serious and urgent task at Cheltenham into a vehicle for some delicate and beautiful images. He began to use colour with confidence. 'We'd learnt water-colour at Architecture School, but in a different way. We were taught to put great washes over our architectural drawings, papers the size of a hearth rug, because that was the fashion in those days. It was really a nineteenth-century fashion, still taught at the Beaux Arts. You never touched the paper with a brush, you touched it with the water on the end of your brush so that the brush never made a mark. It was quite tricky because everything had to be frightfully wet and as everything dries so quickly in a centrally heated studio you had to work at speed with big brushes. But by the time I was working in camouflage, I was rid of the Beaux Arts system, doing small water-colours, and you didn't have to worry so much.' Even so, the lesson about having that bubble of water between brush and paper was an instructive one. The Air Ministry might have been disconcerted to know that he took several of his better depictions of camouflaged airfields with him into civilian life.

Four or five hours a week were spent in flying over the countryside to gauge its appearance in different weather, in all the seasons, and under a variety of conditions. The view from the air taught him not to move about in tall grass near the sites of his deceptions, destroying the smooth shadows and potentially betraying the presence of something important nearby to enemy airmen. These trips, which were vital in the effort to improve and perfect untried methods, were made in any aeroplane which happened to be flying that day, from old Coastal Command Hudsons to bombers towing gliders or Anson bombers and reconnaissance planes. Casson clearly relished the flights despite one hair-raising experience about which Reta wrote home to South Africa in October 1940.

Hugh had a bit of excitement last week. He had to inspect one of his districts from the air, and, in landing, the pilot made a bit of a mess and shoved on his brakes too quickly and the whole of his undercarriage pushed up through the floor. Hugh hadn't realized what had happened and felt nothing beyond a slight jar and proceeded to get out of the plane and found himself gently lifted to the ground by first-aid crew who had rushed to the scene the minute the plane came to rest. Ambulance, doctors, nurses and fire engine, all longing to treat him for something, but he wasn't even suffering from shock.

In addition to concealing the hangars, hedges were grubbed up to make airfields, but then painted on again to disguise the great open space which was now such a giveaway from the air. 'It's amazing how well it worked, especially if you painted a road on too, and sprayed the grass with sulphuric acid in one place to make a yellow field. It became really difficult to spot them at a distance.'

The war had, meanwhile, barely interrupted Hugh's output in other areas of endeavour. Once he had become established

*Cheltenham with its fine Regency buildings was an
appropriate subject for several articles.*

in his camouflage job for the Air Ministry, and had settled in
Cheltenham, he was able to resume freelance journalism at an
unrelenting pace. Now that he could not always rely on quite
so much active support from Reta, who was engrossed with
caring for first one and then two small children, work was even
more demanding. One day at the end of 1940 he had a telegram
from the *Architect's Journal,* saying that their printers' building had been destroyed in the great fire raid on the City of 29
December and would he send copies of his New Year Review
and Astragal column, complete with drawings? All the drawings had to be re-done and the articles copied. And with so
many people in the services, there was, quite apart from his
contributions to the Architectural Press publications, plenty of
other journalistic work available. Newspapers and periodicals
may have become reduced in size and number to a lamentable
extent during the war, but many were stoutly determined to
keep going. In 1943 Hugh had an article about Cheltenham,
'A Planned Regency Town', published in the *Geographical
Magazine,* which was probably recycled from one he had produced for the *Architectural Review* on the same subject. Later
that year a joint effort with Reta was published in *The Ideal*

Home and Gardening, a rather curious article which would be unlikely to make it into print now. Hugh's contribution questioned the viability of women architects, pointing out the difficulties of site work (with the possibility of a dangerous display of legs), the distracting effect women had in offices, but most sinister of all, stating that 'by nature and upbringing they are trained to deal with small things and their outlook is cramped, lacking wide mental vision for large-scale creative work. Generally they make better secretaries than directors, nurses than matrons, employees than employers.' He went on to recount how women get married, have children, don't trust or have confidence in each other . . . and so on.

This was followed by a smart response from 'Margaret Troup', slapping down each of these arguments, without malice but with considerable vigour, and reminding him that the competition for the new Shakespeare Theatre at Stratford-upon-Avon had not long since been won by a woman, Elizabeth Scott. The whole thing must have been some editor's idea of a joke, intent on raising hackles and boosting circulation, but it certainly doesn't seem very funny half a century later. In any case it backfired, because Hugh's article was illustrated with a simply stunning house designed by that distinguished practitioner, Serge Chermayeff, Reta's with an inoffensive but forgettable house by a woman.

Was his point made? Although no architect, male or female, would have the nerve to express such politically incorrect views nowadays, there are still comparatively few women who have attained a prominent position in the profession or produced outstanding buildings.

Hugh made brief visits to London, staying with friends and maintaining his contacts in a world which was to become so important to him after the war, and in March 1942 both he and Reta spent three days in London, staying at the Regent Palace, lunching with friends, taking tea with her Aunt Winifred, going to see *The Man Who Came to Dinner* at the theatre and spending nearly all their clothing coupons on material, some of it for a coat for Hugh. But such self-indulgence was rare, and the pace of Hugh's work unrelenting. Despite an initial resistance, he had even been persuaded by Seton White, Principal of the Cheltenham Art School, to teach architecture there every Wednesday evening. Ronald Green, who entered Hugh's life again after the war, was an art student at Cheltenham at the time and recalls how these evenings under Casson's tutelage brightened the dull week. 'He was a gigantic inspiration, particularly in contrast to the other staff members who tended to be artists who'd run out of steam. He'd rush in in his bright-red braces and beautifully designed watch, eyeing all the girls. It was like someone from another world.'

Reta, writing home to her parents around this time, told them how tired he was, because quite apart from this sort of additional commitment, all his writing was done in the evenings too. He was apparently very upset when, in 1942, several people in one day told him they had assumed he was about thirty-eight, not thirty-two. 'I must say, he's looking ancient these days,' Reta wrote. She spent much of her spare time sewing, as the relatively small allocation of clothing coupons under the rationing scheme to which everyone was now subjected meant they had been wearing most of their garments for three years without hope of renewal and these were beginning to disintegrate under the strain. Hugh had got so thin, his frayed clothes hung on him. Occasionally he spent a Sunday in bed to recover from his exhaustion. (Despite his apparently prodigious energy, he often resorted to this method of recuperation in the hard-working years ahead.)

Meanwhile, Reta's life was virtually confined to coping with the demands of two small daughters (Nicola had been born in 1943), though as was to be a pattern in the future, she also helped Hugh whenever she could. It was she who searched out appropriate illustrations when he lectured on modern architecture at the art school, as well as feeding the old-fashioned slide lantern, and it was she who had photographed Cheltenham to illustrate his article on the subject. 'Hugh is absolutely firm and drives me out whenever the sun appears,' she wrote to her parents, and the article was in fact notable for her marvellously evocative photographs. True to her generation, Reta gave prime importance to Hugh's activities, sometimes at the expense of her own. Meanwhile, Hugh fainted one day after Sunday lunch – he had low blood pressure and he was probably working too hard. When he took to his bed with flu, Reta missed his help in filling the coal hod and burying the rubbish, which was their means of waste disposal.

Despite Hugh's lifelong gregariousness, social life was sparse, though they occasionally had friends from their previous existence to stay. Jean Jackson-Stops, who would always remain a close friend of the Cassons, remembered a weekend visit. 'There were wonderful views from the house at Cleeve Hill; you could see Tewkesbury. They had Carola and Nicola by then, but Reta was not honestly very good with small children. She needed them to be older to really relate to them. Hugh, though, was wonderful from the start. It was bitterly cold, and I remember Hugh and I hanging out nappies together. They froze instantly. My husband was away in the services and I had a baby son, and that weekend I remember as one of the only jolly interludes in the war.' It was Hugh, with his fine singing voice, who, despite an already frantically busy life, would sing to the small girls when they were in bed at night and who, with his usual economy of means, had developed a technique for doing this in a manner which quickly sent them off to sleep.

Visits from Hugh's parents were rare now. With many young schoolteachers, men and women, away in the services, the retired and elderly were being called upon as replacements.

Randal had taken on a job as part-time Mathematics teacher at Winchester College, where he worked from the spring term of 1942 to the spring term of 1944. He was popular with the boys (Geoffrey Howe was one of his pupils), and May entertained some of them at her home. A handwritten note dated 31 August 1943 was carefully preserved amongst her papers.

> Thank you very much for your letter. I am most grateful to you for being so kind to David; it is nice for him to have friends to go to, as in these days I have no home in England. I shall look forward to visiting Winchester again next time I am home; I have very pleasant recollections of my visit in May last.

It is signed B. L. Montgomery, General, Eighth Army, and headed Eighth Army, Sicily. His son David, whose mother had died in 1937, was one of Randal Casson's pupils.

At Cleeve Hill, Hugh and Reta's small circle included potter Charlotte Bawden, whose husband Edward was away in the Mediterranean serving as a war artist, and furniture designer Dick Russell and his family, who had come to live at Torrington for the war years. 'Torrington was some miles away and it was difficult getting there. We went by bus and we had to change buses and so on, but all the same a visit to the Russells became the highlight of our month.'

Reta was never a domesticated woman. Her early years in South Africa had conditioned her to believe that 'others' undertook such menial tasks as housework and cooking and she would not have seen her own mother, who had cousin Aimee as well as several black servants to run her home, engaged in anything other than the lightest duties. For a while she employed a German refugee to help at Cleeve Hill, but life was eased immeasurably after a while by the arrival of Mrs Aldridge, who came three times a week to help with both the housework and the children, and who would very soon become an essential feature in their lives. Hugh continued to do his fair share of the washing up in the household, but Reta was pleased to tell her mother that he would now be able to enjoy his Sundays at home without having to scrub the kitchen floor.

Towards the end of the war, with his job virtually at an end since camouflage was irrelevant in combating the V1s – the flying bombs, or doodlebugs as they were commonly known – and V2s, which were now the main weapons of air attack, Hugh showed some of his water-colours – often of planes crashed by trainee pilots, as well as straightforward camouflage designs – to the owner of a local art gallery, who offered him an exhibition. With permission from the Air Ministry, and 'censored' stamped on the back of each painting, he went ahead, and for the first but far from the last time, found his work was popular. 'It has', as he said, 'a sort of fatal charm which I wasn't very proud of but somehow found I couldn't avoid.' Proud of it or not, he never hesitated to show his work when an exhibition was in the offing.

Reta wrote home at this time, 'I think he's fairly definitely decided to go on the staff of one of the architectural papers after the war. He's received pressing invitations to do so and I think he's really destined to write and illustrate architecture rather than do architecture proper.' For once she underestimated her husband. That sort of work would never be enough to satisfy this multi-talented man. But for the present, with his camouflage work completed, he accepted a job at the Ministry of Town and Country Planning, which he started in April 1944. There, a small research department had been established to work on such putative postwar matters as prefabricated housing and the planning of new towns.

Hugh Casson was essentially an urban person, and although it meant leaving his family in Cheltenham at first, it was a relief to be back in the city for the remainder of the war. Not only did he thrive on the bustle and noise of a major city with all its scope for human encounters and exposure to the arts, but living in London meant he was able to keep in touch with editors more easily and generate a steady flow of the writing jobs he enjoyed. It was now that he collaborated with his architect friend Anthony Chitty to write a book on the housing situation, present and future, under the pseudonym Hugh Anthony. An austere little publication, as befitted the times, *Houses, Permanence and Prefabrication* packed a lot into its sixty-five pages: a history of the English house, an analysis of technical methods available, both at home and abroad, and an exhortation to government to employ standardization and Meccano-type construction in order to achieve the four million homes the country needed. For this was published in 1945, when architects generally were evangelical in their promotion of such methods, believing them to be capable of solving the vast housing problem which had developed during the war years.

By now the driving force of ambition had entered Hugh Casson's blood. Patience Clifford (later Patience Bayne Powell), who worked with him during that period at the London offices of the Ministry of Town and Country Planning, remembers that he often worked late. 'We'd say: "What's all this about? Why don't you stop and come to the pictures?"' But his habit of grindingly hard work was already formed. At the beginning, despite the doodlebugs which were still bringing stress into the lives of so many Londoners, he would often stay in the city during the weekend to finish drawings for one of his journalistic commissions, rather than going back to Cheltenham. Lacking a drawing-board in his own lodgings, he would often end up at Patience's flat in Cheyne Walk, sweeping her work aside to make way for his own. At one period he lodged at the Lewis Casson flat in Swan Court in Chelsea, and he'd take Patience back there for breakfast after they had spent the night at their office, fire-watching together. 'Even at eight in the morning, Sybil Thorndike would be putting on a great theatrical performance,' she remembered.

Patience had now joined that growing bevy of women who were to be known by Hugh Casson's family as his girlfriends. Treated with almost embarrassing physical affection by him on every possible occasion, and the recipients, each and every one, of exquisite little drawings on St Valentine's Day, they were (most of them) accepted by Reta as an inevitable part of his life, though she occasionally felt resentful. Several, including Patience, became her friends too, and she gave little consideration to the idea that some of these relationships may have become more serious. When he took part in *Desert Island Discs* in November 1961, Hugh Casson described himself as the happiest married man in England. The girlfriends probably did nothing more than mop up the overflow of his superabundant capacity for affection. This was likely to have been the case during the period of nearly two years when Reta and the children remained in Cheltenham whilst Hugh was working in London. By June 1944 the threat of doodlebugs had begun to diminish, but Hugh was tired after nights of fire-watching and for a few days he joined Reta, who had taken Carola and Nicky to stay with her friend Jean Jackson-Stops in the Midlands.

At the Ministry of Town and Country Planning, where he was described as a Technical Officer, Casson shared a room with Peter Shepheard (now Sir Peter), who was himself destined for a distinguished career as architect, landscape architect, planner and academic. Their boss was William (later Lord) Holford, and another colleague was Colin (later Sir Colin) Buchanan, who became a cogent force in postwar planning. For about eighteen months, Hugh Casson worked here, largely engaged, in what he always said was a lowly capacity, on the early planning of the new towns (most specifically Stevenage), assessing housing types such as those made of aluminium and the popular prefabs, and writing housing manuals. It was work he found both varied and interesting, and he enjoyed the companionship of the other architects in the office. Reta's life at Cleeve Hill was, by contrast, rather lonely and entirely devoted to caring for her children and the home. When Hugh came for the weekend in February 1945, they spent it erecting a new chicken-house and choosing paint colours for a house they were hoping to buy in London. They would not be able to move into it until the following summer, because it needed bomb-damage repairs, and priority was given to houses which were occupied. Meanwhile, a permit for a new sink, boiler and other essential equipment would probably take weeks to come through. Coupons were still necessary to buy utility furniture which was the only new furniture available, but they had just about enough from pre-war days, and would make do with their old curtains rather than expending precious clothing coupons on new ones.

A month later, Reta was thanking her mother for sending jellies, which were unobtainable in England and were a great treat for the children at Carola's fourth birthday tea. Hugh came down from London that weekend, bringing Patience Clifford with him.

The war in Europe came to an end in May 1945. Repairs were finally completed on the house the Cassons had bought in Sheffield Terrace, a narrow road to the north of Kensington High Street, and on 11 July the whole family returned from Cheltenham to live there. The move, which involved retrieving their furniture from friends with whom it had been stored during the war, was a complicated feat of coordination, but by the New Year of 1946 they were relatively comfortably ensconced. With them came Aldridge, as they called her, who had proved herself invaluable at Cleeve Hill and who was now willing to move with them to London. She would be resident housekeeper, relieving them (most particularly Reta) of a great many tedious domestic responsibilities for years to come. A war widow, she brought two boys with her, one her own, one the son of her dead sister, and though there were occasional difficulties in what was now a large and crowded household, for she was a strong, dominating personality, the advantages,

The large and crowded household in Sheffield Terrace.

as far as Reta was concerned, were inestimable. Aldridge's duties did not, however, encompass the small DIY jobs usually – in those days anyway – undertaken by the man in a household. Hugh was incapable of even changing a power plug. It was Reta who, with great competence, undertook everything of this nature.

Even after the birth of a third daughter, Dinah, the following year, the house in Sheffield Terrace was, or so they persuaded themselves, just big enough for them all. Hugh continued to work relentlessly, with Reta, orderly and calm, managing the organizational side of their domestic arrangements, as she would always do, while Mrs Aldridge took charge of the

children and the household chores. The weather was bitterly
cold that winter – some said the coldest in living memory –
but Reta had managed to ensure they got their full ration of
coal and coke, which meant they had hot water and were warm.
She described England as being in a very low condition, but
'We're used to it,' she wrote stoically to her mother, 'unlike
some South Africans who think it's on its last legs.' She didn't
bother to join the long queues which formed from 6.30 a.m.
one day when there was a delivery of nylons in the shops.
Queuing was still a way of life, almost a social pursuit for
some, and the shoemakers Mansfield advertised one of their
designs as 'A Good Queue Shoe'.

In 1946 Casson made another slim contribution to the solution of the housing problem. His book *Homes by the Million*,
published by Penguin, was a succinct account of how eight
million Americans were housed or re-housed during the years
1940–45. The facts, illustrated by some of the best schemes in
this huge US government project, were spelt out in uncompro-
misingly informative language, and *Homes by the Million*
must have been inspirational to young British architects
returning from the war eager to build a better land; to poli-
ticians too, if they read it. It concludes with what the author
considered a definition of the three fundamental principles of
modern housing for that time:

First, houses cannot be provided on a national scale, in the right
place and for those who need them most, without the direction,
coordinating effort and assistance of the State.

Second, they cannot be provided quickly and cheaply enough
without the reorganization of our building industry on more
modern lines, including the increased use of prefabrication and standard sizes.

Third, houses must be accompanied by communal facilities correctly placed in relation to them.

Some, but not all, of this was to be followed in the years ahead.

During the same period, Casson was editing a series of small books, *Introductions to Architecture*, for his friend and patron from pre-war years, Robert Harling at Art and Technics. To Paul Reilly (later Lord Reilly of the Design Council, but at the time a recently demobilized Army Officer) he apportioned Regency Architecture, to Professor A. E. Richardson, who had expounded with such passion on the subject of Classical architecture when Hugh was a student at the Bartlett, Georgian Architecture, and to Neville Conder, who would one day be his partner (then recently qualified), Modern Architecture. Most young architects – and Hugh was only thirty-five – would have wanted that last one for themselves. Instead, and significantly, he chose Victorian Architecture, writing a longish essay in his usual idiosyncratic style, but investing it with the discernment and lyrical descriptions which distinguished all his work on subjects with which he was sufficiently engaged. He may have settled upon the Victorian period for himself because none of his friends wanted to tackle what was then a deeply unfashionable period in architecture. The project strengthened what was to become an abiding interest, not only in the architecture of the nineteenth century, but in its art too. In the meantime, though, he made no great claims to erudition. As he said in his introduction to *Victorian Architecture*:

Ignorance, it has been said, is a prerequisite of the historian. This is particularly true of anyone who attempts to survey, however superficially, the achievements of the nineteenth century. The material at hand is so overwhelming in bulk and so bewildering in texture and colour that all he can do is pick over the tumbled debris of this vast quarry, and select at random a few stones which, when held up to the light, may reveal something of the nature of the complex mass from which they came. This book does not claim to be more than a handful of such stones, all of them, it should be made clear, dislodged by the pickaxes of previous investigators. Those who look for original research or detailed survey must await those heavier volumes which it is the intention of the author to read as soon as they appear.

Casson's light, easy style and readiness to expound on most subjects was engaging, and his name continued to crop up in a variety of unexpected publications in this immediate postwar period: he wrote about prefabrication, for instance, in a French magazine called *CADRAN*, and later on he wrote a long diatribe about Oxford Street, a cross between architectural assessment, shoppping guide and an early plea for environmental awareness, which appeared in *Leader* magazine. Partly because he needed the money to help maintain his family, but also because he loved to see his name in print and to be caught up in the urgency and *faux bonhomie* of journalism, he continued to write for women's magazines and the women's pages of the national newspapers. These articles were on home-refurbishment projects and he tossed them off with very little effort, though his accompanying drawings gave them panache and reader appeal.

Early in 1946 his life had resumed its pre-war course. With his family now back in London, he rejoined Kit Nicholson, newly returned from naval service, to get their practice going again in premises at 110 Brompton Road in South Kensington. 'The difficulty with private practice then,' Casson said later, 'was that there was virtually no building. You needed a licence, there was a restriction on size of buildings and the use of materials, and although the problems made people use their ingenuity, it was certainly not an easy time. Many young and idealistic architects went to work in the public service. They'd learnt about mutual support for survival during the war, and I think they now wanted to put this into practice to overcome the low quality of existence which we were reduced to, and

Long after Kit Nicholson's death, Casson made this sketch
of him in a note to his son, Tim Nicholson.

help rebuild the bombed cities so that they were better than
they had been before the war.'

Casson and Nicholson chose to remain in private practice.
Kit's circle had grown during the war and several of his new
contacts now became the source of work. He knew Whitney
Straight, then Deputy Chairman of British European Airways,
and Philip Wills, the airline's technical manager and head of
research, was a fellow glider pilot. Kit was appointed BEA's
design consultant and began to establish a useful reputation as
an industrial designer, designing ticket offices for BEA in Paris,
Stockholm and Glasgow, as well as interiors and exterior livery
for the fleet of aeroplanes. For Ferranti, he designed striking
television sets and radios in what was then considered to be a
very modern style. There was also a big sideline in stands for

the exhibitions which were such a feature of British life in these early postwar years, and the beginnings of residential work for people like the wealthy and glamorous d'Avigdor Goldsmids.

Casson's perspective sketches – light, charming and endowing every scheme with a most beguiling insouciance – were once again crucial. The exhibition stands, in particular one he designed for British Tube Investments in about 1948, demonstrated the flair for this sort of work which would help him make such a success of the Festival of Britain. As he pointed out himself, the immediacy (no long-drawn-out procedure as there is with a building) and the theatricality, which are prerequisites of exhibition stands, made designing them a job which perfectly suited his mercurial temperament. But there was also a perkiness about his drawings then, perhaps in order to cheer up the working day as well as serve their primary purpose. People waiting in a sketch of a proposed air terminal at St Enoch's Station, Glasgow, for instance, have an angular jocularity, an engaging air of good cheer, which the Nicholson clients liked.

Hugh, divested of many domestic responsibilities, was drawing and writing wherever he could find an opening, in addition to his work as an architect. Reta wrote home to her parents in 1946, thanking them for some money and telling them that Kit and Hugh between them were collecting quite a bit of work. 'In the meantime, his drawings are in great demand, and he is considered the best freehand architectural draughtsman in the country.' Allowing for a measure of uxorial hyperbole, the Casson reputation was quite obviously becoming established.

That his work was well regarded by his peers is evident from the huge number of drawings he had published in architectural magazines at this time: some to illustrate his own writings, some adjoined to the work of others. In 1946, for instance, a series of his drawings was published in the *Architectural*

*One of Hugh's proposals for the area around
St Paul's Cathedral.*

Review to illustrate proposals for replanning the precincts around St Paul's Cathedral. None of the proposals was adopted, but the drawings stand as a clear and contributory reminder of what might have been, had commercial demands, amongst others, not intervened.

Hugh, who was already displaying his remarkable gift for gathering up appropriate people to work for him, had recruited his 'girlfriend' Patience Clifford, from the Ministry of Town and Country Planning, to work in the Nicholson office. She was surprised at how much responsibility she was given, and what a good atmosphere there was. 'Kit was the more authoritative of the two, the boss, I suppose. They spoke entirely in jokes and puns together, but it was always kindly. There was never any malice or snideness.' Other architects – Gontran

Goulden, Reta's friend from Bartlett days, Robert Goodden and Dick Russell, for instance – had an informal office-sharing arrangement with them, and Neville Conder, Casson's future partner, came for six months soon after qualifying. He loved the place – remembers Casson and Goulden doing a sort of two-man music-hall act at tea-time some days. Fresh out of the Architectural Association school, he shared a devotion to the tenets of the Modern Movement with many architects of his generation. He was startled by Casson's seemingly flippant approach to design in the short period that he worked as a junior in the office. 'I remember my surprise at Hugh's enthusiasm for Lutyens. He probably acquired this from Kit. My generation had not yet got around to allowing credit to Victorians, and Lutyens seemed to group with them rather than with the Arts and Crafts movement, which had already been given a licence of approval by Pevsner. And I admit to being horrified by Hugh's catholic approach to exhibition design: a stand for Berketex was a fibrous plaster rendering of Strawberry Hill Gothic. This seemed shocking to me in a period when the battle for a modern architecture had yet to be won.'

However, it was a desire to work on 'real buildings' rather than a stream of exhibition stands, and not his dismay at Casson's less than purist approach, which drove Neville away to richer and more stimulating pastures at this point. But he would be back.

It was now, even before the Festival of Britain launched him into the public domain, that Hugh began, quite deliberately, to build up a huge circle of friends, many of them already distinguished, others on the same upward trajectory as himself. Reta, after a trip to her home in South Africa, was about to start working again, and their daily routine revolved around work and what their friend Dosia Verney called 'a social life'.

It was Mrs Aldridge who cared for both Hugh and the six-

month-old Dinah when Reta, whose father had died the previous year, returned to South Africa for some months towards
the end of 1947, taking the two older girls to visit their maternal
grandmother. Reta had handed the child over, saying, 'This is
your baby now, Aldridge. You look after her.' Aldridge loved
Dinah from that day, and when the two older girls returned
from South Africa, they felt excluded from her affections,
which all seemed to be directed towards their younger sister.
Their relationship with Mrs Aldridge was to be difficult thence-
forth. Otherwise it was a happy household, with Hugh, a gentle
and loving father, right at the centre of it, despite his growing
outside commitments as well as his 'daytime job' in architecture. He often played with his daughters when they were small
children, though they couldn't help but be aware that his mind
was generally away elsewhere. The playroom at the top of the
house in Sheffield Terrace had his desk at one end, and he
would sit there working while they played noisily at the other
end of the room. But his powers of concentration were phenom-
enal, and it didn't seem to disturb him at all. Peter Shepheard
liked to describe a train journey with Hugh during which they
had an animated conversation about a current architectural
event; at the same time, Hugh wrote his next Astragal column
for the *Architect's Journal*. The
column was every bit as good as
usual, according to Shepheard.

   In 1948, an exhibition of his
water-colours was mounted at
the Architectural Association
School. The subject was buildings, embellished by ancient cars,
the odd alley cat, and a flock
of unwontedly elegant nuns,
painted during an early postwar
trip to Italy. Gordon Cullen, an

*A trip to Italy immediately after the war produced
innumerable drawings.*

acclaimed architectural draughtsman himself, reviewed the
exhibition in the AA Journal, with a prolix concentration on
technique which was presumably dictated by the readership at
which it was aimed. He was interesting on one more general
point, though.

There are some people who can impose character on a drawing in
spite of an almost complete disregard for the shape of the object
represented. Such people as Thurber. Others, like Mr Casson, achieve
their end by a most complete realization of the anatomy of the thing
drawn. Thus four lines portray a dome that is round, stable and
symmetrical, his fifth makes it windswept. This ability is built up
on painstaking observation of volumes, planes, perspective and so
on, and also the courage to have a go. That's the fun of drawing. It is
an adventure, rather like walking a tightrope.

There was perception despite the verbosity here. Hugh took chances with his drawing as he did in so many other ways. By now he was also aware of the exigencies of print. These drawings, delicate and exquisitely detailed though they are, translate brilliantly into the printed images which accompanied Cullen's critique, even on the thin, greyish paper of the immediate postwar period. One, depicting the Villa Medici at Rome, is masterly in its apparently casual and informal evocation of that place.

VI

The Festival of Britain

Hugh was perfectly content with his life in these early postwar years, his work in the Nicholson office satisfactorily balanced by the continual flow of journalism and illustration with which he enriched his income. If real architecture was for the time being hard to come by, the firm's output largely limited to exhibition-stand design, there was plenty of that, and every prospect that soon major postwar construction would begin and that their prospects would be enhanced accordingly.

Then, in the early summer of 1948, everything changed when in a telephone call from Gerald Barry, the man who had been appointed as the Festival's Director General, Hugh was asked if he would consider becoming Director of Architecture for the 1951 Festival of Britain. The reason why he was plucked from the large number of bright, ambitious architects who had come back from the war, anxious to demonstrate their abilities and further their careers, remains unclear, not least to Casson himself. Some say it was because Barry, editor of the *News Chronicle* and the Festival's main propounder, had noticed Casson's writing about architecture in national newspapers (including his own) as well as in a number of recherché publications like the pre-war *Night and Day*, and George Weidenfeld's hardcover periodical *Contact*, in the postwar period. Others surmised that it was because of his reputation as an exhibition designer. Frederick (later Sir Frederick) Gibberd said that he was offered the job first and turned it down as not being sufficiently concerned with actual architecture; he took on the job of designing the shopping centre and market square in the Live Architecture Exhibition at Lansbury instead. Hugh's cousin John Casson even suggested that his father Lewis had mentioned Hugh's name in powerful and appropriate circles. Most likely it was a combination of all these factors, and whatever the reason, Casson, who ventured that it was because he did a lot of things superficially well 'and never quarrelled with people', was, as usual, in the right place at the right time when Gerald Barry telephoned his invitation; it was one he received with excitement and a sense of impending opportunity.

Hugh discussed this offer with Kit over a number of days, and their feeling was that, though it might make things difficult for a while, inevitably if he accepted such an appointment it could – would – mean more work for the practice. It was virtually agreed he should take up the Festival offer before Kit departed to take part in an International Gliding Championship, and on 13 July Hugh wrote to him saying:

Last night after two meetings with Barry and [Herbert] Morrison's secretary I signed up for this 1951 job on ONE condition, that either I was given a considerable amount of designing to do within the 1951 or that if the job was largely 'ideas' rather than 'designs' I should be given the opportunity of doing work OUTSIDE the job. They agreed to this but couldn't say which would be the solution till the job had started off on October 1st. They have no objection to my carrying on private practice 'in my spare time' but say theirs is a full-time job and must have priority, which is fair enough. The salary is £1,500 [some years later he said it was £1,000] – they won't raise it – so I must do quite a lot of work more not to lose on it, and they reckon that all designs must

be ready for tender by 1950 – so next year looks like a busy
year for the boys who get handed any jobs. I've had a week
of terrible indecision but feel – as you advised – I can't NOT
have a bang at it – and if I can't bear it I can always resign.

This uncharacteristically muddled prose almost certainly
reflects the equivocal state of his mind. He was making the
most crucial decision of his career and subconsciously he must
have known it. Happily, it was the right one.

Patience Clifford remembered the day shortly afterwards
which was to deal Casson the only major blow – the only public
one, anyway – he ever suffered. It was towards the end of July
and she had been taken out to an expensive and bibulous lunch
at the Ritz by a wealthy uncle. Returning to the office on this
hot afternoon, feeling relaxed and carefree, she found Hugh in
a state of the most acute distress. He had just received news
that Kit Nicholson had crashed his glider on a mountain above
Lake Como and died shortly afterwards in the small mountain
chapel to which he had been carried. Hugh was devastated. He
had lost a friend and business partner in one shocking blow
and Patience had the unenviable task of trying to comfort him
as he assimilated the full horror of what had happened.

Reta was away with the children, staying at the small coast-
guard's cottage, one of a row, at Needs Ore in Hampshire which
the Cassons had recently started renting as a holiday home on
a permanent basis. They had heard about it through a cousin
of Hugh's, and it made a perfect retreat away from the pressures
of London. Situated on the Beaulieu estate, it was fairly remote
but with a splendidly wide view across the Solent to the Isle of
Wight, and it was to remain in use by the Cassons, their friends
and their children for a great many more years. A few days after
hearing the dreadful news of Kit's death, Reta wrote to tell her
mother in South Africa and to say that Hugh had decided to
join them for a short holiday at Needs Ore as they had planned.

The few days he had at the office were harrowing for him, with letters of sympathy pouring in from friends and clients in huge numbers. Apart from his personal grief over his loss of a man he described in a despairing letter to Kit's wife, EQ, as his greatest friend, without whom architecture would no longer be fun, it had thrown a tremendous burden on him coming just as he had accepted the Festival job. Reta wrote, 'He felt that he would have to give up 1951 [the Festival] but everyone has been so insistent that he shouldn't that he is now undecided, but how he's going to solve the problem we can none of us see.'

It has to be said that the hideous tragedy which had struck the Nicholson family – EQ was left with three young children – was both an end and a beginning for Hugh Casson, the time when he really grew up and ceased to occupy a comfortable number-two position in the practice. Until now, Nicholson, his one-time tutor, had been present to face and fend off the problems which always affect a business. Now, not only was Hugh about to embark on his work for the Festival of Britain – he did decide to go ahead with it – but he had to find a means of holding together the practice which he had thought to leave in Kit Nicholson's more experienced hands whilst he was away. Apart from the usual plethora of exhibition stands and domestic work, there was an important new job in the office. Kit had just designed the structures laboratory at Wexham Springs in Buckinghamshire for the Cement and Concrete Association, and it had to be built. By now, fortunately, Neville Conder had rejoined them, attracted by the idea of working on real buildings rather than exhibition sites.

There is a haziness surrounding the ensuing arrangements. But they focused on two people. Neville Conder – still young and with only a year or two's experience since he qualified – and Patience Clifford. It was they who took over, and between them they resolved Hugh's difficulties. Conder remembers no partnership agreement being drawn up until some years later, but the two young architects saw the Cement and Concrete Association job and others through to their conclusion, 'and, along with Hugh, we shared the bank balance at the end of the year,' said Conder. 'It had become an office-sharing partnership of three without even a letter of agreement and with all three either acting independently or paired with one another according to the whim of the moment. Hugh, however, was largely absent, being a full-time employee of the Festival Office.'

Conder saw this incident as the first example of Hugh acting as impresario. 'And I personally profited from it. Sometimes throughout his career, Hugh gave out work to people because they were there; sometimes because he recognized a talent to nourish. I got to be executive architect for Kit Nicholson's Laboratories because I was there. Definitely not because this recent schoolboy had the knowledge or skill.' Conder has been remarkably generous and perceptive in his judgements about Hugh Casson. In this case, though, I think he is wrong. His performance to date, both as a student and working in the Casson office, had revealed him to be intelligent and conscientious, quite apart from his obvious design abilities. Casson believed he was leaving the office in capable hands, and his confidence was justified.

In any case, he had no option. His work at the Festival Office had become overriding. Any expectation of keeping the architectural practice going in his spare time proved to be quite meaningless, even for somebody prepared to work at the pace Casson did. All his energies, his imagination, his time and his interest were now devoted to the Festival of Britain. From the moment he joined the team (most of its members part-time to date) that first autumn, when no site for the main Festival had yet been chosen and the two full-time designers – himself and James Holland – worked from an unheated attic in Cadogan Gardens, Casson was entranced. The Festival's ultimate success was to bring him fame, supreme self-confidence, job offers which boosted his architectural practice – and a knighthood. All of these were deserved. But they were earned rather more by his considerable journalistic facility with words, his bubbling fount of ideas, his energy, his charm, his exquisite little sketches and his gift for choosing and managing people than by any outstanding design talents. And there were those few, as there always are in such cases, who were resentful and bitter at the end of it all, feeling that their own substantial contributions had been undervalued in the glow of Casson's more ephemeral talents. It was people such as these who would always be irritated (and deceived) by his jokey, light-hearted approach.

In September 1945, the idea of a Festival had been suggested in a letter to *The Times* by the journalist John Gloag, who thought the year 1951 would be an appropriate date since it was the centenary of The Great Exhibition of 1851, which had spawned the Crystal Palace. Gerald Barry immediately seized and promoted the idea with great enthusiasm in his own newspaper, and was then appointed Director General. Because he was the editor of a left-wing newspaper, and because the whole project had blossomed and come to fruition at a time of Labour Government, the idea of a Festival, 'this tonic to the nation' as Barry called it, was lambasted by the largely Tory press. Determinedly disregarding its morale-boosting potential at a time when the national spirit was at a postwar low ebb, and when people in the cities, in particular, were tired and shabby and depressed, it poked fun at the forthcoming frolic, deriding it as a waste of money and publishing letters from those of its sourpuss readers who were eager to ride that particular bandwagon. It wasn't just the press. Hugh Casson wrote many years later: 'The Establishment suspected it was all a smoke-screen for advancing Socialism. The Left decided it was middle class; the academics that it was populist; Evelyn Waugh that it was pathetic; Sir Thomas Beecham said it was imbecilic;

Noel Coward that it was not worth more than a mild giggle.'
Admittedly it was turning into a nationalistic affair. The idea
of a world trade exhibition had perforce to be abandoned when
it became clear that work on such a scale would consume a
third of the constructional labour of London for several years.
This would have been disastrous at a time when there remained
so much war damage to make good, so many new schools and
hospitals to be built.

The Design Group, charged with the pressing task of drawing
up an outline scheme for the Festival, averted its gaze from
what could have been dangerously debilitating comments.
Apart from Casson, its chairman, it comprised Misha Black,
an experienced and talented exhibition designer, the architect
Ralph Tubbs, James Gardner, who had been the coordinating
designer for the successful Britain Can Make It exhibition in
1946, after army service when he had worked on camouflage,
and the designer James Holland, who had spent the war at the
Central Office of Information.

Casson was always grateful for the enthusiastic but non-
interfering support they received from Herbert Morrison who,
as Lord President of the Council, was the Government minister
in charge: Lord Festival, the press called him, and the *Evening
Standard* launched an assault on 'Mr Morrison's multi-
million-pound baby'. Morrison loved London, and he was
determined to give that city in particular a joyous event to help
eradicate the memories of war, always with the rider that this
was never in any way to be politically motivated. 'I don't want
to know how it's going,' he told Casson at a meeting early on.
'Just get on with it, and come back if you're in real trouble.'
The shrewd appointment of Lord Ismay, a fair and decisive
man, as Chairman of the Festival Council successfully sab-
otaged the criticism of some influential Conservatives, in particular Ismay's old friend Winston Churchill, who had been
vociferous in anti-Festival sentiments up to then. Pug Ismay

had been his Chief of Staff during the war and could be accorded nothing less than respect and support.

By November 1948 the desolate twenty-seven acres of land alongside Waterloo Bridge, mountainous with the rubble from bombed buildings which had been dumped there, and divided almost into two halves by a railway line, had been established

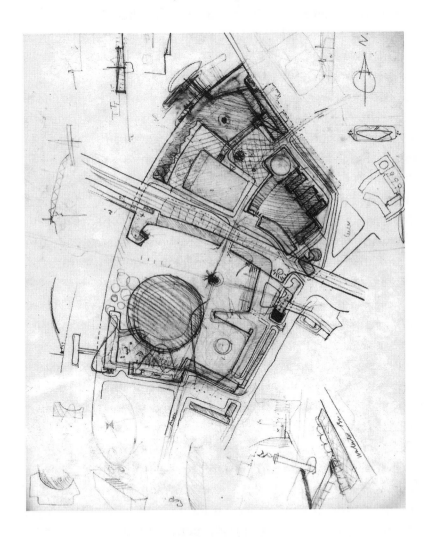

Casson's original suggestion for the layout of the Festival of Britain site.

as the main Festival site. On the day the decision to use this site was announced, as James Holland described later, 'Hugh Casson and I were set to produce for press release that very evening bird's-eye impressions of how an exhibition might fit into this site . . . and the final layout differed very little from the cockshy sketches we produced in a few hours and which were published in *The Times* next day.' The LCC undertook to clear the site, and to build an embankment along the whole of the river front.

Battersea Park was to host a funfair, an escort carrier, the 16,000-ton *Campania*, was converted by James Holland into a travelling exhibition which would tour British ports, and other events were planned for locations throughout the country. The main themes on the South Bank were to be The Land and The People. The People of Britain would be downstream of the dividing railway line where the Festival Hall, built by the old LCC, was already under construction, and where there was the Shot Tower which was the site's only retainable feature. The Land of Britain was to be upstream, its great central area filled by a major structure, the Dome of Discovery.

The Dome's young architect, Ralph Tubbs, was told by several firms of structural engineers that his building would be impossible to achieve in the time. Sir Ralph Freeman of the old-established engineers Freeman Fox, who had been consultants for the Crystal Palace at the 1851 Exhibition and had also built Sydney Harbour Bridge, presented no such difficulties. Hugh recounted, 'Ralph Tubbs and I went to see Sir Ralph Freeman, a tiny white-haired man of about seventy-six. He heard what we wanted, and said, "It's absolutely no problem. Leave it with me. I'll get something out by the end of the month." And he did.' Sadly, Sir Ralph died suddenly in March 1950, well before the Festival opened, though Freeman Fox carried on with the job under the able direction of his son.

The work was to be allocated so that each zone would be

designed by a different architect and different display designer, under the Design Group's guiding hand. Some of the zones would be open to competition, and each member of the Design Group could, if he wished, choose his own zone. Tubbs had chosen to design the Dome of Discovery with its great 365-foot span, Misha Black the River Restaurant and the decoration of the Bailey Bridge which would link the site to the North Bank, and Casson (whose particular charge was the downstream part of the site) the area around the Shot Tower, including a new boathouse for the barge dock, which was to be filled with a display of small marine craft. (Neville Conder remembers Casson's boathouse as revealing the only hint in the whole exhibition of the New Brutalist style of architecture yet to come, and agreed that this was probably one of Casson's few leaps into the architectural vanguard.)

Those were the bare bones of their decisions. The timescale was hair-raisingly short, and it remained to choose the architects and designers who would contribute. For those at the receiving end, it must have been rather like waiting for the telephone call when a prime minister appoints his cabinet. As it turned out, most of the unknowns who were summoned to these jobs from the Festival Offices, by now located in Savoy Court, had their future careers ensured. Young, just back from the war and hungry for work, they were presented with a glorious opportunity if they got on the list. Those who complained that these were jobs for the boys had right on their side. Inevitably, the chosen were friends, colleagues and acquaintances of the Design Group. How, short of throwing everything open to competition, could it have been otherwise? And despite the best of intentions, the setting up of competitions became an early casualty of the stringent time programme. Only two survived: the vertical-feature competition (such was its name), which resulted in the brilliantly simple and appropriate Skylon by Powell and Moya, and the 51 Bar which overhung the river and was won by Leonard Manasseh. Cost-cutting requirements resulted in Manasseh's winning design being swiftly reduced in size and simplified.

But the boys (a dearth of women in the main jobs) performed well, and though Sir Albert Richardson, the notoriously reactionary Professor of Architecture at the Royal Academy (and later to be its President), when shown the scheme by Casson dismissed it as a disaster, the project was now on course for immense success. Ground down by restrictions, tired of standing in queues for goods which the shops were still finding it difficult to supply, depressed by the de-mob suits which had been handed out to them on return from war service, struggling with the coal shortages which left their homes ill-heated and uncomfortable, and with many essential foods, like meat, still rationed, as well as inessentials like sweets, the British were becoming restless. They disliked the rubbery Spam which constituted a staple of their diet, and were sick of being exhorted to Make Do and Mend, and of their movements being restricted by petrol rationing, which did not cease until 1950. The scars of wartime bombing were still only too evident in their cities, and they were battered by bad news surrounding the Berlin Air Lift and the Korean War. They wanted to push it all into the background. They were, as their Labour masters had gauged, in the mood for a party. There had been little relaxation in their rigorous existence since 1939, and they were more than ready to have some fun. Morrison resisted all suggestions that the Festival should be deferred or even cancelled in view of the Korean War and Britain's commitments: 'I quite agree that there is plenty to be anxious about in the state of the world, but we do not know how long this anxiety without large-scale war is going on . . . and . . . in this situation, which may continue, it is profoundly important that we should keep the self-respect and morale of the British people on a high level.'

Graphics for the Festival were entrusted to Abram Games,

who had produced some famous posters for Shell and BP in the 1930s, had done propaganda work for the Ministry of Information during the war and was already establishing a reputation as one of Britain's wittiest and strongest graphic designers. He was an inspired choice. In particular the logo he designed for the Festival, which now appeared on everything to do with the event from brochures to souvenirs, was a most potent and memorable symbol. It instantly signified 'Festival of Britain', and for many people it still does.

Richard Guyatt was another successful designer who had done camouflage work during the war and knew Hugh Casson slightly. So he was 'one of the boys', deputed to work on the interior of the Lion and Unicorn Pavilion along with its architects, who were two more of Casson's old friends: Robert Goodden and Richard Russell. Guyatt (who eventually became Professor of Graphic Design at the Royal College of Art and then its Rector) remembers Casson at that time as 'an absolute sparkle, fizzing away like a rocket. The pavilion we worked on was first called the Communication of Ideas, which was hardly inspiring. It was Hugh's idea to change it to the Lion and the Unicorn and use it to demonstrate the essential eccentricity of the British Isles.' This turned out to be one of the most successful pavilions at the Festival, and its designers somehow managed to express abstract ideas about the British attitude to life, their love of free speech, their eccentricity and the amusement with which different social groups regarded each other, by means of a wide-ranging line-up of artefacts.

Reta Casson, leaving Carola, Nicky and Dinah in Mrs Aldridge's charge, was now working again, much to her own relief. She started after Dinah was born, first working mornings only, and gradually increasing her commitment until it was full-time. 'To have both Aldridge and me in the house together was ridiculous. There was insufficient for both of us to do, and I was beginning to feel that if I didn't get back to work soon I never would.' For some months she worked for a firm called Cockade, designing exhibitions, then, after her trip home to South Africa with the two older girls, Richard Guyatt employed her as an assistant for his work on the Festival's Lion and Unicorn pavilion (although she would return to Cockade when the Festival was over). 'Apart from being a very good architect, she always provided a rock-steady background for Hugh whilst he was out in front fizzing away, telling jokes, being amusing.' Reta was a good architect, but once again it was interior and exhibition design with which she was involved rather than construction of buildings.

The Festival was Hugh Casson's all-consuming occupation. Peter Shepheard, who had worked with him at the Ministry of Town and Country Planning, saw him in a slightly more sober light than Richard Guyatt had. Shepheard was a landscape architect as well as an architect, and Hugh presented him with the job of landscaping the downstream section of the exhibition. 'We were at one in thinking the spaces between buildings were as important, or even more important, than the buildings themselves. He was the one who had all the bright ideas, you know. And he offended no one. He made concept sketches of most of the buildings himself. The architect Jane Drew, of the husband-and-wife team Fry and Drew, was appointed to do the Waterloo Bridge entrance building, one of the few women who played an important role in the Festival. Hugh looked at her first design and said, "Jane, you can't possibly do that." He gave her a sketch of how he thought it should be, and she, who was not an easy lady, apparently complied without making too much fuss, because it was a Hugh-type building which emerged.'

In recounting this, Shepheard knew he was presenting just one example of Casson's almost legendary ability to smooth people's ruffled egos, gently persuading them that his way was right and leading them along his own chosen path. It would be

*The preliminary artist's drawing of the wigwam structures
which marked several entrances to the Festival.*

naïve to think he did this without personal toll. In fact, his
stomach, which had always been weak, suffered considerably
from the effects of stress, and he regularly departed for the
Festival office carrying a bottle of milk to soothe an incipient
ulcer. 'Dyspepsia,' he said, 'is the occupational hazard of all
exhibition designers.' In public, though, he retained both his
equable demeanour and his idiosyncratic manipulation of
words. Someone remembered him at one difficult meeting of
the Design Group instilling a new rigour into his tired colleagues by remarking, 'I feel the hot breath of cold feet around
the table.'

Casson was an astute man, sensitive to the opinions and
suspicions of others, and he wisely forbore from handing a
major commission to his own practice. His erstwhile colleagues, working to maintain the firm while he was otherwise
engaged, were presented with two appropriately low-key projects: the display design for the Schools Section, which was
housed in the Fry and Drew entrance building, and for the
Design Review, an exhibition of British products selected by
the Council of Industrial Design. Other architects who participated, with a comcomitant boost to their careers, included

Jim Cadbury-Brown (the Main Fairway), Brian O'Rorke (the Countryside and Agriculture Pavilion, comprising an open-sided Dutch barn with a sixty-foot span), Architects Cooperative (Raw Materials Pavilion), Arcon (the Transport Pavilion), Wells Coates (the Television Pavilion), Edward Mills (staff accommodation), and of course Basil Spence (Sea and Ships Pavilion), who was later to design Coventry Cathedral and become Sir Basil.

The Festival of Britain job demanded and got every ounce of Hugh's energy and time, and it was also significant in encouraging him to exploit an endemic ability – never distorted or even enhanced by professional training – to speak in public. One of his Festival duties, assumed, rather than required, was to tour the country, awakening people's interest in the forthcoming event, and this he did with a verve which developed into passion as the months passed and he became more deeply engrossed in his task. His first major appearance at the RIBA was to describe in exhaustive detail, to a huge audience of his peers, the buildings which were then nearing completion on the South Bank. This was almost certainly his first important speech in public, though he had made an unwonted sortie into political campaigning when he addressed a sparse group in a lock-up shop in a back street in Cheltenham on behalf of the Commonwealth Party during the war.

It seems feasible that Casson's desire to speak or perform in public had genetic roots. Quite apart from the evident rhetorical skills of his uncle, Lewis Casson, there were many actors manqués in the family, and his own parents were addicted to amateur theatricals from their days in India. His beautiful speaking voice – perhaps a little too light for effortless projection to the back of large halls, but none the less attractive to listen to – must have helped. And he had soon trained himself to speak rather than read, because, as he said, 'You don't listen for very long to people who read from a manuscript because you feel they are walking a path where they have already carefully trodden the grass down, and if they saw something unexpected like a snake or a poppy they wouldn't be able to cope with it . . .'. Casson himself was adept at scooping up unexpected happenings or responses and incorporating them seamlessly into whatever he was talking about. In February 1951, with the race to finish the Festival site on time nearly over, Reta accompanied him to Dublin, where he gave a lecture to the Irish Architectural Association, sponsored by the British Council, and then he went up to Belfast to visit the Festival office there. They both enjoyed the wonderful food in Dublin, which contrasted deliciously with their plain diet at home, where the meat ration in particular was minute. Eggs had become more plentiful, but Reta knew they would become less so by the following winter and was grateful for the tins of dried egg in the food parcels they were still receiving from South Africa. Thanks to her family, the Casson cupboards were well stocked compared with some, and the time had finally come when she could write to them and say she thought they could manage without the monthly parcels.

At four a.m. on 3 May 1951, a day of sunshine and showers, the contractors' huts and a formidable amount of rubbish were finally cleared from the South Bank site. The Festival was ready to be opened the next day. Hugh and Reta Casson drove in their 1927 grey Rolls Royce to the Service of Dedication and the Opening Ceremony, which was going to be performed by King George VI from the steps of St Paul's Cathedral. Hugh, in a top hat, and Reta, looking elegant and aloof as always, were wildly cheered by the immense crowds clutching Union Jacks and interspersed with policemen which lined the streets near the cathedral, where the carriageways had been cleared of all unauthorized traffic and sprinkled with grit. The cheerers had no idea who the couple were, and might not have been very interested if they had known, for it was the results not the means they were applauding and already there was a whiff of success in the air. The Cassons walked up the steps into the cathedral, where every seat was soon taken. The Prime Minister and his cabinet, the Lord Mayor of London, diplomats, dignitaries, service people from all three armed forces, representatives from the professions and the trades, and members of both Houses of Parliament were present, the great and the unknown together. Soon the whole Royal Family arrived, and after the church service, culminating in the singing of 'Jerusalem', King George VI formally performed the opening ceremony of the Festival from a canopied dais on the steps, looking out over the crowds below. 'I see this Festival as a symbol of Britain's abiding courage and vitality,' he said, and his words were broadcast by radio worldwide. The dais, its requirement somehow overlooked until the very last moment, had been designed by Casson, the working drawings were prepared by his young architect assistant Leslie Gooday, who stayed up all one night to finish them, and it was built in a twenty-four-hour spurt of frenzied activity. Some architects, exhausted by the workload of the past two years, might have panicked at this last-minute demand. Casson, adrenalin running, turned to with apparent sanguinity. Gooday remembered other occasions when they worked all night, 'but I'd never have refused to make that extra effort for Hugh. He got the very best out of us all.'

That evening there was a concert – the first – in the new Festival Hall, which was now completed on its site alongside the Festival. The King unveiled a small commemorative plaque in the entrance hall, and the audience then enjoyed a programme of triumphant and magnificently performed British music in what seemed a startlingly modern building: it included Sir Malcolm Sargent's arrangement of Arne's 'Rule Britannia', Vaughan Williams' 'Serenade to Music', Elgar's Pomp and Circumstance No.1, and the Hallelujah and Amens of Handel's *Messiah*. The audience was suitably impressed by the new auditorium and jubilant to be present at this great national, even nationalistic occasion. The architecture critic from *The Times*, whilst approving the Hall's interior, had reservations about the exterior of what was to become a building much liked by the general public. He judged the hanging panel of stonework, high up in the centre of the riverfront, as not having a happy effect. 'It disturbs the scale of the rest of the façade, and the eye does not easily reconcile itself to so large a mass of masonry apparently poised over the centre of a wide opening.'

The Cassons thought the Queen 'in a pink crinoline dress' looked wonderful, but they were still preoccupied by a multitude of small problems which were bedevilling the contractors on the South Bank and which had to be resolved before it opened to the general public the next day. They stayed there until midnight with Hugh doing his last rounds, and left the place a hive of industry with work continuing all night. The next morning they were back at nine-thirty to find, as is the way with exhibitions, that all was now spick and span and ready for the first visitors. Later in the day, despite rain and mist, many members of the Royal Family and a group of VIPs were given a special tour of the Festival site. Reta waited in the Lion and Unicorn pavilion with the children, all three dressed in dark-green jackets and pleated skirts made by Aldridge's sister, whilst Hugh took Princess Marina, Duchess of Kent, and her children on a conducted tour. The small Princess Alexandra whom he escorted then grew up to become one of his favourite members of the Royal Family, and like others she received several Casson water-colours as gifts.

On that day in 1951, it soon became evident that the Festival was going to be successful. Reta wrote to her mother: 'The girls were thrilled to see their father talking to all those important people. Hugh has had a great triumph, and in spite of the fact that he keeps saying that it's not him but equally his colleagues, nevertheless he is king pin.' And *The Times* reported: 'Nobody expects an exhibition to be completely ready on opening day ... but few rough edges were apparent anywhere.' The flood of visitors – the 250,000th, a Frenchwoman, was recorded on 11 May – complained only of the low quality and high cost of food in some of the restaurants, a matter which was soon dealt with. There were queues for several exhibits, notably the Dome of Discovery, but after their wartime experiences, the British almost relished a queue. Indeed they occasionally invented one. Two Scandinavian visitors, pausing to consult a guidebook, found that a queue of about twenty people had formed behind them. It remained there, as they moved on.

By the time it closed on 30 September, the South Bank site had been visited by eight-and-a-half million people. But no one, it was realized only two weeks before this date, had made a film to record its existence. David Astor, editor of the *Observer*, which was then particularly well respected for its arts coverage, proposed that his company should fund this last-minute enterprise. So a tour of the exhibition, with Hugh Casson as guide, was made into the film called *Brief City*, which is still occasionally shown to students and professional audiences. It starts in a dramatic way, after the exhibition has closed and the whole site is empty save for two figures, Hugh Casson and leading *Observer* journalist Patrick O'Donovan, standing in the driving rain with the wind flapping at their overcoats. Then it switches back a week or so. The exhibition is in full swing. And there is Hugh, small and nimble as a monkey, long overcoat flapping, trilby hat at a jaunty angle on his head, leaping on to plinths, striding along the walkways, eagerly and energetically leading O'Donovan through the crammed site which had occupied him for nearly three years, had taken over his family life and invaded his household, so that his daughter Carola's chief memory of that time is of being dragged protesting around the South Bank construction site on Saturday mornings. The film is immensely revealing of this free and light-hearted spirit which contributed so much to the Festival's success. The travails of the previous two years were not mentioned in the narrative which accompanied the tour, and Casson spoke only of pleasure and fun in his light, friendly voice, which by now was becoming quite well known on radio arts programmes.

He made no mention of the bad weather, the strikes, the shortage of materials (particularly wood), the difficulty of accommodating construction materials on such a constricted site, the long evening meetings of the Design Committeee which usually culminated in dinner at an Italian restaurant, the time factor, the terrible dilemma which faced them in the autumn of 1949, when the pound was devalued in September and the Festival budget was cut from twelve million to eleven million pounds in November following a general public-expenditure cut ... Public condemnation had gathered force. In December, a furious letter to *The Times* had proclaimed:

A halt must be called to the present proceedings. The aerial view published looks like nothing so much as the top of a derelict gasometer planted in a field surrounded by a lot of shacks, put down apparently without thought or design ... the whole thing is just a mess.

None of these was important now. But Peter Shepheard was to retain grim memories of that budget cut and of being called upon to reduce his landscaping schemes at this point. 'Landscaping was the first to go, with stone being replaced by concrete, gravel by Tarmac. I remember a whole building was cut out and I had to landscape the resultant blank space with flagstones, a pergola and flowerpots. Quite late in the day, Hugh decided we should have a bandstand. The first design was judged to be too modern. He wanted something more traditional and Gaby Epstein produced one with a roof painted in pink-and-white stripes. Freeman Fox didn't think the structure was safe. Hugh asked whether it would go plonk and collapse or whether there would be slow decay. Freeman Fox predicted slow decay – so it was built. Hugh was absolutely the queen bee. The whole Festival project wouldn't have got off the ground without him.'

The going had been hard, though. A bout of chicken-pox which felled Hugh Casson at one point had been utilized as 'thinking time', of which there was precious little, though he had made it his business to increase the number of his 'propaganda' talks on the forthcoming jollification as the opening day approached: Oxford, Cambridge, Durham, Cheltenham, Liverpool were all visited, despite his increasing fatigue. The weather had been atrocious, they were facing absolutely new problems which none of them had experienced before. And there were innumerable wild-cat strikes. The comic catch-phrase 'everybody out' was no joke to those working on the Festival, especially when on occasions the electricians withdrew their labour and the site was blacked out. The diplomatic handling of workmen became a new skill for designers and architects more used to dealing with servicemen trained to instant obedience. It was a skill which would stand them in good stead in their future careers.

Meanwhile, at Festival of Britain Council meetings, it had been decided that in all publicity material, emphasis would be put on gaiety and enterprise. These were to be the keynotes. Some felt daunted at the prospect. Hugh, it appeared, did not, though his life was becoming increasingly onerous.

In July 1950, shortly after the death of Ralph Freeman, when there was worry amongst officials (subsequently proved completely unnecessary) that his son might not have time to cope with the pressures of the job, and it looked as though the deadline was in danger of being missed – public records reveal that some architects were falling behind in their production of drawings – the architect Howard Lobb (already involved as chairman of one of the advisory councils) was appointed Controller of Construction to help speed progress. A less level-headed man than Hugh Casson might have resented this as a slight to his own capabilities. Casson wisely accepted the appointment calmly, went to Needs Ore with Reta where they spent a weekend cleaning out the cottage for a tenant, and thereafter worked in harness with Lobb without any apparent qualms, though Reta remembered several being expressed in the sanctity of their own home. All these matters were in any case pushed aside once the Festival had opened, in the euphoric climate of achievement. There were few distractions for people in this utilitarian postwar period: no smart restaurants, limited foreign currency for holidays abroad, no leisure centres such as those which became prevalent during the ensuing years. They flocked in their thousands to this bright, modern attraction, situated so close to the centre of London. Doubts about its success were forgotten.

Hugh Casson afterwards put the relative smoothness with which such a huge, unwieldy job was achieved down to the fact that most of the people in charge had just returned from the services: they were used to working in teams, used to taking orders and used to solving unexpected and peculiar problems. None was regarded as insuperable. Everyone buckled to as they'd been required to do in the services, shouldering whatever responsibility came their way, and achieving seemingly impossible ends. They had – on a nepotistic basis or not – been carefully selected. As Casson commented years later, 'Barry said to me: "Architects can be tiresome and quarrelsome. I cannot have people who quarrel. The time element is too short to cope with prima donnas or others of difficult persuasion."' The amiability factor was vital and seems to have operated well, with Casson's sense of humour constantly invoked to ease tension. One of his friends swears that the telephonist in the Festival Office answered the phone with the response 'Festering Britain', though this sounds suspiciously like one of Hugh's own inventions, as was his instruction to an assistant that all Misha Black's memos – which became copious as the tense months progressed – should be put in a file marked Mishallaneous.

The fact that the planning and management of the whole enterprise were – as specified by its directorate – in the hands of professionals such as architects, engineers and designers, rather than administrators and contract managers, has rarely been commented upon. But it speaks well for the solid organizational skills, in addition to their creativity, which the professions were able to muster in those days. It is not to their credit that in the intervening years, architects, while boasting of their iconoclastic and questioning approach, have allowed themselves to be shoved aside, their role diminished and their confidence diluted by consultants of diverse and sometimes dubious skills.

Twenty-five years after the Festival closed, a cool look at its success and influence was taken in an exhibition at the Victoria and Albert museum, and in an accompanying book *A Tonic to the Nation*, edited by Mary Banham and Bevis Hillier. It was a cogent reminder of what the South Bank site in particular had been, recalling the bright newness of it all, the fresh paint, the trees spangled with red and white lights at night, the uplighters set into the Fairway where people danced to the music of Geraldo's Embassy Band in their overcoats because it was so cold and wet, and the fountains which seemed to symbolize the gaiety and optimism which abounded, particularly Richard Huws's bucketing water feature. Paintings and sculpture by major British artists adorned every area, though, as Casson explained, the architects had generally had to be guided in their selection. 'Most of them had only heard of the really famous artists like Henry Moore and Graham Sutherland, but we pushed them in the direction of many others: John Piper, Epstein, Lucien Freud, Barbara Hepworth, Ben Nicholson, Josef Herman, Victor Pasmore and Keith Vaughan.' Feliks Topolski, by now a British citizen and with a fine record as a war artist in almost all the areas of combat, held regular Thursday salons at his Little Venice studio where a disparate collection of the great and the good would gather, Hugh amongst them, these salons culminating in one glorious 200-strong party for Picasso. Now Topolski was commissioned to make a dramatic painting, sixty feet long and twenty feet high, depicting the Cavalcade of the Commonwealth in an arch of the Hungerford viaduct over Belvedere Road. (A year or so later, with his old studio in Little Venice demolished by an unassailable Council bent on replacing it with a public lavatory, he was granted a lease on the arch next door. This was glazed with windows from the temporary annexe to Westminster Abbey which was erected for the Queen's Coronation in 1953, and he worked there until he died in 1989.)

The restaurants and cafés, the specially designed furniture and plant-holders, the Bailey Bridge which brought pedestrians across the river, the Shot Tower which was the single link with the past, and the decorative designs based on crystallography which had been conceived by the Festival Pattern Group, made vivid evocations of that almost-forgotten event which was not – as it surely would be now – blighted by graffiti, and where there was no vandalism or bad behaviour.

Veiled in, though certainly not obscured, by all this finery were the buildings, and it is they particularly which twenty-five years after the event were, at the time of this exhibition in 1976, the subject of rather supercilious dismissal. Twenty-five years was long enough for the forces of reaction to have gathered, not long enough for the Festival to have assumed its rightful place in the history of architecture and design.

The buildings were likened to others which, by 1951, had

already been built in the USA and in European countries (not-ably Italy). Serious commentators said that they were deriva-tive, lacking innovative stature of their own, and contributed little to the future development of architecture in Britain. They failed to acknowledge that most good architecture carries allusions to the work of other generations, and that no one was claiming masterpiece status here, even for the Dome of Discovery. Hugh Casson, who was incapable of being supercili-ous on any subject, nevertheless opined that there was nothing revolutionary in either the layouts or the buildings, several of which were based on standard Dutch barns, their workmanlike structure suitably embellished and concealed. 'The language in which the Festival was put over was really late thirties, which none of us in England had seen. So to ordinary people it seemed more novel than it was. But in fact it was a pretty straight development of steel, aluminium and wire, bright colours and masses of plate glass.'

As usual he was seeking to please, to be in step with his peers, and he did add that this had not been the view of the public. 'They just thought it was terrific,' Misha Black said, in talking about archi-tecture and the effect of the Festival. 'What had pre-viously been the private pleasure of the cognoscenti suddenly, virtually over-night, achieved enthusiastic public acclaim.'

Casson was adopting an over-simplistic and unwon-tedly humourless view when agreeing with critics. The

The symbol of the Festival of Britain 1951 designed by Abram Games.

Festival did not produce any world-shattering architecture, but much of it was inventive and progressive, and there was a bold demonstration of fresh and technically accomplished exhibition design. An architect who was a student at the time remembered making countless visits to the site (thanks to a free pass he had been given by Katz and Vaughan, architects to the Homes and Gardens pavilion). Well versed in what was happening architecturally in the rest of the world, as keen architectural students invariably are, he was nevertheless intrigued and excited by the home production, citing the Dome of Discovery – then, at 365 feet, the biggest single span in the world – the Transport Pavilion with its roof made of stressed skin steelwork, and Basil Spence's Sea and Ships building as extending the existing boundaries of construction techniques and aesthetic convention. He remembers the 'largest sheet of glass in the world', which was erected in the Power and Production Pavilion with the aid of a newly developed vacuum sucker, and best of all the Skylon, simple, dramatic, symbolically aiming for the stars, and designed by architects Powell and Moya, who were only a few years older than himself. It was inspirational. He was one of many – architects, designers and even manufacturers – for whom design thinking had been quite dramatically shifted into a new gear. The last nail had been banged into the coffin of the war and they were being made aware of all the new possibilities which stretched before them. Having come to maturity in wartime, they accepted that the multiplicity of materials used in Festival buildings, which had been judged by some commentators to result in a displeasing bittiness, was due to continuing shortages. What they probably did not know was that the Design Group had considered and rejected the idea of standardizing the buildings from a kit of component parts. Casson explained afterwards, 'We knew the risk that coherence and homogeneity would be more difficult to obtain the way we eventually opted for, but were confident that the chances of visual excitement would be more probable. And anyway part of our brief was to demonstrate structural and technical innovations, and the use of new materials. Shortages meant we had to use whatever we could get, so it was difficult to achieve much continuity. One of the most interesting technical experiments was in the tension-stressed concrete footbridge which Maxwell Fry and Jane Drew designed to go from Waterloo Bridge to the Festival Hall.'

The strong primary colours which had been disliked by some gloomy commentators were a reaction against the all-pervasive khaki, navy and grey colours the British had endured for so many years. It was only the cynics and certain professional critics well versed in the craft of abuse who picked over these details in search of deficiencies and failures. The architectural critic Reyner Banham gave the Festival a remorseless (and sometimes flippant) scrutiny during the 1975 Tonic to the Nation exhibition and reassessment. But he conceded, 'It was a turn on. It is striking how many of that generation (people who were teenagers in 1951) have told me in recent months that it was the Festival that turned them on to modern architecture, or made them want to be architects for the first time. It was a preview of the human environment as a zone of enjoyment and its design as an occupation of pleasure.'

Regrettably, it has to be admitted that the Festival's influence on design in its wider manifestations was not entirely beneficial. Those who emulate new ideas rarely do so with the same amount of ingenuity and skill as their progenitors, and such was the case now. Awful sub-Festival products began to appear and continued to do so for many years. Particularly unattractive were the textile and graphic designs based on crystallography which had been such a feature of the exhibition. In unskilled hands they looked horrible. And the spindly metal legs which had been a characteristic of Festival furniture, and particularly of the very successful chairs designed by Ernest

Race, and which had been a direct result, according to Casson, of the need to economize on materials, appeared looking grotesquely inappropriate on lesser designs throughout the furniture industry. The description 'very Festival of Britain' entered the national vocabulary, and it was generally used pejoratively.

But all this was in the future. Back on 3 May 1951, Casson had rushed into his office before setting off for the opening ceremony. There he found a roneoed letter on his desk informing him that his services were no longer required, and there was a similar one awaiting all members of the planning and design staff. Casson's sense of humour saved him from being overly shocked by this insensitive and untimely document. He laughed at the lack of imagination demonstrated by the civil servant from whom it came. He liked to mention it whenever the subject of his part in the Festival came up in conversation. He knew though – they all knew – that no further public cash could be expended on unnecessary salary bills. And their job was done. In any event, Hugh Casson had a healthy architectural practice awaiting his return. Better still, he was soon to receive an adequate demonstration of the gratitude which was felt for his work; there was recognition that it had far exceeded the call of either duty or his monthly pay cheque.

There were many distinguished contributions to the Festival of Britain, and they took a variety of forms: practical, intellectual and creative. The Architecture Council, the Science Council, the Council of Industrial Design and the Arts Council all participated. And there was a formidable array of committees and panels. There was Ian Cox, Director, Science and Technology, who mapped out the story which was to be told. There were the writers like Laurie Lee and Stephen Potter who put it into words. There was a large number of artists, designers, architects and landscape architects whose work was manifest on the South Bank, at the Battersea Pleasure Garden, and in Poplar where the Exhibition of Live Architecture had been constructed. There were the engineers Freeman Fox, who had made Ralph Tubbs's spectacular concept for the Dome of Discovery practicable, as well as overseeing the engineering works for the whole site, and there were the contractors. There were contributions from a lot of people to events all over the country, which though less sensational and of less interest to the media, helped to make the whole show a national endeavour. It was, however, to result in only one immediate knighthood (Gerald Barry had been honoured some time previously), and that was conferred on Hugh Casson in the 1952 New Year's Honours List, following the exhibition's closure.

Casson deserved his singular honour. His charm, his drive, his work as a publicist, his powers of leadership had, way beyond anyone else's, driven the Festival preparations along to their successful conclusion. He received his knighthood with glee, and kept a copy of *The Times* in which it was listed for the rest of his life. Establishment recognition was something he always relished. Reta, now Lady Casson, found her new title embarrassing, particularly when it was incorrectly used and she became Lady Margaret. 'I didn't want it because I could see it was going to be a bore in my professional life. But I couldn't be too vociferous because of course for him it was wonderful.'

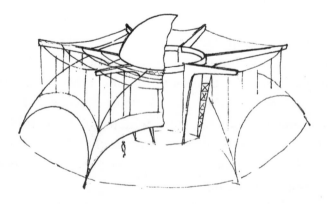

Proposed design in canvas for the first 'dome'.

VII

Taking Off
in Another Direction

His contribution to the Festival of Britain had made Hugh Casson a high-profile figure in his own country. Not only had he led the South Bank design team, but he had talked and written about what was going on with a lucidity and wit which endeared him to people used to regarding architecture and design as arcane subjects, not for the likes of them. Hugh made it clear that these were subjects for everyone, and perfectly accessible ones at that. Reta, who nerved herself to give two large parties during the Festival summer, wrote in August to tell her mother that Hugh had been made a Royal Designer for Industry. 'He is quite a famous little man now. You can hardly open a paper without seeing something about him.'

If there were murmurs about him being a lightweight, these tended to be from members of his own profession who mistook clarity for lack of depth, who persisted in judging a good architect (which he was) by the criteria of a great architect (which he was not), and whose mistrust was mixed with a considerable helping of sour grapes. The intelligentsia generally made a more penetrating assessment of his capabilities, and putative clients – both corporate and private – were bewitched by his fame and charm. Borne on this wave of acclaim and goodwill, he returned to practice.

Neville Conder, in tandem with Patience Clifford, had held the fort with admirable tenacity whilst Casson was engaged elsewhere. A slightly austere and sardonic man, lacking the social graces which Hugh Casson had so assiduously developed, he was to do so for the rest of his career. Patience Clifford got married very soon after this, became Patience Bayne-Powell and departed for a life of domesticity; though she remained a friend, and the three little Casson girls were bridesmaids at her wedding.

The building for the Cement and Concrete Association laboratories at Wexham Springs which Kit Nicholson had designed before his death was complete. Conder said, 'This was a big building of technical complexity and I didn't particularly like the design. But it had character. In fact, it was Hugh's job of course, but I ran it whilst he was organizing the Festival architecture. And that was to be the pattern of our life.' There was other work in the office now and, as a result of Casson's fame and popularity, innumerable enquiries, some making direct offers of work. Casson was also, as Conder has pointed out, in the position of pushing work towards other people, a practice in which he delighted.

From now on the major projects in the office assumed a design rigour from which they rarely departed. Casson's more personal projects may sometimes have displayed an element of whimsy, an ambiguity of intent, even a softness of touch. The jobs attributed to Casson and Conder and run in that office were, with perhaps one exception, of a no-nonsense order which at least paid lip-service to the original creed of Modernism. There was, though, a strong feeling in the office that each building should set its own style. An article by Robin Boyd was published in the *Architectural Review*, saying in effect that a new empiricism had come into being, and that now the functional creed was qualified by the mood of the occasion, a fact which should be accepted and acknowledged. Conder remembers introducing the concept of 'the mood of the occasion' into their office parlance and aspirations, but he also remembers that it was Hugh who was so good at establishing such a mood, indeed insisting that there was always something deeper than material need to discuss. 'His sensibility and wisdom would influence a whole job, sometimes by one phrase dropped into a conversation.'

This burgeoning post-Festival practice did not, however, proceed in an entirely straightforward manner. Simultaneously with supervising its new growth, Hugh took off in yet another direction, obviously certain that once again Conder would cope. This chapter, then, is concerned with the early years he spent as Professor of Interior Design at the Royal College of Art, with his concurrent work as an architect lurking slightly in the shadow of a glamorous lifestyle.

The story really begins in 1948, when Robin Darwin, egregious and genetically endowed scion of two famous dynasties, the Darwins and the Wedgwoods, became Principal of the College. In what was now a postwar period of innovation and renewal, he set about revitalizing a somnolent backwater, lacking in either vigour or respect. Fresh – or rather stale – from its wartime evacuation to the Lake District, the College desperately needed change. Darwin, a painter himself, believed firmly in the principle that fine arts and applied arts should be taught in the same school. He envisaged a place where artists and industrial designers worked alongside each other, to their mutual enlightenment and benefit, at the same time pursuing specializations which would make them valuable to all sections of industry. This would be a place which was respected and supported by that industry, and one which would educate its students to a singularly high standard. Other College heads before him had shared these aims, but perhaps none with Darwin's determination. The College was now freed from Civil Service management, and newly established as an educational charitable foundation, with a Council sharing the responsibility for its finance. The time was right for visionary ideals to be realized.

True to his provenance and generation, the Eton-educated Robin Darwin started by invoking the services of talented friends and acquaintances, and those in the design network braced themselves in pleased anticipation. The boys were about to be called upon again.

Casson had known Darwin slightly during the war, as both were employed in camouflage, though in different departments. The two men, as well as being the same age, shared what *The Times* was to call 'an ability to choose the best men and get the best out of them'. In some cases this meant nothing more than choosing people they liked and whose company they enjoyed. Some of the people Darwin had brought in to help vitalize the College, most of them the practising designers and architects he favoured, were then chosen by Casson to work on the Festival, notably Professors Goodden and Russell, who had designed the Lion and Unicorn Pavilion, and Professor Richard Guyatt, who had been responsible for the interior.

Darwin had been immensely enthusiastic about the involvement in the Festival of 'his' people and came to regard this notably successful pavilion as a Royal College of Art trophy; which in some ways it was. It inevitably strengthened his acquaintance with Casson, and when, in 1951, he decided to start a new Department of Interior Design at the College, Casson, with his recently acquired star quality and reputation for being a mover and achiever, was the obvious choice to head it. Originally, Darwin had intended this to be a school of architecture, but he failed to get RIBA support (and therefore Ministry of Education funding) for such an establishment, so he settled instead on a Department of Interior Design with an architectural approach of a type which is now common but was then extremely rare. There were architects and there were interior decorators, and neither camp had much regard for the other. This school aimed to train a new breed of professionals, people who did not just choose colours, fabrics and furniture, but who designed interiors with a background of structural knowledge and all the respect for proportion, space, light and materials which architects gave to buildings.

Casson, with Reta as his Senior Tutor, was to bring energy, architectural abilities and, above all, his brilliant reputation to the project. As it turned out, though, this closing of the gap between architecture and design did not really occur during Casson's tenure as Professor, despite his enlisting distinguished architects as lecturers and tutors on a part-time basis. It was not until John Miller took over from him some twenty-three years later that the course on offer acquired real architectural weight, and students who already had degrees in architecture began to enrol in any number.

Hugh Casson had always worked at a punishing pace, but not in such a focused and blinkered manner as to be labelled a workaholic. His commitments were too diverse for that, with his energies always divided between writing, broadcasting, painting and whatever was officially his main activity. This was the case now. Here he was, senior partner in a growing architectural practice based in Old Brompton Road. At the same time he was taking on other onerous duties a mile away in Exhibition Road, where the RCA was then scattered around a number of sites. He never, in all the years he was a partner in Casson Conder, had an office at the firm's premises. Michael Cain, who started work for the practice in 1952, said, 'He was always a visitor to the office.'

Instead, he shared a small room with Reta at the RCA, and from there he ran a practice within a practice. It was one which dealt mainly with smallish, personal projects, most of them more glamorous than the day-to-day meat of architectural practice. Hugh, for instance, designed the Coronation decorations for the City of Westminster in 1953; deliciously light and whimsical, embodying all the gaiety of the Festival designs,

Sketch ideas Casson produced for Westminster City
Council's Coronation decorations in 1953.

and with the sturdy practicality which he, better than anybody, knew was essential. He prowled the streets for hours before committing himself to paper on this job, counting the lamp-posts, discovering that most of the many statues related to war, and deciding to fill the hands of all these erstwhile Generals and Field Marshals with posies. 'The decorations had to reflect history, religion, pageantry and the basic greatness of this country, but they had to be feminine and light-hearted too. That's why I used a Rose and Crown motif.' It was all a charming and typically Cassonesque tribute to the young Queen for whom he was to work so much in the future. Swaths of lights spangled the trees, the street-sweepers had flowers in their buttonholes, lamp-posts were painted pale blue, and there was a great heraldic feature across Parliament Street, designed by Robin and Christopher Ironside. Made of cast aluminium, this was polished to bright and satin finishes, with parts tinted in delicate shades of gold, copper and green. Eros was given cover in an aluminium cage with a coronet-shaped top, the whole lot spray-lacquered gold, and sparkling with tiny lights which outlined its shape at night.

Despite Hugh's contribution to the gaiety of the occasion, the Cassons were given only mediocre seats along the route of the Coronation procession. And these came about as the result

Hugh drew this little sketch of the stand in Hyde Park from which he and Carola watched the Coronation in 1953.

of a ballot amongst RIBA Council members (an extraordinary extra commitment Hugh had been persuaded to take on at that time), because Westminster offered them none. Reta decided not to go at the last minute, so Hugh took the twelve-year-old Carola with him and they started out at six a.m. to reach their seats in Hyde Park, near Marble Arch, although the procession did not pass by until after the service at three p.m. Like thousands of others, they got cold and wet in their unsheltered seats, but the atmosphere was euphoric, and Hugh was pleased with his decorations which were attracting almost universal approval.

Hugh Casson never disguised his partiality for interior-design work. Temperamentally, it suited him to perfection, because it was quick and immediate, unlike the hard grind and long-drawn-out programmes associated with the construction of a building. Paradoxically, like many of his generation, he was equivocal about its worth. 'Interior design is regarded by serious architects as a form of pastrycook work. It's fiddling around with things you're going to tear out again in five years' time. And that in a way had the same sort of attraction for me that theatre design had, that at the end it was torn down and you never saw it again. Buildings continue to ooze your blood until you drop or they fall down. So I liked the slightly temporary aspect of interior design.'

Uncharacteristically, he did not foresee the future. Long after he had retired, a much younger generation of architects had no option but to tackle interior-design projects with enthusiasm – and relief. During the great recession which hit the construction industry harder than most during the late eighties and early nineties, it was a case of accepting interior-design work or going out of business. Once resigned to this fact, many performed magnificently and restaurants, hotels, shops and office interiors benefited from architects' dependence on this discipline for their livelihood. Interior design had become respectable.

When Casson was in practice, certainly during this fifties period, the pressure for architects to concentrate on interiors was not so acute. Nevertheless, in addition to all the new buildings Casson Conder was commissioned to design, Hugh was offered a plethora of interior-design work, and he generally accepted it with alacrity.

This phenomenon was probably set in motion by the most prominent job of them all, which started in 1951 just after the Festival of Britain opened. Gordon Russell, then Chairman of the Council of Industrial Design, had been asked by Prince Philip to recommend a designer who could work on the Royal Yacht *Britannia*, and he recommended Casson. Thus began Hugh's long working relationship with the Royal Family. When news of the commission became public, it must certainly have triggered the quantity of interior-design work which now followed. In 1952, for instance, he was appointed coordinating architect of the interiors in the seven-storey Time Life Building, on the corner of New Bond Street and Bruton Street, which had been designed by the architect Michael Rosenauer. In planning these interiors, Hugh's job was to demonstrate the wide range of talent amongst British artists, designers and craftsmen of the time. This project, on which he worked with his old Festival colleague Misha Black – now a partner at the Design Research Unit – reinstated Casson in the role of patron he had so enjoyed at the Festival. Other Festival of Britain veterans were involved too, but it was Hugh, in what Neville Conder dubbed his role as impresario, who brought in a galaxy of artists: Henry Moore, Ben Nicholson, Lucie Rie and Hans Coper, Geoffrey Clarke and many more. On the design front, things were more difficult and good products – particularly furniture – of British provenance were not so easy to find. Designs from Scandinavia and the United States were enjoying cult status in Britain, while indigenous designers and, crucially, manufacturers were still recovering from the war. But contributions from furniture designers R. D. Russell and Ernest Race displayed a strength which presaged the admirable work several generations of British designers would achieve in the future.

The only room which Casson Conder designed *in toto* was the cafeteria, and with Misha Black they worked on the London director's office. The conference room was by H. T. Cadbury-Brown. Considering the difficulties with which everyone still had to contend, these were rich and beautiful interiors which attracted extensive coverage in the design press when they were opened in 1953. So the Casson caravan continued to roll.

Never able to resist extending his activities into a new area of design, Hugh was intrigued to be approached by Roy Midwinter in the early fifties. Midwinter, scion of the old-established ceramics firm W. R. Midwinter, had modern ideas acquired during a sales trip to the USA in 1952, and began to commission freelance designers (Terence Conran was one) to give his wares the fashionable 'contemporary' look. Hugh did two ranges, Riviera in 1954, Cannes in 1960, both of them depicting scenes as light-hearted and cheerful as they sound. I do not personally think that the light, airy Casson style suited the curved ceramic shapes devised by Midwinter; something bold and assertive would have been more appropriate. Hugh was always disparaging about this project himself. Nevertheless, both ranges sold well and are now collectors' items.

The College office was joined in 1954 by Ronald Green, whom Hugh had taught over ten years previously at Cheltenham Art School. Now an architect, Ronald Green gradually took a lead role in the jobs Casson was handling from the College, was made a partner in 1962, and remained with Casson Conder until he retired. Small and neatly built like his boss, he had a complementary sense of humour, he drew well, and he did not apparently resent working in the shadow of the other's dominant personality. Casson – who when interviewing him for the job had demanded whether he could handle money responsibly – had again found a man on whom he could rely. Green, like Conder, was resigned to Casson leaning over his board at the end of a hard day's work and saying tentatively, 'Don't you think that would be improved if it were just a little more . . . ?' or 'Have you tried so and so . . . ?' 'He was,' Green said, 'rarely wrong and the irritating thing was he invariably hit on the very fault you had been trying to conceal from yourself. But the main thing was he always supported what you did. So your confidence grew overnight.' The man Green had found so inspiring when he was a young art student proved to be the most exhilarating colleague, and one to whom his peers instinctively deferred. Green remembers groups of erudite and eminent people having meetings in their office, some of them clients, some members of the boards and committees with which Hugh was increasingly involved. 'But Hugh would automatically assume the position of chairman because he was a natural chairman, this puckish little fellow.'

Hugh Casson was never destined to join the ranks of 'commercial architects', those who work for and under the dominance of property developers, and who enjoy handsome financial rewards, sometimes sacrificing the quality of their work as a consequence. On one occasion in the fifties, he came close to doing so. He – or an Australian architect called Robin Gibson who worked in the College office at that time and who did most of the drudgery – put immense effort into obtaining planning permission for a building which would eventually become Castrol House. Once permission was obtained, the developer who owned the site pressurized them to produce a fast-track building, since by now Castrol were waiting in the wings to become its occupants. Casson baulked at this, decided such developer work was not his *métier*, and telephoned Frank Gollins, of the well-regarded firm of architects Gollins Melvin Ward, to bequeath him what was by the standards of most architectural firms a covetable job. Happily, Gollins's appointment resulted in a good building.

As Ronald Green commented with some admiration, Hugh was really the last gentleman amateur, and this developer-directed project was just not his type of work. More in his line was the work the College office did for his friend and neighbour Edward Norman Butler, who was general manager of Martin's Bank and who shared out the bank's considerable construction work between three firms of architects, one of them Casson Conder. It was for a major reconstruction of the bank's city office that Ronald Green had been taken on, and he enjoyed doing this from his perch in the RCA rather than at the low studio-like building in Thurloe Place where Casson Conder now had their main office. 'Apart from anything else, it was good to be rubbing shoulders with all these artists and designers, and often bringing them in to work with us. Geoffrey Clarke, for instance, made a handsome grille for the bank building, and then went on to do his major work on the stained-glass windows at Coventry Cathedral.'

Hugh liked his involvement with these prestigious projects. At the same time, he kept close tabs on what was happening in the main Casson Conder office. Neville Conder is resolute in his assertion that such tabs were kept. 'This was a period of real partnership between us. Although, obviously, I spent more time on the bigger jobs in the office than he, he had a disproportionate influence on the work.' As usual, Casson was working well past conventional office hours, and would often appear in the main Casson Conder office at about six o'clock in the evening to become involved in projects which were on the boards there, as well as appearing in the mornings with conceptual ideas he had drawn up overnight. Some employees didn't like having their evenings hijacked in this way, but they rarely complained; or at least, not to their seniors.

Casson's journalism might have been expected to diminish

under the onslaught of other commitments. This did not happen. Work for the Architectural Press continued and he became a directing editor of the *Architectural Review*, sharing the credit for several notable and well-received issues. In June 1955, the architectural critic Ian Nairn produced an issue entitled *Outrage*, which was a polemic against the iniquities of postwar developments, coining the word Subtopia, and later on Casson himself, from the position of authority due to the Professor of Interior Design at the Royal College of Art, was responsible for a fat issue of the *Review* entitled *Inscape*. This, in the face of many architects' views to the contrary, convincingly promoted the concept of interior design as a serious and important subject.

A prophet in his own land as well as abroad, Casson was, from the Festival of Britain onwards, frequently invited to give speeches on architecture, planning, art and design. The composition of his audiences varied, but whether it was a hallful of eminent professionals such as the Council for Visual Education, or the General Dental Council, to whom he gave the Sir Wilfred Fish lecture, or a gathering from a local amenity society, he rarely refused a request to speak. His network of friends was eager to capitalize on this fact. In 1956, at the instigation of Sir Bernard Burrows, who had married Reta's great friend Ines Walter and who was now British Ambassador in Turkey, the British Council invited Hugh to speak about British architecture to an audience in that country. Lady Burrows remembered years later that he gave a wonderfully enthusiastic lecture which he illustrated with drawings, made as he spoke. 'He was so quick thinking and able to react to the mood of the audience.'

Never one for polemical ranting, Hugh did in his temperate and amusing way promote the views he held dear. These were not the contentious opinions of a radical, and his audiences were never roused to fury or explosive debate – he would have hated that – but they may have been swayed nevertheless by his gentle rhetoric. In December 1960, for example, an address to the Farnham Society on the subject of Town Sense was notable for an early exposition of the idea that modern buildings can be felicitously slotted into an old (in this case Georgian) setting, and that old does not necessarily mean beautiful any more than new inevitably means ugly. An audience of over five hundred people listened to what he had to say and the talk was so enthusiastically received it was later printed in booklet form. It included this passage:

In our natural respect for the past we often become over timorous about the future. Humility and discretion are admirable, cowardice is not. We seem to be too often obsessed by the need to be in keeping – and thus avoid the enriching opportunities of contrast or fantasy. Look, after all, at the visual violence of a Salisbury Cathedral or a Telford viaduct and picture if you can how these abrupt dynamic structures would have survived the present obstacle race of local-authority approval, amenity protests, public inquiries and angry letters to *The Times* that today beset any large-scale building project.

This was almost prophetic in its description of a long and worrying period, fast approaching, during which Casson was to be assailed on all sides by the people of Bath and a bevy of other interested parties.

There is an immediacy about broadcasting which suited Casson's temperament to perfection, and he was in steady demand for both radio and television. Architects had not prescriptively taken part in arts programmes then (some do now), but Hugh was often a member of *The Critics* on BBC radio. This, incidentally, alerted him to the prevailing ignorance about architecture even amongst otherwise well-informed people. 'I always used to choose a building to discuss. It was very interesting that these highly educated and sophisticated critics, who could talk for twenty-five minutes about an obscure stained-glass artist or fifth-rate poet, would find it hard to name a single building, and certainly no architect. They'd never heard of any architect apart from Christopher Wren or Le Corbusier. They simply had no critical sense when it came to talking about a building, in particular a modern building.' Some of his own broadcasts may have done a little to ameliorate this situation, though, as he knew, he was pushing on slack rope during the fifties and sixties. Things would not begin to improve to any real extent until well into the 1980s. Meanwhile, in architectural circles it was said that Casson was the only present-day architect whose name was recognized by the general public.

In the early fifties, the most exciting project for the Casson Conder partnership (still an informal one with nothing written down) was an invitation to participate in a limited competition at Cambridge. Casson said later that they were asked to enter because of the Festival. Before that, he maintained, nobody knew who he was. The Casson Conder 'partnership', incidentally, was in name only. They did not have a proper agreement until 1956, and then it was at Conder's instigation. Hugh Casson would probably have been happy to drift along, two gentlemen working together as partners who had no need to put their arrangement in writing. Lutyens had a similar disregard for formality, bringing to all his associations, according to his biographer Christopher Hussey, 'his peculiar innocence of which one aspect was his assumption that no legal agreement was needed to ensure that those with whom he had dealings would be actuated by impulses any less virtuous than his own.' Casson was similarly innocent. Conder, fortunately, was also actuated by perfectly virtuous impulses.

The master plan for the Arts Faculties on Sidgwick Avenue was exactly the sort of job to set a small practice on its feet. Any firm of architects invited to compete for it was going to make a ferocious effort to win, and Casson and Conder – both

*This was part of a large development in Sidgwick
Avenue which Casson Conder planned and
designed for Cambridge University over a period of
more than thirty years.*

still young in the architectural world, where success rarely
comes early – were no exception. In later life, Casson dismissed
the other competitors as being too weak to offer much real
threat, but this is yet another of his light-heartedly self-
deprecating statements which has little foundation in fact. He
and Neville Conder determined to sweep the opposition aside.
They did, and this was essentially the job which set their
practice *en route* for expansion. The future was clearly marked
out and it would be a successful one.

Casson devoted much time to winning and executing this
job, time which must on many occasions have eaten into that
which he properly owed to the RCA. Darwin, with his thick
dark hair and heavy spectacles, was not a man known for his
bland good humour and tolerance of other people's iniquities.
He was either unaware of the demands of an architectural
practice (which was unlikely, for his piercing eyes missed
little), or wanted Casson for his new department so badly that
he was prepared to suffer this split interest. With the devoted

support of his wife and several colleagues, including of course Neville Conder, Hugh Casson managed such a seemingly impossible balancing act for over twenty years. Darwin encouraged his senior staff to run practices in their own disciplines in conjunction with teaching duties, indeed he demanded that they should do so. He felt, rightly, that in this way his students were being taught by people with vital, hands-on experience. Only rarely did he become sufficiently exasperated to demand more of the time – officially four days a week – for which Casson was being paid, and then he invariably allowed himself to be appeased by Casson's silver tongue and Reta's calmly emollient personality. In return he got the high-profile professor he and his College wanted. After all, as he himself once said, 'You don't get good designs from the sort of person who is content to occupy a small back room: a man who won't mix because his interests are too narrow to allow him to, a man who is prepared and, by the same token, only desires to eat, as it were, in the servants' hall.' No wonder he cherished Hugh, who was the very opposite of everything this didactic and socially fastidious man abhorred. For as his friend and colleague Richard Guyatt said, 'Hugh's centre of gravity was outside the College.' Reta, as Senior Tutor in the department, was crucial to the balancing act, though she, like Hugh, was running a small private practice of her own at the same time, and the two of them seemed to swap or even share jobs and staff with quite hair-raising insouciance. But it worked.

In those early years at the Royal College, Hugh and Reta assembled their first group of students, four in all. This mixed bag – two ex-Architectural Association students, an embroideress called Joyce Conwy Evans (who later worked for Hugh for many years), and Julia Trevelyan Oman, who was preparing to embark on her career as a theatre designer – had been gathered up from an exhibition of the best of National Diploma in

Design work by art students across the country. As Casson said, 'It was a terrific gamble. And as there were no interior designers being taught elsewhere, my wife and I went round choosing people we thought had a sense of invention. You know you do or you don't respond to people's work.' This apparently casual method of selection would make students in today's competitive climate cringe, but the Cassons were skilled at spotting genuinely creative ability, and anyway a considerably more orthodox selection process was adopted once the Department had become established. Eventually, its reputation was such that it could take its pick of those clamouring to enrol, and now that interior design had become a recognized subject in a number of art schools, these would often be people with a first degree in the subject.

For the present, though, it was new and untried but underway, with Hugh as titular head and inspiration. Reta did much of the work, helped by one other full-time tutor, John Wright, and many of their friends who came in and out as visiting lecturers: Natasha Kroll, who was much admired for her display work at Simpson's in Piccadilly; Dorothy Goslett from Misha Black's design firm, DRU, who taught business methods; Terence Conran, who came one day a week for a year or so until other matters began to absorb all his time.

Later on, prominent architects like Peter Smithson and James Gowan were employed at various times on a part-time basis. The ethos in what must have been an unusual place in those early days was relaxed and very typical of both Hugh and Reta's approach to work. 'We believed,' Reta said, 'that every student should develop in his or her own direction. They came from such diverse backgrounds – engineering, fine art, architecture, crafts – it was useless to push them along just one particular route.'

These were glory years for the Royal College of Art, with Fine Art, Fashion, and Graphics and Illustration at their peak.

Robin Darwin, with his black moustache and enviable connections, pursued a reign of autocracy, if not terror, but Casson had established a durable line of communication which held fast (apart from one traumatic rupture), and the two men remained friends. The interior designer Jo Pattrick, another close friend of the Cassons, confirmed that this was probably largely due to Reta's influence. Robin thought a great deal of her, and she made sure they had a good relationship with him. After all, they *had* to.

Despite his irascibility and blatant snobbishness, Darwin had a kind streak too, and a genuine fondness for his mercurial Professor of Interior Design. The painting he made of Hugh during this period, which hung in the Royal Academy Summer Exhibition in 1957 (and again in the RCA Centenary Exhibition of 1996), is both laudatory and perceptive. Hugh in his turn respected Darwin's energetic reconstruction of a school to which they were both devoted, and told without any malice the story of the painters' table in the Senior Common Room. 'There was a distinct *froideur* if any of us from more lowly disciplines attempted to sit there at lunchtime. And this was an attitude encouraged by Robin, of course.'

The late Carel Weight, who was Professor of Painting at the Royal Academy for many years, admitted to having had a love–hate relationship with Darwin himself. 'You never knew when he was going to erupt and pounce on somebody. But Hugh always seemed able to quieten him down. At staff or Council meetings, this low voice would gently intervene when Robin was ranting, and somehow the steam was gone. Hugh was very much a peace-maker.'

In 1953, Hugh Casson added a further sphere of creativity to his amply full life: stage design. It seems barely credible now, in our society of high professionalism, that Casson's first theatre commission had come from his uncle, Lewis Casson, in 1926 when he was barely sixteen. Lewis was directing a series of

Grand Guignol short plays at the Coliseum, and wrote to his nephew, who was then at Eastbourne College, asking him to design the set for one of them. 'It was a very conventional set. It had a studio window and a stove with a crooked black pipe. Anyway, he took the design, which I thought was extremely noble of him, and it was used more or less as I designed it.' He didn't touch the theatre again as a designer for many years. Then in 1953 the approach came from Glyndebourne. They wanted him to design the set for Gluck's *Alceste*.

This invitation was just one of many Hugh received in the early fifties. It was one of the most welcome, although immensely daunting. When he went to Glyndebourne for a first visit, the small, intimate nature of the place, as it was then, combined with its experimental approach to opera, engaged Hugh's enthusiasm immediately and enabled him to overcome his nervousness – even terror, he said – at this new challenge. Naturally, he had never even considered saying no to the commission, and he swiftly adapted to what he described as 'wooing' the technicians with whom he had to work, rather than telling them what to do as he would have done on a building-site. The set for *Alceste*, which all takes place in a temple, had a monumental statue of Apollo in the middle of the stage (made by Casson's friend Christopher Ironside) and an expanse of gentle, shallow steps. It was appropriately dramatic in concept and was judged a success.

Hugh designed another opera, William Walton's *Troilus*

and Cressida, in the 1950s, this time for Covent Garden. On 19 July 1954, Moran Caplat, then general manager of Glyndebourne, wrote to him when he heard of the Covent Garden appointment:

> I am sure you will make a wonderful job of *Troilus and Cressida* and I'm delighted that once again the National Opera House [as it then was] has seen fit to follow Glyndebourne's lead.

The architectural nature of the sets required for this Walton opera – a temple with great columns surmounting an acropolis, a Roman interior, and a besieged camp, which Casson designed rather like a concentration camp with a look-out tower on which a soldier was silhouetted against the sky – make it clear why an architect was chosen to do the work. The director, George Devine, a decisive person of immense integrity, became a friend, but the opera was not a great critical success, and – for whatever reason – Hugh was not invited to do another Covent Garden set.

He did more work for Glyndebourne, though, beginning with Monteverdi's *L'Incoronazione de Poppea* in 1962, again with a classical set, with steps, columns and a magnificent classical façade. Despite his good singing voice, which he still liked to exercise – his daughters remembered, exactly as his Cambridge friends had done, that he nearly always sang when sitting

*Hugh delighted in his connection with Glyndebourne
over the years, and made these informal sketches for an
appeal brochure put out by the opera house.*

at his table drawing – Hugh claimed that he, unlike Reta, was
not very musical. But he loved this opera and considered hearing
the concluding love duet be-
tween Poppea and Nero to
be one of the top musical
experiences he ever had.
Some years later, he chose it
for his eighth disc when he
was on *Desert Island Discs*
with Roy Plomley.

Casson also designed several sets for the theatre over the
years, all of them slotted in amongst his other responsibilities,
none especially memorable except the one he did in 1959. The
first night of *The World of Paul Slickey*, by John Osborne, at
the Palace Theatre, was one of the most unpleasant evenings
of his life. His sets were not the problem. Based in a newspaper

office and a stately home, these were largely comprised of bold, striking black-and-white drawings. Particularly effective were those in the Victorian–Jacobean stately house, where a four-poster bed was dramatically hung with red curtains, and the hallway had a broad, shallow flight of steps climbing away into the distance. The trouble was that the play, a musical, was salacious and in dubious taste, and whereas, somewhat to Casson's surprise, it had been greeted without a murmur in south-coast resorts like Bournemouth, it evinced ear-splitting boos, catcalls and shrieks of 'get off' in London. John Osborne departed the stage in distress, subsequently decamping to Italy with the Australian costume designer Jocelyn Rickards, and the play came off after a very few days. Milton Shulman wrote in the *Evening Standard* on 6 May: 'By far the best thing in this embarrassing evening is the vigorous and imaginative music of Christopher Whelen and the elegant simplicity of Hugh Casson's sets.'

Throughout his life, Casson tackled most projects with aplomb, his confidence growing as he worked, even if it meant breaking new ground about which he had initially had doubts. This innate confidence seemed to desert him, though, when he was designing for operas or plays, much though he enjoyed every production, and despite the critical acclaim with which his work was invariably greeted. He never ceased to feel like a junior recruit to the theatre, and once said that if somebody had asked him to go and hammer up some curtains at the back (this was years later when he was President of the Royal Academy), he wouldn't have hesitated to do so. 'I don't think,' he said, 'that stage designers in those days were very significant people, except for a few famous ones like Cecil Beaton.' In some ways he was right. More recently, designers trained in the specific skills of stage design have used their expertise as well as their imagination to electrify the public and thus make names for themselves, with sets of huge technical accomplishment and dramatic impact. It is unlikely that they feel at all like junior recruits.

In 1954, Casson had received an invitation from the British Council. A small group of suitably accomplished people was to tour China for the purpose of reopening cultural relations with that country now that it seemed to be going through a period of relative stability under the leadership of Mao Tse-Tung. Unlike certain others, who had refused the offer to participate because they disliked or disapproved of those already invited, Hugh accepted with alacrity. As he said then, 'I don't care who is with me. I'll survive that for the experience.'

In the event, his travelling companions were A. J. Ayer the philosopher, who was a professor at Oxford, the poet and Greek translator Rex Warner, the geologist Hodgkinson and, most memorably for Casson, the painter Stanley Spencer. He liked them all, and despite the exigencies of postwar travel to an as yet remote and mysterious country (they stopped at both Prague and Moscow *en route* in addition to several less romantic places), and despite the pangs of homesickness which assailed him from the beginning ('In Prague the knife of homesickness is given a further twist by the poignancy of a tiny homely label, "Thrupp & Moberly", on the sill of the taxi door'), he was fascinated by everything he saw. The hilarious, undergraduate mood with which this distinguished little group bore the hardships as well as experiencing the delights of their journey must have seemed curious to their hosts. Only Spencer was aloof, a solitary person in his own world, often reading the Bible, who played hymn tunes on the piano in the airport dormitory at Irkutsk where they spent an uncomfortable night. Casson contributed illustrated articles to both the *Observer* and the *Architectural Review* about his experiences on this trip, and eventually these were published in book form under the title *Red Lacquer Days* by the Lion and Unicorn Press. For some reason, his fellow delegates were therein described as the

Sketch made during Hugh's visit to China.

Poet, the Painter, etc. rather than by name, but years later Casson recalled Stanley Spencer at that time, carrying an unfurled umbrella and a shapeless shopping bag, as 'a most grotesque figure, in his long Ulster with a huge yellow woollen scarf wound round his head against the cold, his pyjama cord showing at the foot of his trouser, because he kept his pyjamas on under his clothes for virtually the whole trip as far as I remember.' Speaking about the trip to a large audience at the Architectural Association on his return, Casson paused theatrically after mounting the platform, and gazed around the audience for several seconds before saying, 'I think I can safely say I am the only person in this room who has slept with Stanley Spencer.'

Casson's contribution to the cultural bridge, speaking to architects and students on the contemporary architecture of the West, was valuable: he was able to talk knowledgeably about the new towns which were then rising in Britain and the prefabrication methods which were being exploited to speed construction. Apart from a National Day parade, which the British group (sickened by the great procession of guns and troops) opted out of halfway through, there was no overt political element to the expedition, and they absorbed the wonderful cultural treats contained in the Chinese cities they visited for day after heady day. 'In lovely weather – warm sun, cold breeze, clear blue days and Mediterranean nights – the week passes crammed with sightseeing. At our request we eschew factories and clinics, mines and blast furnaces. For us, day after day, are spread out the delights of temples and gardens, of palaces and lakes, of secret courtyards and absurd pavilions with delicious elegant names: the Palace of Pleasant Sounds, the Studio of Pure Fragrance, the Hall of Vast Virtue, the Pavilion for Watching the Spring. All are beautifully kept, affectionately restored, crowded with visitors – soldiers strolling with linked fingers, old ladies tottering on misshapen feet, pale-faced Europeans hung with light meters and scribbling in notebooks, parties of schoolchildren in scarlet scarves.' At a time when both Russia and China were unknown to most Westerners, it was a memorable experience which Casson vividly evoked in *Red Lacquer Days*.

Both Reta and Hugh were often away, either on working trips such as this one to China, or on holiday. Even when the girls were young enough to expect family holidays, they were generally packed off to Needs Ore, certainly for the long summer holiday, where they met and played with other children who were staying in the group of coastguards' cottages. Conditions there were fairly basic in the early years, with no electricity – lighting was by oil lamp – and only two buses a week into the nearest town. Aldridge, who didn't drive, would be in charge, with the parents only appearing at weekends, or maybe for one week during the whole holiday. The two older girls' mild resentment at this state of affairs was not helped by the fact that they continued to be in constant conflict with Aldridge. They were aggravated by what they saw as her increasing concentration on Dinah and her evident boredom with the simple cottage life, which caused her to vent her

Needs Ore, with its boats and wide shingly beaches,
was a peaceful escape place for the Cassons.

irritation on them. There were frequent disputes. Even Dinah occasionally adopted the prevailing mood of rebellion, enquiring one night when she was aged six and Aldridge was listening to her say her prayers, 'Shall I ask God to make you less bossy tomorrow?' But Mrs Aldridge was a conscientious and reliable

woman. Nicky remembered that when she had acute appendicitis in 1952 and both parents were away, Aldridge insisted on staying at the hospital with her overnight, not a normal procedure in those days. In any case, whatever her defects, the Cassons were entirely dependent on Aldridge to maintain their busy lifestyle. Hugh, in particular, swept away any complaints from the girls, saying they were exaggerating. 'Any sign of trouble or emotional involvement and he'd be off,' said Nicky. 'He just didn't want to know.'

When the whole family was there, Hugh drew Reta walking along the beach with Mrs Aldridge and the children.

It was at this point that the two elder Casson girls began to register their parents' overwhelming involvement with activities away from home. Eventually, when the few years immediately following the Festival had driven their parents' level of activity, both working and social, up to an almost insupportable degree, the girls were sent to boarding school at Cranborne Chase in Dorset, Carola going first in 1954, Nicky a year later, and then Dinah in the 1960s. Reta was loath to put too much emphasis on the discord, but explained to her daughters that they were sent mainly because she had not wanted them to come home from school each day to Mrs Aldridge's unalloyed influence and its concomitant lack of stimulation. Boarding school provided the ancillary pursuits which would have been lacking at home, for even when Hugh and Reta were there, they were working, or they were entertaining friends. It was certainly not a home where life revolved around the children, and in any case this was a family for whom boarding school was still considered the norm.

The children were reasonably happy at Cranborne Chase. Nicky liked her parents visiting the school in one of the succession of old Rolls Royces which they drove for a number of years, Hugh dressed in a duffle coat or something equally casual. Even though this was now the late fifties, his Festival of Britain aura was still plainly visible. 'It gave me a great lift at school to come from what the others saw as this rather bohemian background with mildly eccentric parents. All this had a certain cachet at Cranborne Chase. Once Father came and gave a talk at the school. He would write to us regularly too, although I always felt they were breathless letters written with his diary open in front of him to give him a list of things to write about, because you were in a long line of letter recipients.' Many years later, Harrison Birtwhistle, who was Head of Music at the school and a favourite of Dinah's, was commissioned by the Cassons to write the music for Dinah's first wedding.

All through the fifties, during those early years at the Royal College of Art, Hugh Casson utilized his draughting skills as a working tool for demonstrating ideas to colleagues and clients, although he still found time to make paintings for friends – and even to sell – as he would do for the rest of his life. He continued to develop the techniques and tricks of his craft with almost feverish application whenever he had a spare moment, watching with professional interest the work being produced by his painter colleagues at the College and informing himself on the work of masters from the past, most particularly the Victorians. But he could never have restricted himself to the life of an artist, or even to that of a portrait painter for which, with no training in life drawing, he was hardly well equipped. 'Like most architects I have a sort of technique for drawing people, what you might call standard people, who we put into drawings to show how high the building is. One practised at drawing little standard people when I was younger and I suppose I became reasonably good at it, though now of course you can buy ready-made ones on sheets of paper from art shops. But I greatly miss the experience of having done life drawing, that wonderfully fierce discipline. Quoting Robert Frost, who said, "You don't play tennis without a net," I feel unless you've mastered the disciplines, the rules of the game, you can't be really liberated. But I'm afraid I'm just self-taught.'

Somehow, though, trained to it or not, he managed to capture the quintessence of people to embellish his drawings in a way which is difficult to analyse. Even had he been a portrait painter, it is perfectly obvious that the calling's inherent loneliness would have defeated him. Somehow, as with most things he did, he managed to turn his art into a social asset, never investing it with the solid number of working hours which would have kept him away from other people and other work, drawing interest and acclaim because of his skill, and showering his efforts on friends, colleagues and even acquaintances in a profusion which was as endearing as it was unusual.

VIII

A Real Passion for
Architecture

Despite his major excursions into other activities, and despite the senior position he held at the Royal College of Art, the architectural practice in which Hugh was senior partner, Casson Conder – and the smaller office he ran from the College – continued to thrive and prosper.

The architect Tim Rendle had started working for Hugh Casson at the College in 1952. In those early days, the new Interior Design Department was ineptly slotted into the old Western Galleries of the Imperial Institute, which it shared with other departments of the College and with the aeronautical collection of the Science Museum. Hugh and Reta occupied an office near the entrance, there was one other office for 'the assistants', and the students were in accommodation a considerable distance away, upstairs and through the textile department. Time-and-motion-study consultants would have blanched at this bizarre arrangement. But Rendle, like others, became absorbed immediately. 'On my first day, shy and inexperienced and ready to sit at the feet of the master, I was whisked off in Whitney Straight's Rolls Royce to his house, the Aviary, in Osterley Park, where Hugh was architect for some major alterations. I was just thrown in to get on with it. Hugh was marvellous at delegating – quite reckless really. And being at the College presented the most wonderful opportunities. Hugh brought in students and staff from other departments on every possible job: furniture and textile designers, sculptors, potters, silversmiths, mural artists.'

When the Western building was about to be demolished in advance of a huge development by Imperial College, the Department was moved to a house in Cromwell Road. Here, Rendle remembered one of the students, Cephus Howard, setting up a practice room in a top-floor studio for his group The Temperance Seven, which was soon to become so popular and well known. Ronald Green saw the group's piano passing his office windows as it was being hauled up the outside of the building on ropes. Such renegade activities took place, if not with Casson's permission, at least with his passive acceptance. He liked the general aura of eccentricity with which his Department was surrounded in the wake of this and similar episodes.

The fifties were years of achievement and expansion for the Cassons. The house in Sheffield Terrace was – always had been – too small, with Reta complaining while the Festival was still on that they were bursting their bonds, and her chief preoccupation now was finding a new home. After much searching, she finally settled on a lovely idiosyncratic house in Victoria Road, w8, designed at the turn of the century by an architect for himself, which had wide, white panelled corridors, a generous staircase which wound its way up through the three floors, and spacious rooms. They moved in on 16 October 1952, and this is where they lived for the next twenty-eight years, along with their growing children and Mrs Aldridge. Her sons, well liked by the Casson girls, were old enough to have left home by now, but they came back each Christmas, and were included in the amateur theatricals and square dancing which were generally a feature of the seasonal festivities.

Dosia Verney, a wartime friend who now lived close to the Cassons in London and later worked on the administrative staff at the RCA, says, 'I don't think they ever had an evening on their own. They were always busy or out. Not that Hugh had any hobbies, he wasn't that sort of man. But he took on so many jobs. He never said no to anything. You know, I think it was a form of ambition in a way.'

Sometimes there would be dinner parties, with Mrs Aldridge doing the cooking for a group of the Cassons' friends. These were convivial affairs, although Aldridge would clatter pans in the kitchen if they lingered at table too long. During the years that the College occupied the Cromwell Road building, there would be big, noisy parties at Christmas time. All the Cassons' friends and their friends' children were invited and the large common room was extravagantly decorated for the occasion. Any child who was present, like the Topolskis' son Dan, grew up with vivid memories of those parties and of the boisterous and happy time they had there. Even Reta's aversion to parties seems to have been in temporary abeyance.

Often Hugh and Reta would have separate engagements, and – particularly during these Royal College years – both had special friendships which smacked of an 'open' relationship, though there was never any question about the happiness of their marriage. Robin Darwin was a great admirer of Reta's and he often came to the house, perhaps for drinks at the end of the working day, which may have partly explained his indulgence over Hugh's frequent absences from the College on other business. Reta was passionately keen on music, and would go to concerts and recitals, frequently with Gontran Goulden, her friend from the Bartlett days, who shared her musical tastes. She made trips abroad, either holidays with friends when Hugh was busy, or on official business to set up exhibitions she had designed or to judge competitions.

There were nearly always lodgers in the house in Victoria Road, with Reta lamenting in the summer of 1953 that in addition to all her other duties she had to get the lodger's room ready. 'But it will be a financial asset.' One of the first was Susan Einzig, a young and talented illustrator who had come

to England as a girl of sixteen, without her parents, to escape
the Nazi regime in Germany. Einzig, a likeable but slightly
lost soul, led a bohemian life with London's artists' community: John Minton, Lucien Freud, Francis Bacon, Robin
Darwin ... Through an originally slight contact with Hugh,
she ended up as the Cassons' lodger, occupying a front room
overlooking the street and becoming deeply attached to them
during the three years she was there. Determined to have a
child, at a time when the single mother was generally considered an embarrassment in society, even by her own louche
friends, she disregarded Reta's warning about the heavy responsibility she was making for herself, the damage to a
burgeoning career, and went ahead. When her daughter Hetty
was born in 1954, it was the Cassons who gave Einzig immense
moral and practical support, although she had by then left their
house; at their own suggestion, they became the little girl's
godparents and helped to surround her with affection and care.
The Cassons were busy. They had increasingly important connections – Einzig once took an early call from Buckingham
Palace on the single phone at Victoria Road – but they remained
her closest and kindest friends. 'I was nobody but they were so
good to me. It was always they who kept in touch.' Others tell
a similar story. David Leather, son of Hugh's sister Rosemary,
remembered how kind Reta was to his sister Sarah when she
was ill, taking her to live at Victoria Road, and Carola confirmed that her mother offered shelter to many lame ducks.
'Although of course it was Aldridge who had to cope.' By now
though, the mid-fifties, the house had become a quieter place
during term time as first Carola and then both the younger
girls were away at school.

In this period, Hugh contacted Eileen Duveen, whom he had
met on the cruise he and Rosemary had taken when he was at
Cambridge. Perhaps his memory of her had been revived by
the publication in 1948 of her father's *Plain English: A Guide*

to the Use of English, which received such critical acclaim. When he was designing the opera sets at Glyndebourne, Hugh began calling in to see her at the house in West Sussex where she lived with her husband. Or he would take her to lunch in Brighton when he had meetings there, or invite her to lunch in the Senior Common Room at the Royal College of Art. Sometimes Reta sat just a few tables away. It was perfectly overt, little more than Hugh's abiding desire to embrace all and sundry, to draw them in to the great spread of his affections.

Reta freely admitted the marked divergence in their personalities which was obvious from the beginning of their relationship and which became increasingly apparent now. Hugh enjoyed social life and big events, and she did her best to enjoy them with him. Sometimes she did, but it was not easy as she was not naturally outgoing. If she was walking along the road and saw somebody she knew slightly coming towards her, she would cross the road. Hugh, on the other hand, would rush across to speak to them. And spotting an acquaintance when he was driving, he would hoot until Reta begged him to stop. He helped her to be less shy, and so did her teaching at the RCA. 'I enjoyed a lot of the social life which I would never have had if it hadn't been for Hugh and his achievements. We got into areas of friendship which I have had a great deal of pleasure from. But I would never have sought it. I have only followed Hugh's lead.'

With his personal life a happy one, Casson took seriously his duties at the RCA, even if he made them less of a burden than might have been expected. His devotion to writing and painting was also being fully exploited and it is easy to overlook his commitment to architecture. This was nevertheless the main drive of his working life. In 1952, he and Conder had their first meeting with clients at Cambridge University. It may be simply coincidence, but could also be an indication of their similar design thinking that the two architects, coming from

different directions, turned up wearing the same somewhat
outré tie. They were as embarrassed by this incongruity as two
prep-school boys on an outing.

The fundamental thinking on planning which related to
Sidgwick Avenue, original and unusual, was Casson's, and it
was based on precepts he had evolved while establishing the
Festival of Britain plan with its different architects and changing briefs. It remained valid well into the 1990s, when Sir
Norman Foster (now Lord Foster) produced ideas which neg-
ated its principles. The architects recognized from the beginning that the original plan was unlikely to be implemented as
drawn up, because the buildings they had incorporated would
only be built as and when there was money available. This
meant the construction timetable was likely to drag on over a
long period. As Conder commented years later, 'The archives
of Cambridge and most universities are endowed with grand,
unbuilt long-term development plans prepared by distinguished architects. They are there rather than on the desks of
building officers because, though conceived to be built in
stages, they nevertheless aimed to produce finite architectural
effects. All such plans need a Napoleon and only have a hope
of realization if all the money is available at one time.' So
Casson's idea was that each completed building should create
opportunities but not obligations for future generations.
There was implicit recognition that, money apart, needs and
architectural tastes would change and that other architects
would be involved on the many buildings which the plan
encompassed.

This pragmatic and flexible approach was to characterize
much of the firm's future work and the plan was warmly
approved by Nikolaus Pevsner on its publication in 1953. The
practice went on to design a number of the buildings which
the University required on the site. First, apart from a small
lecture-hall block, was the stone-faced building housing the

faculties of Modern and Medieval Languages, English and Moral Science; this contained four libraries, as well as seminar and study rooms. With its painstakingly detailed flat stone façade and broad clerestory windows, this was the one formal building, which it was intended others would group around 'like dons seated around the High Table'. Raised on columns like many other buildings of its period following the diktats of Le Corbusier, who was then at the zenith of his influence, its interior embraced the loose-fit principle which allowed for a flexibility of arrangement and possible future changes. But the university's ancient courtyard tradition was dissipated in the long, uncontained views which flew away in all directions beneath the stone columns. This building was completed in 1961, the first major work of a young practice. Neville Conder, who was the executive architect, would have winced at Casson's apparently flippant remarks years later when commenting on the effort involved in embarking on this large project in view of their relative lack of experience. 'We were lucky. Nothing fell down and I don't think anything leaked much. If you have good builders who say, "Well, I wouldn't do that if I were you," you learn as you go.' As Piers Rodgers, who was then Secretary of the Royal Academy, once said, 'Hugh was one of those people who is absolutely determined not to let the effort show.'

During the fifties and sixties, these early years of the partnership, it was still possible to buy land and build a house in Britain, though this became more difficult with each succeeding decade due to shortage of land and the high cost of construction. Casson had built houses with his father's inheritance before the war, and had written numerous articles on the subject, as well as contributing to a book, *Weekend Houses, Cottages and Bungalows*, which was published by the Architectural Press in 1939. He was therefore a popular and obvious choice to undertake the potentially difficult task of house design. But, with large projects regularly coming his way, these small house jobs, demanding tact and patience as well as design skills, and not particularly profitable, were welcomed without a great deal of enthusiasm, and they were undertaken by the individual partners rather than going into the main office. In Casson's case he was helped by Reta and by Ronald Green, and those jobs he agreed to take on were, with the rare exception, not for Mr and Mrs Nobody in the suburbs, but for clients with famous names and ample money. Despite his immense niceness, there is no denying that Hugh Casson had a penchant for such people. So there was work on houses belonging to the d'Avigdor Goldsmids, the Whitney Straights and the Cazalets, and new residences for Lord Montagu and members of the Sainsbury family.

Edward Montagu, Lord Montagu of Beaulieu, was Hugh and Reta's landlord at Needs Ore and he, along with other neighbours, had become a friend, part of the relaxed and undemanding life they were occasionally able to enjoy there. One night at a party, he asked Casson if he would be interested in designing the beach house he had decided to build, a haven to which he could retreat from the formality of life in Palace House, Beaulieu. This beach house was to be on a splendid seaside site and for a client who, despite his love of old buildings and the care he lavished on his estate (he became Chairman of the Historic Buildings and Monuments Committee in 1984, and Chairman of English Heritage in 1985), was positive in his approach to modern architecture. He said at the time, 'I am a complete Modernist as far as building is concerned. I want a contrast to Beaulieu and I love modern furniture.' It was an irresistible project, even though there is only a small profit in jobs of this size for architects with substantial overheads; and by now Casson Conder were established at 35 Thurloe Place with a staff of about fourteen, and large jobs on the drawing-boards. But if Hugh liked the rich and famous, he positively revered the aristocracy, and this was a job close to the small holiday home he loved.

It turned out well, a flat-roofed, single-storey wooden building raised on concrete pillars, with a central brick fireplace and large windows looking out across the sea. On its completion in 1957, Montagu, helped and guided by Reta, filled it with modern furniture, and in 1961 he and his new wife Belinda

Hugh sent an illustrated letter of congratulation to Lord and Lady Montagu on the birth of their son Ralph in 1961. Heading the letter is a sketch of the Beach House at Beaulieu.

asked Hugh to design an extension. He still uses it as a peaceful retreat, and is amused to remember the landlord–tenant relationship which, long after the building was finished, linked him quite firmly to his architect. Despite his sparse free time, Casson acted as a kind of uncrowned king of Needs Ore, much respected by the other tenants and writing to the landlord on their behalf if they had a complaint: like the time when two concrete bird-baths appeared outside one cottage, 'which appear to look as though straight from Neasden', Hugh wrote crossly, or when one tenant wanted to name his cottage The Chief Officer's House, or when a battered caravan appeared on the east promontory, threatening to obscure the wonderful view across the Solent. The bird-baths disappeared, the offending house name was dropped, and Montagu was able to assure his tenant that the van had been placed there by English Nature in order to mount a twenty-four-hour watch on thieves who were stealing terns' eggs from this important nesting area; it was soon replaced by a low, unobtrusive canvas hide. Conversely, when Montagu, unasked, cut down gorse which was also threatening his tenants' view, he was amused to receive a Casson letter of approval and thanks. That cottage and its surroundings meant much to Hugh, which was why he acted as its protector. The Cassons happily lent it to friends such as Susan Einzig, who would take her small daughter Hetty there for holidays.

The d'Avigdor Goldsmids also commissioned Hugh to do residential work at this time. He had already extensively remodelled the Jacobean mansion on their large country estate, Somerhill, in Kent. Now they asked him to convert their London house in St Leonard's Terrace. Ronald Green told a macabre story about something which happened at the London house soon after its completion. Lady Goldsmid had an 'ancient friend' to tea, who sadly fell from top to bottom of the stairs, and was found to be dead. 'Whatever did you do?' cried Lady Goldsmid's architects. 'Well, I phoned Harrods,' replied this ingenious woman who was also one of Hugh's ubiquitous 'girlfriends'.

Hugh's desire to please people with gifts of his water-colours and drawings was well known. The extent of his munificence became apparent when, many years later, Rosie d'Avigdor Goldsmid showed me the bedroom in the flat where she now lived in London, every wall crowded with first-rate Casson water-colours. 'He used to give them to me as birthday presents, or to thank me for a party. I think I've got the best collection in the country. Oh, Hugh was a wonderful man, but, darling, it was no more than a loving friendship. The fact that he was never my lover made the friendship more precious.'

Rosie Goldsmid did not know Reta quite as well, 'because of course she was busy with her three little girls'. In fact, the shy Reta of those days, for whom even informal social contact with her neighbours at Needs Ore was an ordeal, found this rich and racy world not to her taste at all, and left it to Hugh to enjoy. Which he did.

Hugh Casson once said, 'The best artists don't waste time being likeable,' and though this generalization is open to challenge, it was essentially a criticism aimed at himself and his dedicated amiability, rather than a belief arrived at after long consideration. As with so many other things – architecture, writing, teaching – Casson became a competent artist, even a good one, but never a great one, a fact which pained him more than his failure to reach the heights in other areas. Nor was this through any lack of effort or application. From his days in the art room at Eastbourne College, he spent many hours of his life drawing and painting, and even now with his myriad other responsibilities both at the College and at Casson Conder, a whirlwind of finished work issued from his hands on an almost daily basis. His father was a reasonably good painter in oils, and though, for Randal, art was a hobby about which he never became as obsessive as his son, he frequently exhibited with local art groups in Southampton. (At Christmas in 1940 he had sent Reta a cheque from the sale of his first picture, for the child she and Hugh were expecting.) The young Hugh grew up in an atmosphere where it was normal, even desirable, to spend time making pictures, and from childhood until well into his eighties, when his eyesight failed, he rarely stopped. Yet, unlike many artists of considerably less talent, he never ceased to be aware of his own frustrating limitations.

This may explain the irritation he was wont to express at the cliquishness demonstrated by his artist colleagues during the Royal College years, the way they had their own table in the Senior Common Room 'and didn't like other people sitting there'. Such behaviour rankled, but conversely he came close to accepting it as his due. Judged by his own exacting standards, he wasn't quite one of them.

It is difficult to imagine Hugh Casson devoting the time and concentration needed to making an oil painting, and he never did. He once said to Conder, 'It takes too bloody long.' Conder, a skilled draughtsman who took to painting seriously after his retirement, was a man who understood the complexities and technical difficulties involved in producing any worthwhile picture. He thought it would be surprising if Casson ever spent as much as a whole morning on a water-colour. The very essence of his style was produced at speed. It became a conceit

Like so many other friends and colleagues, Joyce Conwy Evans received her share of illustrated thank-you notes.

early on to decorate every letter he wrote with a drawing or, more usually, a water-colour. Some were of a high quality, and many were framed by their recipients. A supremo in the art of thank-you letters, he wrote them instantly on returning home, whether from a grand event or a simple supper with a friend, 'without even taking off his coat, and sitting at the kitchen table', Reta recounted. Joyce Conwy Evans, the ex-student who worked with him for many years, said, 'That was one of the pleasures of his particular gift, and it was something I copied from him, remembering to send thank-you notes, and decorating them with my own drawings.'

People expect architects to be able to draw or paint well and some – though by no means all – do. But even when they practise their art for relaxation rather than professionally, it is too often in a stiff and unyielding style which immediately identifies their calling, especially since the subjects tend to be buildings or ruins of picturesque charm. Casson's schoolboy efforts have not survived, but he was well tutored in the techniques of draughtsmanship when he was at Cambridge by Harold Tomlinson, the man who insisted his students used fountain pens, forbade rubbing out and demanded that every one of their architectural schemes was drawn in perspective and in three dimensions. Hugh said later: 'I of course learnt how to draw plans, section, elevations. But I was absolutely well informed because of him about when something hit something, an occurrence you can't always see in plan or elevation. Would it be awkward? Would a little bit stick up or drop down? In a way, it's been a slight snag because I get hypnotized by drawing rather than designing. If you're quite good at drawing in this way, as I was, you alter the drawing you're doing to make it look nice and cheat on the facts you see. If you're a bad draughtsman you don't notice whether the drawing is nice or nasty, you just get on with the work. I've always been hypnotized by skill in quick drawing, which makes things, buildings usually, look better than they are.' (Other architects are guilty of this practice; few are so ready to admit to it.)

From his earliest days as a practising architect, the time when drawing and painting took their grip as a major activity in his life, Hugh worked freely, lightly, and with an awareness of when to leave well alone, which were all strong characteristics of his work. Look at drawings he did as a young man in the thirties, or in the fifties, and they are very similar to those he was producing as a man of eighty. But not quite. All his life he worked at perfecting the economical line, eradicating the superfluous, indicating rather than overpowering with detail, avoiding the tight, overworked look which tends to blight architects' drawings in particular. This applied whether he was making a perspective drawing of an architectural design, intended to convince a client of that design's suitability, or whether he was making a charming and romantic sketch of some lovely scene which would end up in an art gallery or hanging on a friend's wall. He particularly liked the work of his friend Feliks Topolski, who had made the portrait of Reta just after their marriage. 'He did this very loose drawing. I was rather frightened of Feliks because his skill and fluency were really quite breathtaking, especially the work he did as a war artist.'

Casson also professed to find Ben Nicholson 'frightening'. He too often said that he was frightened of people. What he really felt – certainly in the latter case – was awe in front of major talent he did not himself possess. Similarly, on the Arts Council trip to China, it was the withdrawn Stanley Spencer around whom he circled with nervous fascination, Spencer whose moves and moods he watched so closely, Spencer whom he mentions again and again in *Red Lacquer Days*.

Michael Cain, talking of the postwar years at Casson Conder when Hugh was so often called in to make the firm's presentation drawings and water-colours and perspectives, said that the rest of them all set up perspectives for him. But this is a straightforward, technical task which is not too difficult even for an architectural student to perform, and the more able of them often do; one architect, who worked in the Casson Conder office as a student after completing his first degree, remembers being pressed into service on several occasions to set up Hugh's perspectives.

There were many required. In addition to the small jobs for high-profile clients, a stream of other, more ambitious projects was being undertaken by Casson Conder during the late fifties and early sixties, and it was a time when Hugh Casson, despite his job at the Royal College of Art, was at his most active architecturally. The King George VI Memorial Hostel in Holland Park, which was completed for the Youth Hostels Association in 1959, was amongst the most interesting projects. Holland House, a Jacobean mansion, had been partially destroyed during the war and had then fallen into neglect; only its fine gardens were maintained as an exceptionally attractive public park. Now the remaining East Wing of the house was to be restored by the then LCC, and Casson Conder were commissioned to build an extension so that the whole complex could be used as a youth hostel. Comprising two dormitory blocks, a low brick one emulating the warm red brick of Holland House itself, and a five-storey block faced in artificial stone, they formed a courtyard with the house. This job in its idyllic London setting was naturally mulled over by the press when it was finished, but it was generally acclaimed and is still, over forty years later, a pleasant place for young people visiting London to stay.

There was a small headquarters block built for the General Dental Council in Wimpole Street in 1960. Not one of architecture's blazing statements, this is nevertheless a quietly distinguished building which is modern in concept and yet, with its well-proportioned and appropriately shaped windows, slots in

effortlessly amongst the substantial late-Georgian buildings of
Wimpole Street. It received a Civic Trust Award. It is interesting to note that whilst the practice received nine Civic Trust
Awards during Hugh's time – which are given to buildings for
the contribution they make to the townscape or street scene –
they only received three RIBA awards, which are given for
architecture *per se*, and do not necessarily pay as much attention to the impact (positive or otherwise) a building makes on
its surroundings.

Norman Foster remembered with surprising clarity the short
period when he worked in the Casson Conder office. As an
architectural student at Manchester University, he was in
search of a summer job in 1959 to gain work experience, and
like many other aspiring students of the time, he wrote to
Casson Conder at Thurloe Place. Unlike most of the others, he
was taken on because it was already evident from his work
portfolio and his committed attitude that here was a person of
outstanding ability. Casson Conder, and Hugh in particular,
always had an eye for the high-flyers.

Foster remembered the office with affection. 'I'd looked at
the buildings they were doing and thought this would be an
office where I could learn something. I was right. It was an
extremely civilized and enjoyable experience working there
and I really did learn. Unlike many of the offices I'd had experience of in Manchester, they had a real passion for architecture,
wanting to talk about it and live it all the time. Unfortunately
that's not true of a great many architects' offices. Obviously
we all have to make a living and try to avoid going bankrupt,
but you can actually separate the architecture from that commercial imperative, which is what happened at Casson Conder
under Sir Hugh's influence. They really cared about the details
and the way in which buildings were put together.' This was
an approach which greatly appealed to Norman Foster, who
went on to become renowned, amongst much else, for the

exquisite and thoroughly worked-out quality of his own detailing.

Because of what he described as the lowly nature of his position in the office, he had little close contact with Hugh at the time, though he remembered that both Neville Conder and Michael Cain were able to scribble their own initials on a drawing much like Hugh's. 'His style was emulated by everyone, including myself. I was and still am a great admirer of his drawing. I think I still do characters that bear a close resemblance to his when I'm putting people into a drawing.

'Because of building the Law Faculty at Cambridge in the 1990s, I went back and forward to Cambridge a lot and had a chance to look at the Casson Conder development in Sidgwick Avenue which is close by. I worked on some of the detailing of that complex during my time in the office. I still like it and it's weathered well.'

Another building Norman Foster remembered and admired from that time was the youth hostel in Holland Park, though he hadn't seen it for many years. Hugh Casson would have been surprised but delighted to hear that this unassuming building created such a lasting impression on the summer student who was to become one of Britain's greatest architects.

Like so many others, Foster talked of Hugh's charm, 'but he was one of those rare people who was *genuinely* charming. It's not a slick word when applied to him because it was an essential part of his nature.' He also, having just bought a copy of the Festival of Britain catalogue at a second-hand bookshop in Bath when I spoke to him, was able to take a long-distance view of the work done then, and was intrigued by how good it was. 'I was only sixteen in 1951, and even going to the centre of Manchester was an adventure, never mind London, so I never saw the Festival. But looking at those images, it still looks so fresh and exciting. A great deal of that must have been due to Hugh.'

IX

Difficulties at
the Royal College of Art

The incident which was to mar Hugh Casson's years at the Royal College in the sixties might have been accepted as nothing more than grist to the mill in some architects' offices. For Casson, it was deeply upsetting, and though he was not a man to bear grudges, it probably rankled for the rest of his life. The problem was that this 'last gentleman amateur', as Ronald Green described him, was treated by people he had regarded as his friends in a manner which implied they did not trust him. He was bitterly hurt.

It started in the late fifties when the College, scattered haphazardly around what Christopher Frayling in his history of the RCA has called 'a collection of shacks and mansions' whose only common denominator was that they were in South Kensington – and this included the Interior Design Department, by now at 23 Cromwell Road – needed a new building. It was to be constructed on the site in Kensington Gore which the College owned, but which unfortunately could only be developed in part at this stage, with the remainder not to be available for another twenty-five years.

In typically nepotistic manner, Robin Darwin decided that its design should be an inside job. Such a route would never have been taken in more recent times when architects are required to compete, often financially as well as creatively, for even the smallest of jobs. But it made sense then, as the College was reasonably endowed with architectural talent of its own. Even so, the architectural press reared up to demand a competition for such an important building on such a prominent site. Its pleas were disregarded. Three architects were appointed to share the job, an arrangement which might have led to friction, but which in those less competitive times and with the supremely civilized people involved, was perfectly expedient.

The three Darwin chose were Casson and two of his old friends – H. T. Cadbury-Brown, who as well as having a small private architectural practice was a lecturer in sculpture at the College, and Robert Goodden, who had trained as an architect but was in fact Professor of Silversmithing and Jewellery. Several years previously, Goodden had been charged with forming a schedule of accommodation needs for those departments which were to be housed in the new building: all the departments of industrial design, and the College's administrative offices.

Cadbury-Brown explained the individual contributions of this triumvirate as he recalled them. 'Robert Goodden obviously wasn't going to be the lead architect, and Hugh was doing work then which wasn't quite radical or modern enough, so he seemed happy to let me do it, though he did lovely little concept sketches.' It seems more likely that Casson, far from questioning his own architectural abilities, was too engaged elsewhere to take on the hard graft of designing this complicated building in detail, let alone being executive architect for the job. But in typical Casson fashion, he was happy to act as adviser and overseer, and above all to lend his name to the work. However, it was Jim Cadbury-Brown who shouldered the main burden of the job. 'Hugh was one of the most generous people in the world,' he said. 'Without Hugh I would never have got the job. Robin was a capricious man and sometimes you were in the doghouse, sometimes not. But Hugh was never in the doghouse.'

Darwin had come to terms by now with Hugh's frequent absences from his College office, particularly as they were often during the College vacations. The Casson girls tended in middle age to focus on their parents' frequent absences abroad during their childhood. But they weren't entirely excluded from these trips. In 1961, while the new College building was under construction, Dinah and Nicky spent a holiday with Hugh and Reta at the British Embassy in Istanbul, guests, along with their parents, of the Burrows. It was a heady experience

Sketches made during a Greek holiday.

for two teenage girls. Reta found it hard work living up to the Embassy's standards, although 'we did our best', and they managed to fit in adequate bathing and sightseeing between the inevitable lunch, cocktail and dinner parties to which they were invited. On another occasion, Carola and a school friend accompanied Hugh and Reta on a cruise around the Greek Islands. There was an occasional trip to Paris, a couple of holidays in Malta. Inevitably though, when the purpose of his trip was to lecture, to judge a competition or to act as a paid consultant, Hugh went alone or with Reta as his sole companion.

In late 1961, the reinforced-concrete building Cadbury-Brown and Casson designed for the RCA, and built to a limited budget, was complete. The first phase in a large development which was intended to join all the scattered buildings on one site, it was a studio/workshop block, with administration and a large auditorium occupying the ground floor, and those departments which were to be housed in the building each allocated one of the floors above.

The Royal College building was reasonably well received and, considering the sensitive nature of its site – opposite the Albert Memorial and astride the leafy purlieus of Kensington Gore – it was lightly treated by those who make it a point of honour to condemn any new building. If there was something rebarbative about its black concrete frame and black engineering-brick walls, looming sombrely over the greenness of Kensington Gardens, which caused some to grumble, they probably did not realize that the dark shades had been chosen in deference to the soot-caked bulk of the Albert Hall next door. This whole point was lost when the Albert Hall was cleaned a year or so after the College building was opened, revealing it in polychromatic splendour, and reducing its neighbour to a sullen contrast. But eventually, as the years passed, the granite wall cladding was perceived to give it a certain grim grandeur alongside the red-brick rotundity of the Hall. Anyway, the students were happy in their splendid modern studios, and the architects were almost immediately instructed by the College to begin their research for the next, rather complicated stage of the development.

The trouble which now arose had been incipient for some time, however, and it concerned the track along which window-cleaning cradles were moved. During the course of construction, holes for the supporting beams, or in the canti-lever which was to support the beams, were made in the wrong place. Remedial action was taken, involving the use of dowels as well as bolts, though permission for the additional cost was not obtained from the College Building Committee at the time. That was not the end of the matter. Window-cleaners subsequently refused to use the cradles because they believed the bolts to be unsatisfactory. The College decided to take action of its own and to spend more money grouting in the bolts, but when two bolts were found to be broken, it was advised there was danger of the whole beam coming away from the cantilever and crashing to the ground.

There was more emergency action and beams were strapped to cantilevers with steel-wire ropes, a remedy only guaranteed for six months. At this stage a member of the College Council, engineer Alfred Whitaker, was consulted, and on his advice a firm called Cradle Runways was called in to fit twenty-four sets of suspension bolts and plates in stainless steel and to reposition and fix twenty lengths of runways beam. Another £2,000, a considerable sum in the early sixties, was to be spent, but this would resolve the trouble once and for all.

From the time the problems arose, the College had been indicating that it would expect the architects or engineers, Clarke, Nicholls and Marcel, to be responsible for the costs involved. The letters exchanged on the subject seem, all these years later, to have followed a desultory course. Exchanges were polite, although attitudes hardened slightly on both sides as the months passed. Reading them from a distance, it does seem that the fact that there were three architects involved – all operating from different addresses – may have compounded problems, as did the fact that whereas most relevant correspondence was addressed to Cadbury-Brown as the executive architect, Hugh Casson was considered lead architect by the principals involved. There was much 'copying' of correspondence – solicitors and insurance brokers were notified – but apart from indicating that they rejected culpability, the architects appear to have let matters drag on. The College's main complaint was not that mistakes were made but that, as registrar John Moon wrote in a letter to Casson on 20 April 1966, 'it is not right to expect the College to have to pay to put these mistakes right'. The engineers, Clarke, Nicholls and Marcel, insisted all the time that they were waiting for specific details of negligence to be spelled out by the College. And solicitors to the architects' insurance company insisted that the next move should be up to the College, and that the architects should take no initiative for the time being. The College solicitors could apparently only make this next move by instituting a definite charge of professional negligence, which the College was loath to do. It seemed that impasse had been reached, though the architects and engineers did talk amongst themselves of offering some sort of financial compensation.

After a long silence, those acting for the College, who included Duncan Oppenheim, Chairman of the Council, Anthony Lousada, Council member and solicitor, John Moon, the Registrar, and Robin Darwin, must have lost patience. Robert Goodden had long since dropped from the equation, since his real involvement was to act as a link between the other two architects and the College, but on 28 April 1967, a writ alleging negligence by Hugh Casson, Cadbury-Brown and the consulting engineers Clarke, Nicholls and Marcel was served on the architects' solicitors.

Casson was in Canada when the writ was served, but was notified immediately. His shock at this turn of events was perhaps ingenuous. He had headed a well-known firm of architects for years, and he must have known the rigours and rules of business. But the gentleman amateur described by Ronald Green was an ever-lurking presence, and though he reacted with dignity and restraint, he felt he had been treated shabbily by men who were his friends and was deeply hurt. Not only that, but news of the writ had reached the press, and about a week later the *Evening Standard* carried a large headline to the effect that Sir Hugh Casson was being sued for professional negligence.

This struck hard. As Hugh said in a letter to his own solicitor, who had so far not been involved, 'we are irreparably defamed whether we defend, win or lose'. He was particularly enraged to discover that a writ was apparently public property, a fact which the College solicitor had not warned his colleagues about, probably because, except in a deliberate leak to the press (which this obviously was), no such details can become public property until a case is set down for hearing. The College men were just as dismayed by the ensuing publicity as Casson and Cadbury-Brown, as it did not put them in a very brave light.

As to Robin Darwin's part in this furore, it seems to have been one where, as in running the College, he trusted others to do their jobs without fully acquainting himself with their methods and intentions. He was mortified by the publicity, and genuinely sorry for the damage he realized may have been done to the Casson Conder practice. (Whether he cared quite so much about Cadbury-Brown's reputation is not clear.) He wrote two long and sympathetic letters to Casson in exculpation of his own part in the proceedings, explaining that according to Anthony Lousada, his office had indeed warned the architects' solicitors that the writ was impending, and had been told they 'had instructions to accept service'.

The affair blew over remarkably quickly now, driven to its conclusion by the shock all parties had suffered. The following notice was issued to the press on 7 June 1967:

It is announced that the Royal College of Art, Sir Hugh Casson, Mr H. T. Cadbury-Brown and Messrs Clarke, Nicholls and Marcel have reached agreement on the claim in respect of which the College recently issued a writ necessary to prevent the possible running of the Statute of Limitations. The College have withdrawn the writ and all allegations of negligence.

The claim covered a technical error which was subsequently corrected and was small in comparison with the total building costs involved. No damage to life or property was caused by this error.

The confidence of the College in the architects and consulting engineers is unimpaired and they are being re-employed in connection with the further buildings by the College which are at present being planned.

The architects and the consulting engineer duly contributed £1,650 to the cost of remedial work (most of it paid by the engineers), and the matter was closed. But it rankled, and though Hugh Casson had known Anthony Lousada for years, he was never able to meet him again with anything more than polite reserve until Lousada's death in 1994. There was no longer any question of friendship between them.

There was no room in the new Darwin Building for those members of Casson Conder's staff who had been working at the College with Hugh. They moved into the firm's main office in Thurloe Place. But Hugh and Reta kept their office in the Interior Design department. It was in a room with a fine view of the Albert Memorial, and Casson continued his daily visits to Thurloe Place.

Another building, a smaller one, for which Casson Conder were responsible during the early sixties resulted in no problems, and was much admired. It was a small commercial building with a Lennard's shoe shop at ground level which was slipped into the heart of Chichester, just a few feet away from the medieval Market Cross, and it demonstrated Hugh's belief that it is possible to fit a good modern building into an old setting if you do so with care and restraint. Built to a very small budget, it has white-painted stucco walls with a black-painted aluminium roof, and despite being unequivocally modern in its simplicity and lack of decoration, it causes offence to no one, fitting in, as the critic Ian Nairn confirmed, 'as though there for a couple of centuries'.

Two interior-design jobs for which Casson was responsible while he was at the Royal College gave him lasting satisfaction. One was the new Royal Yacht *Britannia*, the other was the P&O liner *Canberra*, which was finished and set off on its maiden voyage to Australia in June 1961. The *Canberra* was being designed at the same time as Casson was involved in constructing the new College building, but he managed to be deeply involved with all aspects of the work.

'It was a wonderful opportunity to work on this P&O flagship, and it was particularly interesting because P&O were noted in those days as having a very conservative Scottish management. I went to see the Chairman and he said, "I have no advice for you, except to remind you that on P&O ships, drinks are brought to you at the table. You do not sit at the bar. People who sit at the bar become nuisances. That's all." I thought his approach was surprisingly austere, but it went right through management.'

Uninhibited by this daunting interview, Hugh drove ahead in his by now familiar impresario mode, allocating tasks, employing artists, directing operations and ultimately drawing another major job to a successful conclusion. 'We were only a small firm. We couldn't have done it all. So I did what I did at the Festival and at the Time Life Building, gathered together a core of designers, architects, painters and sculptors who we enjoyed working with, and everybody had a section. I remember the painter Julian Trevelyan did some wonderful stainless-steel inlay on the main stairs. He was such a fine artist, and a very amusing man, dark-green face, looked as if he'd been assembled rather than born. Anyway he was excellent.'

Hugh Casson should have given P&O more credit for daring. They were about to make a break with outdated ideas, and Hugh himself, who had just completed his work on the *Britannia*, was part of this new vision. It was quite a radical step, and a beneficial one, to have brought in an interior architect so early in the ship's design. P&O were working in an original way which paid off. The *Canberra*, designed by the young naval architect John West, with whom Hugh got on well, was abreast of and in some ways ahead of advanced thinking. West had convinced the company that there should be an emphasis on passenger needs and comforts, and with its aft engines freeing up space and allowing for easier planning of both cabins and public rooms, this was now possible.

Under Hugh Casson's overall guidance, interior design of the cabins and crew's quarters was passed over to Barbara Oakley; John Wright, who worked with Casson at the Royal College of Art, was given the tourist-class public rooms, while Casson took charge of the first-class public rooms with Tim Rendle as associate in charge of the job. After seeing the keel laid in Belfast, they also did a certain amount of work on the superstructure, largely on the appearance of the ship above the waterline. Philip Dawson, in his book *Canberra: In the Wake of a Legend* which was published in 1997 said,

His work had the effect of softening the ship's lines, particularly in the details of the afterdeck openings and in the shape of the bridge and officer accommodation housing, as well as reducing any possible discord between new features such as the aft funnels and superstructure aerodynamics and the more traditionally nautical elements such as the hull lines prescribed by longstanding shipbuilding experience. It would blend the influences of convention and modernity with a tailored smoothness of line and form which would look 'right' in the public's eye.

Inside, working within the quite restrictive and necessary confines of naval architecture, they produced a good contemporary interior, particularly in first class, where ceilings were nearly all white and kept as flat and unbroken as was technically possible, with the carpeting the rich blue-green of the Pacific. With a beautiful sweeping spiral staircase whose white terrazzo treads and aluminium-clad balustrades rose through three decks, a bar whose sculpted shape was emphasized by being clad in dark Indian laurel (there was the usual row of bar

Joyce Conwy Evans was amongst those who worked with Hugh on designs for the P&O liner Canberra, *and made this drawing of designs for the musicians' uniforms.*

stools, despite the Chairman's admonishments), more Indian laurel in the lounge and artwork by such luminaries as Robert Buhler, it all had the comforting aura of a sumptuous masculine club: appropriate, it seemed, for the first-class passengers. (Things were more austere, though still carefully designed, in the second-class section.) However, this was an era when teenagers had just been invented, and it was in the Teenagers' Room that Casson had his most adventurous coup.

'John Wright, who did the room, had lined it with wood boarding, and we asked David Hockney, who was still a student at the RCA, to draw all over the walls with a red-hot poker. He wrote a lot on his drawings in those days, and he drew from top to bottom, side to side, all the way round the room. It looked simply wonderful. It was the largest Hockney in the world, but after about three voyages, teenagers, encouraged by David's writings, had added their own graffiti which weren't very attractive or funny, so it was boarded in.' It fact it seems more likely that this early Hockney was destroyed. The curator of P&O's art collection could find no trace of it.

Tim Rendle afterwards emphasized Casson's very close personal involvement with *Canberra*. 'Dealing with a company as large as P&O, this was essential and expected. We both attended her trials, and I remember looking down at the vast expanse of the engine rooms in the bowels of the ship and thinking: this is the clever part, the serious part. We're just putting the meringue on top.' Carola remembered that *Canberra* dominated her late teens. 'My father and mother talked about it interminably, and he drew the ship endlessly at the time when he was working on the exterior.'

Hugh's projects were always the dominant feature of home life in Carola's memory, which refutes the impression – too often stated as fact – that Hugh flitted across the surface of his work without any deep involvement. A long lecture about the design of *Canberra*, which he gave some five years after she was built, demonstrated how deeply he was involved in every minute detail of her interior design, and how all-embracing was his knowledge. Once, when *Canberra* was in dock at Southampton, Hugh and Reta took a group of students from the College all over her, explaining every aspect of their work.

It was sad to see *Canberra* before she was decommissioned in 1997, her unmistakable and unusual silhouette thankfully intact, but her once-handsome interior blurred by a surfeit of crenellated pelmets which hung from the bulkheads between public spaces, heavy velvet drapes and frilled cushions. The original clear colour schemes were now murky and dismally inappropriate for an ocean-going vessel.

Another interior which Hugh completed in 1963, and which was torn out only a few years later, was the bar and restaurant at the top of the 32-storey Hilton Hotel in Park Lane. Tim Rendle appeared again in charge of this job, and his predilection for sombre splendour was evident in the curving serpentine wall covered in brown tiles to give acoustic absorbency, the purple and blue patterned carpet and the huge curved black-leather sofa which accommodated up to twenty people around the central circular open fire. It was a dramatic concept which did justice to the spectacular view, but it outclassed the clientele, and in the manner of some interiors, it was shortly redone in a less demonstrative fashion.

Speaking about the Hilton Hotel years later, Casson condemned its siting in such a sensitive position as one of the three architectural mistakes made in London since the war. The others, he said, were the removal of the Euston Arch, and the selling off of County Hall. He pointed out that all three happened under Conservative governments. 'The Hilton was turned down by Westminster City Council. It was turned down by the Royal Fine Art Commission. But it was given permission by Anthony Eden on threat from Conrad Hilton that he wouldn't come to London if he wasn't allowed to build it. Well, a more sophisticated person than Eden would have realized that Hilton couldn't afford *not* to come to London and that he'd have gone to another site, but the political decision was that he should have this one.' This simplistic version of the planning procedure involved may have some truth. It ignored the fact that Casson accepted the commission to work on the Hilton, sensitively positioned though he may have considered it to be in retrospect. The Royal Family's objection to having their Buckingham Palace gardens overlooked probably coloured his later view.

Hugh Casson was ever the realist, sometimes to the discomfiture of his more timid colleagues, and as he once said, 'Every piece of architecture is a battlefield, it really is. The battle is fought over money, over materials, and it is fought with yourself, about misjudgements you have made.' The building which now caused his practice one of its biggest battles was the Lady Mitchell Hall, the part of the Sidgwick Avenue development on which they were working from about 1960 onwards.

Modern architecture has been a contentious subject for centuries, and certain members of Cambridge University who had not liked the earlier Casson Conder work on the site which by now included another faculty building, formed a powerful lobby against the new design when it was announced. Some, led by the Professor of Archaeology of the time, H. W. Plummer, indulged in the type of abuse – hyperbolic, inaccurate and, in many cases, ridiculous – which the more obsessional opponents of modern architecture can claim as their own. One man said the design was 'a monstrosity, suggesting a wind tunnel, a shoal of sharks and a primitive stockade', though another group, which included Noel (later Lord) Annan and the Professor of Architecture, Leslie Martin, rallied to its support: 'Many of us can agree in our admiration for the architecture of the past without believing that the best solution of our present problems is a faint-hearted and uninspired imitation of earlier periods. We ask members of the Regent House to join us in voting Placet.' A vote was held, and Regent House – in effect, the Senate – narrowly rejected the plan by 109 votes to 82. Fortunately, Casson Conder's immediate clients, the Sidgwick Avenue Building Committee, stood firm, declared their support and dissuaded the architects from resigning. Nevertheless, in view of the Non Placet – the Regent House had expressed itself not pleased – the scheme was radically altered and, in the view of Michael Cain, who was now a partner at Casson Conder and the man in charge of this project, much improved. 'There had been a request for less aggressive materials, so it was now a brick rather than a concrete building with rough-ribbed cladding, and the sharply triangular roof lights, in fact the whole silhouette, was changed.'

Following this there was a further vote – reported in the *Sunday Times* of 21 May 1961 – and this time, despite Dr Plummer saying that 'As far as I am concerned the buildings already up are monstrosities and if the scheme were completed it would be a complete disaster for Cambridge,' and calling for a replacement of the architects, it went in their favour. Lady Mitchell Hall was on course for construction, and the architects had survived an unpleasant onslaught.

Leaving aside the question of architectural ability, designing new buildings for historic settings requires considerable nerve, strength of purpose and the confidence to remain courteous and accessible under attack. Fortunately, Hugh Casson was able to muster all these characteristics and became adept at inspiring his colleagues to follow suit.

Lady Mitchell Hall seats 450 and it is adaptable for theatre, film or music, providing stores and dressing-room facilities. Despite the major redesign and its good facilities it is, in my opinion, a building which with its various extrusions, its lack of symmetry and its unwieldy shape against the skyline, must still lay itself open to misanthropic comment. Stylistically, it falls in no particular camp, certainly not that of New Brutalism, which was favoured by some architects at the time (which would have received an even more rancorous reception), and it falls short of the polished and improved Modernism which various distinguished architects were attempting. What Casson Conder were aiming for, of course, was a building which would fit that 'mood of the occasion' they favoured. Personal predilections aside, in February 1965 it was described in the *Financial Times* as a highly successful building.

The original Sidgwick Avenue site plan was revised to respond to new site boundaries and different requirements, and from now on other architects worked there too: James Stirling won the limited competition for the History Faculty (which also raised local ire), Cambridge's own Professor of Architecture, Leslie Martin, designed the Music School, and Norman Foster's glisteningly purist and unequivocally finite Law Faculty, completed in 1995, took the site into a new and exalted realm of architectural quality. But as Casson Conder, over a long period of time, designed the Department of Oriental Studies and the Faculty of Classics and Museum of Classical Archaeology, pleasant, unassertive brick buildings with aluminium roofs, the Cambridge development provided a steady background of work in the office for years to come.

Ironically, it was Hugh Casson's early success, his management of the Festival of Britain team, his talks about architecture on the radio, his articles in which he had dealt with the subject intelligently and with a solid background knowledge which came from extensive reading and research, which led to his work as an architect occasionally being treated dismissively. Because of this dazzling public image, professionals and lay persons alike assumed that he should be regarded as a great architect. He should rather, as he himself willingly acknowledged, have been judged at the level of an able and productive practitioner. In that group he, and the Casson Conder practice, could hold its own. As it was, despite performing well in the higher echelons of middle rankers, they rarely received the amount of approval which was their due. There was a determination amongst their peers to consider them alongside the great – and find them badly wanting. Nor was there ever any likelihood of their being leaders in a stylistic sense. Hugh Casson frankly admitted that his convictions were too weak to have taken him down the innovative road followed in the postwar years by such British architects as James Stirling and, later, Norman Foster and Richard Rogers. 'Not being a dogmatic person means I'm probably not tremendously convinced about style or anything, so I'm a pretty middle-of-the-road designer.' All the same, during his later years at the Royal College of Art, the sixties and early seventies, Casson was probably at the height of his powers as an architect.

The strange, disconnected way in which the practice was run must have put a strain on Neville Conder at times. Much of the work was his responsibility, despite Hugh's frequent interventions and advice, but the kudos almost inevitably went to Hugh. The press, ignoring Hugh's pleas to credit Casson Conder, or Neville Conder alone in respect of certain jobs, almost always wrote of 'Sir Hugh Casson's' buildings. Even architectural journalists, who should have known better, tended to adopt this sloppy shorthand when attributing a building to the firm. And the glamorous invitations, the overseas lecture tours, the work for the Royal Family, the fun were Hugh's.

This caused tensions, not so much whilst Conder was married to his first wife Jean, who was an architect, because then the families were friends and would sail together at Needs Ore, and entertain each other in London. But after Jean and Neville were divorced, and he eventually remarried in 1972, things changed. Wives rarely like to see their husbands pushed aside

Sunday
at
Notting Hill Gate
Tube Station

M. C. Casson
1928

The deco style was in fashion when Casson made these drawings just before
going up to start his Architecture degree at Cambridge.

Drawings of crashed aeroplanes were the subject of his first
exhibition in wartime Cheltenham, 1940.

Casson drew this design for an Arthur Sanderson and Sons stand at the Ideal Home exhibition when he was in partnership with Kit Nicholson in 1948.

Casson gave innumerable drawings to his friend Rosie d'Avigdor Goldsmid. When her birthday in 1952 coincided with the sell-off of artefacts from the Festival of Britain site, his sense of humour found the occasion irresistible.

Westminster Council asked Casson to design their street decorations for the Queen's Coronation in 1953. Colour was an important factor, with this image of a train crossing the freshly decorated Hungerford Bridge over the Thames as an example of its imaginative use.

Casson designed this shining and decorative emblem which was made by Christopher Ironside to hang above Whitehall for the Coronation.

Buckingham Palace
Ante-Room & H.R.H.'s Audience Chamber

Above and below: One of Casson's first commissions for the Royal Family was to design Prince Philip's study and library at Buckingham Palace, with the Prince an active participant in every decision. Neither of the two rooms has been much altered from the original concept.

Buckingham Palace.
H.R.H.'s Audience Room & Library.

Above: Casson drew this scheme for the Royal College of Art building, though the porch area was subsequently somewhat amended.

Below: *Canberra*'s first-class Meridian lounge with its rich blue-green colour scheme is entered via a dramatically sculptural staircase.

Lighting was also a feature of the Pacific dining room, with overhead illumination from a cluster of fibreglass cylinders.

Windsor Castle.
Suite 240/246.
Main Bedroom – MB/2.

AC.

Casson refurbished a number of guest suites at Windsor Castle over the years, and his ideas were always presented to the Queen in the shape of delicate water-colours, such as this one depicting a bedroom scheme.

Somerhill June 1960 — A Christmas Fantasy for Rosie with much love from Hugh

Casson presented his friend Rosie d'Avigdor Goldsmid with
this romantic drawing of her daughter's twenty-first birthday ball in the
courtyard of their Kent house.

Ferry. Venice

Elegant images of Venice figured in many
of Casson's sketchbooks.

Casson was a trustee of St John's Smith Square, designed by Thomas Archer, and this is one of many drawings he made of this beautiful baroque building.

Another fine building which featured so largely in his life was Burlington House, home of the Royal Academy of Arts.

in any respect and Susan, Neville's second wife, found it upsetting. The two men remained on excellent terms at work, but personal friendship, weekends in the country and social visits in London came to an end.

Conder's position was far from unpleasant, however. Inevitably, he enjoyed a large measure of autonomy in running the office, he was able to seize upon the interesting jobs which Casson's renown brought their way, and as he avowed from the quiet hindsight of his retirement, it was with unvarying support and encouragement from his partner. There was rarely any major shortage of work, and the Thurloe Place office, next door to the Venice restaurant where the partners often lunched, and close to the V & A, was a happy one.

At the College, Casson continued to interweave his various commitments with a skill and apparent ease which verged on the miraculous. He loved his link with youth and he was popular with his students, treating their concerns with the complete attention (sharpened by knowledge acquired over decades of practising architecture) which he brought to everything else. John Miller, the architect who worked as a tutor at the College on a part-time basis from 1962 and who would eventually replace Hugh as Professor, did not consider that Hugh was a great teacher in the generally accepted sense. 'But he had a flair for choosing bright and original people. He was not a bit didactic, and in a curious way he helped them just by his presence. I remember the entrance examination we evolved to select the students. It was Hugh's idea to hold it over three days, with a written paper, an essay, a design project and then a party. The papers we set them really tended to be rather frivolous, in fact one of the pleasures of the job was setting those papers, but somehow because they were amusing they encouraged the students to relax and give of their best. Hugh liked to give them nicknames which made them memorable. One very beautiful Danish girl was the Danish Pastry.'

There was always a certain restraint in Casson's involvement with 'the boys and girls' as he called them. He kept a
pocketful of sweets which he would hand out to them in an
avuncular fashion, but he never indulged in the type of effusive
camaraderie which some teachers, particularly during the
sixties and seventies, were inclined to do with a consequent
lack of dignity and respect. Reta, by her very nature, could
never have crossed the boundaries of intimacy. They were both
warm and friendly with their students but, as Hugh said, 'we
didn't coax their affection by constantly having them round
for beer and sandwiches at number thirty-three or anything
like that. Although I think some teachers find it easy to do
that, I never did.'

There was another side to all this *bonhomie*, however.
Terence Conran, whose career as a designer, retailer and res-
taurateur was eventually to reach tycoon level, was still struggling to get established in the early sixties, and accepted a job
teaching for two days a week in Casson's Department at the
Royal College. Reta remembered him as being an able teacher
but one who she was convinced was out of kilter with their
ideas and who thought he knew more than they did. 'There
was a slight air of contempt . . .' She chose the wrong word,
because Conran was not contemptuous so much as dis-
appointed at what he found in the Department. He had taken
the job because he needed the money, but also because it
satisfied a deep evangelical need. Despite his engaging sense of
humour, Conran is and always has been serious about his work,
and has a fervent commitment to the cause of design and
design education. The way in which the school was being run
affronted his own professionalism. Liking and admiring Hugh,
as did everyone else, he deplored his continual absence from
the College which he thought resulted in a general sloppiness
and lack of discipline amongst the students. 'They could do
exactly as they liked, and of course they enjoyed the freedom

which included not bothering to go to the College if they had something more amusing to do. Sometimes I'd turn up to teach and only two or three students were there, or sometimes none. It was all just terribly badly organized, and it was impossible to be effective. But of course when Hugh *was* there, when he stood up in front of a group of students and talked, he was inspirational. He would have been the most brilliant teacher if he'd given more of his time to the job.'

Conran remembered discontent amongst other teachers too. 'But everyone loved Hugh. No one complained.' Despite all this, it would be no exaggeration to say that Hugh was revered by many of the students who regarded him as a role model for their own careers. When he was in the building, the atmosphere became instantly more vibrant. There was, as one ex-student recalled, 'a buzz in the air'. They kept in touch with him for years after they had left the College, and he followed their progress with genuine interest, most especially drawing attention to his past connection with those who achieved distinction, such as James Dyson the designer and entrepreneur, Anton Furst, production designer for such films as *Batman* and *Company of Wolves*, interior designer Ben Kelly, and John Redmond, who became Professor and Director of the College of Art and Design at Monash University, Melbourne. Perhaps Conran's teaching years coincided with a period when Hugh was exceptionally engaged elsewhere, or maybe, in his own dedication to an orderly routine, he misinterpreted the Cassons' more serendipitous ways.

Many students in the Interior Design Department – along with people from other disciplines at the College – were brought in to work on Hugh's architectural schemes. One of the most unusual must have been the refurbishment of guest suites at Windsor in the early sixties. This was one of his many projects for the Royal Family, and the Queen was keen to keep one of the suites, situated in a tower, as a monument to fifties design. When the time came to choose pictures to hang there, Casson went to Windsor with a large number of British paintings from that period for a meeting with the Queen and Anthony Blunt, not yet revealed as a traitor, who was Keeper of the Queen's Pictures. Alan Davie, Barbara Hepworth, Ivon Hitchens, Carel Weight were all represented, and from them the Queen and Prince Philip made what Casson considered a good selection. Blunt, haughty and disdainful and one of the few people Casson ever admitted to disliking intensely, contributed nothing to the occasion. 'He was virtually looking out of the window the whole time, making it clear he thought the whole lot was junk. He was really only concerned with French art of an earlier era. But I thought it was so rude to the Queen.' There was no pompous huffiness in Casson's reaction, however, and he could see the humour surrounding the encounter. 'I think Blunt thought I was a ludicrous little upstart architect who didn't know a Renoir from a Mercedes.'

Such diversions lightened the solid weight of large-scale building works with which Casson Conder – including Hugh – were much involved at this time. Several jobs were won in competition, and competitions, as usual in architects' offices, were worked on out of normal office hours. Fortunately, this was a time when Hugh, drawn away by so many other activities during the day, was best able to be present. He would do concept sketches on a short roll of tracing paper, but Neville Conder never remembered seeing him use a T-square or parallel rule. The National Westminster Regional Bank Headquarters competition, which they won in 1964 and which led the firm into the field of headquarters office blocks, produced an original building, and they had all worked on it throughout a number of weekends. In Conder's view it was fundamentally 'a Hugh building' and none of them would have arrived at the particular solution they did without him.

The solution he spoke of resulted in a sober, dark-grey riven-

granite exterior which envelops the reinforced concrete structure. There is a wonderfully rich interior, achieved by the
lavish use of white marble, gold-coloured carpet, teak joinery,
black leather and stainless steel. M. J. Foden, the project manager, remembered that when the banking hall was just a great
void, Hugh and other members of Casson Conder spent two
days in Manchester, working on the interior details, including
the addition of a magnificent stainless-steel clock. Hugh's
enthusiasm engendered a real desire amongst the contracting
team to produce a building of quality, though Mr Foden recalled
how Hugh would sometimes arrive on the train from London
without his tie, 'so that we had to go and buy him one'. Forming
a handsome addition to the reburgeoning city of Manchester,
the National Westminster Bank Regional Headquarters
received a RIBA Award when it was finished in 1970. As
Conder said, other major headquarters buildings followed,
including one for W. H. Smith in Fetter Lane, London, and
another for Benn Brothers, publishers, at Tonbridge, Kent.

Because of their perceived success at Sidgwick Avenue, there
was a great deal more university work over the years. For
instance, the practice transformed an over-rigid plan for the
University of Birmingham into a more relaxed arrangement
which was responsive to changing needs and capable of completion stage by stage; here they also designed a number of
buildings including the students' refectory, a staff house, the
School of Education, and a computer centre. In Belfast, they
designed the Department of Microbiology for Queen's University, to fit in with their own development plan, and in Oxford
there was a block of student bedrooms for Worcester College.
All these were decent academic buildings, less assertive and
demanding of attention than work in similar situations by
such acclaimed architects as James Stirling, Denys Lasdun,
Richard MacCormac, or even Powell and Moya, but good for
their purpose nevertheless, and meeting the practice's avowed

aim of designing to suit 'the mood of occasion'. Casson was
happy with them. He would not easily have faced the public
scorn aroused by such a controversial building as, say, Lloyd's
of London.

Another diversion which Hugh Casson became involved
with – indeed, actively sought – was the designing of a house
for John Sainsbury and his fiancée Anya (now Lord and Lady
Sainsbury). Sainsbury, engaged to be married and keen to build
a country home, had found a marvellous site overlooking
Romney Marsh. Because it bore the remains of a wooden house,
planning permission would not be refused. Sainsbury, like
Montagu, had a taste for things, including buildings, which
were fine and modern. He asked a friend who was at the time
Hugh's secretary at the Royal College if she thought her distinguished boss would recommend 'some talented young architects' who might be interested in designing a house for him.
He was asked to lunch at the College with Hugh who, a short
while later, rang him with some names. To Sainsbury's surprise, but pleasure, Casson (now fifty-four) asked if his own
name could be added to the list. He was offered the job.

Revelling in the glorious site to which he was now introduced, Casson also liked his young clients and spent a lot of
time with them to find out exactly what they wanted. Sainsbury said, 'He would sit between us, talking and sketching at
the same time, eliciting all the details about how we intended
to use the house, drawing Anya at the kitchen sink, me reading
the paper. He was almost too obliging in meeting our demands.'

Long, low, and weatherboarded, the house emerged, evocative of its era, with open planning, large windows and a flat
roof. Ronald Green remembered hearing John Sainsbury insist
that Hugh Casson should work on the building himself. He did
not always do so, of course, and perhaps he handed the detailing
and supervision work over to a younger person in his office too
readily. But despite a few problems during what is always an

anxious time – the house was initially set out at the wrong level, for instance, and later on door handles had to be researched by Sainsbury's works department because Casson Conder had failed to specify any that were suitable – the final result was a pleasure to all concerned. The Sainsburys lived there for many years, during which time Casson extended the house twice, and though they eventually moved to a grander establishment, it remains in the family and the Cassons remained their friends.

The two older Casson girls were now grown up. Carola had trained as a typographer, and in 1962 she went to live in New York with Adam Ritchie, whom she married the following year. She had been anxious to get away from England, where the Casson name was so well known as to inhibit all her actions and to become a factor – sometimes a negative one, sometimes positive – whenever she applied for a job. She and Adam remained in New York until 1966, when they came back to England and their son Joshua was born. Nicky went to secretarial college, and then joined Carola in New York for a year. Dinah, after leaving Cranborne Chase, went to art school in London.

From the early sixties, when the older girls had left home and Dinah had interests of her own, Hugh and Reta spent two or three weeks each summer in Majorca with Whitney and Daphne Straight. The Straights, whom Hugh had first met when he was working for Kit Nicholson just after the war, and for whom he had done the work on their London home so clearly recalled by Tim Rendle, were wealthy and well connected. Whitney Straight, who, after a brilliant war record, had been Deputy Chairman of BOAC and was now Chairman of Rolls Royce, was a handsome and ebullient man with many interests, including modern architecture, and a wide circle of friends. The house at Formentor – designed by a Spanish architect with Hugh acting as consultant – was luxurious, other

*For many years the Cassons took an annual holiday with
the Whitney Straights at their luxurious house
at Formentor, Majorca.*

guests were exotic, and there was a magnificent motorboat to
take them on expeditions around the island. The entertainment included parties aboard Greek shipowner Niarchos's
yacht, and drinks with the King of Greece. The Cassons were
perfect house guests, Hugh lively and funny, with talk of a
busy working life to entertain other guests, Reta elegant and
quietly charming. They were asked back regularly for seventeen or eighteen years. In Hugh's case, these were also active
holidays when he drew and wrote, as well as relishing the
social activity. They came to an end in 1979 when Whitney
died and Lady Daphne sold the house.

The Cassons celebrated their silver wedding in November
1963, right in the middle of their period at the Royal College,
with a series of three cocktail parties – not their favoured form
of hospitality, but it seemed the only way in which to include
their huge number of friends.

In January 1962, Hugh's mother May Casson had died. She

was a gentle soul, loved by her grandchildren, who had usually been taken to see her on their way to or from Needs Ore, and her death was shocking for Randal, who lived alone afterwards for several stoical years. In 1964, though, he came to live with Hugh and Reta at Victoria Road. Hugh wrote to his sister-in-law, Freda, at Christmas time that year, describing Christmas lunch at Victoria Road 'with Pa 83, Aunt Kitty 80, Aunt Sybil 82, Uncle Lewis 86, all blissfully yacking away at each other'. They also visited the Aunt Jo of whom Hugh had always been so fond, in Croydon. Fortunately Nicky and Dinah were both in and out of the house, or Hugh and Reta might have despaired under the weight of all these elderly relatives.

One of Aldridge's duties – apart from helping with the Casson grandchildren, beginning with Joshua in 1966 – was caring for Randal, and this she did with great kindness until his death in August 1972, aged ninety-four. He was cheerful and independent to the end, frequently going away to stay with Rosemary in Liverpool, taking his morning walks in Kensington Gardens, talking to his grown-up granddaughters who were all devoted to him, and listening to music on his record player. He regularly exchanged mathematics problems with a pen-friend and occasionally with Dinah, who had done mathematics at A-level. He loved conversation, despite being very deaf, and Dinah met him on the stairs one very hot July day to have him boom at her, 'Just like Christmas in Mandalay.' He would sit in his room during the day, but join Hugh and Reta for dinner if they were at home. Nevertheless, it was Aldridge on whom he mainly relied for companionship, and Aldridge was with Reta's sister Freda in the house with him the night he went upstairs to collect a new record, and was found dead shortly afterwards, sitting in a chair with Fauré's Requiem in his lap. Hugh and Reta always treated Randal with unfailing kindness and courtesy: he was one of the numberless family members, friends and colleagues who filled their waking hours.

But Reta felt guilty after his death for not having devoted more time to him. It seems obvious, though, that in his quiet, self-effacing way, he was happy enough being part of life in this busy, animated household.

Reta's cares and duties were by no means entirely concerned with work or with her admittedly busy social life. She worried endlessly about her daughters now, more so perhaps than when they were children, and these cares were particularly manifest in the long letters she wrote to Freda, who with her husband Leon Levson had left South Africa in 1962 after she clashed with the political masters of the apartheid regime, and was now living in Malta. There was worry about Nicky, who had been seriously ill in 1959 and again shortly after her marriage to the photographer Ian Hessenberg in 1967. (Hugh was not at his most helpful when somebody was ill, tending to fade into the background or treat the whole affair with a less than kindly flippancy. Sarah Leather remembered him calling up the stairs to Mrs Aldridge, who was ill with flu, 'Aldridge, do you want a brandy, a banana or a sleeping pill?') Reta also worried about Carola's marriage to Adam Ritchie, which was failing. And she spent an inordinate amount of time looking after repairs to the property Freda owned in London, finding tenants on behalf of its absentee landlady, and even searching for people to go and stay at the holiday flat Freda owned in Malta. The Gontran Gouldens went, and so did the Casson girls at various times, but as Reta explained, it was difficult to find suitable holiday tenants amongst their friends. When Leon died in 1968, Hugh wrote a letter of condolence, but it was a fairly conventional one, and it was Reta whose letter was staunchly supportive and loving; Freda was one of those people who would stay at Victoria Road when she was in England, and she came now for a short time.

In the summer of that year, all the students in the Cassons' department at the Royal College were invited down to Needs

Ore for a day, and shown around the Beaulieu Estate, with those who would be leaving that term invited for lunch at the Cassons' cottage, and the rest joining them for tea. Despite the amount of work involved, Reta was relieved and pleased that the day was so obviously a success, and Hugh was in his element. But all this was in addition to Reta's normal work at the College, and it is understandable that she often wrote to Freda late at night or before she rushed off to work in the morning, and complained that she was tired.

Hugh regarded all familial problems and domestic duties with apparent serenity, confident that Reta would cope. He devoted his immense energy and enthusiasm to the mainstream of his life, which was work. There were times, though, when Hugh's delegation of responsibilities verged on the immoderate. At the beginning of one College year, for instance, they were embarking on a new course, with more new students than ever before, and new secretaries working in the department, so it was, as Reta wrote to her sister, 'quite a sweat. Hugh wisely skipped off to lecture in Germany.' This was Reta employing irony rather than ire, but Freda would have taken the point.

It was around now that Hugh was engaged in designing the building for which he is probably best known. It is quite different from anything Casson Conder had done before or has done since. It captured the public imagination in a way very few new buildings do, and it seemed, in one job, to epitomize all the ideals Casson liked to talk about. It is the Elephant and Rhinoceros Pavilion at London Zoo, which opened to the public in March 1965. He had worked with Solly Zuckerman, who was Secretary of the Zoo, during the Festival of Britain period. Now Zuckerman had ambitious plans for expanding and reorganizing the Zoo, and in 1956 he had asked his friend Casson to draw up a development plan. Money was, as ever, a hindrance to progress, and so it was that the Elephant House,

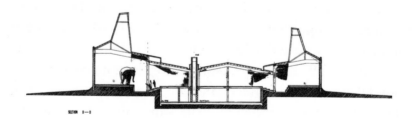

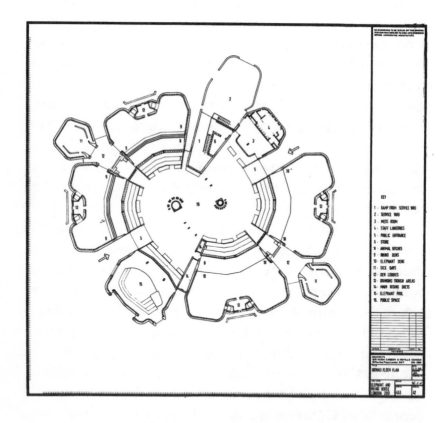

*Plan and elevations of the Elephant and Rhinoceros
Pavilion at London Zoo, a building which Neville Conder
described as 'absolutely Hugh's'.*

not started until some years later, was the first building to be completed.

Neville Conder has said that 'of all the major partnership buildings, the one that is most absolutely Hugh's is the Elephant House. I detailed it, but by then the main lines had been set because I was engaged elsewhere when the concept was worked out by him.'

The very idea of such a building intrigued Hugh to an unparalleled degree, and Neville Conder thought its strong and unusual shape sprang from a comment he made early in the design stage: 'You can but humiliate elephants by making them stand in a straight line.' This empathy, and advice from Desmond Morris who was on the Zoo's client committee, led Hugh to house the elephants in linked circular pavilions which surrounded the main public-viewing area and from which, for safety reasons, they were separated by a wide, dry moat.

Viewed from this central position where the light level was kept low, the animals were dramatically silhouetted against light flooding down from the tall lantern lights which give the roofline of the building its idiosyncratic shape. With the tree-like structure of the central area, these viewing pens assumed the appearance of sunny clearings in a forest, and there were one or two waspish comments when the building opened about the suitability of 'exhibition design techniques' in such a situation. But, clad in bush-hammered concrete, a rough grey surface which can't fail to invoke an elephant's singularly heavy skin, this was a building with an appealing element of fantasy. It was described in the *Financial Times* as both romantic and functional. Neville Conder said, 'I don't think Hugh set out to create a visual analogy to animals gathered round a watering hole, but he noted it and allowed it to stand.'

A very different aspect of Hugh Casson's architecture, but one he instinctively found beguiling, was concerned with

conservation, memorials and follies. In much of this he worked
with Stuart Taylor, a Casson Conder partner whose interests
also lay in this direction, and who was, when classical details
were demanded, able to ensure that they were completely
accurate. 'Gentry work,' Conder called it, and certainly some
of it emanated from that group of charming, civilized and
well-heeled aristocrats (or even members of the Royal Family)
with whom Hugh loved to consort. There was the white-and-
yellow-painted memorial arch at Polesden Lacey dedicated to
Mrs Ronald Greville's father, William McEwan; a summer-
house in the Savill Garden at Windsor; the restoration in 1965
of Winchester public library, which was a handsome 1838
building; and several wooden buildings destined for rural situations which were commissioned by such clients as the
National Trust and the Royal Society for the Protection of
Birds.

One conservation project which many Londoners use as a
cut-through from Haymarket to the National Gallery, probably
without even wondering who was responsible, is Hobhouse
Court, where existing buildings were converted and small new
ones of a quiet, modern demeanour added to provide office
suites, shops and galleries. Still well maintained, with its
attractively landscaped central courtyard intact, and nothing
either flamboyant or demanding to spoil the overall harmony
(no curtain walling, no synthetic cladding), this is one of the
partnership's most sensitive and successful restoration jobs; it
received a Civic Trust Award.

X

The Likeable Proselytizer

By 1970, Hugh Casson was moving into the last years of his tenure at the Royal College of Art and, one would expect, towards retirement. Meanwhile, he showed no sign of loosening his hands on the reins. He was totally engrossed in his work: at the College, at the two architectural offices he headed, and with his activities as a communicator and an artist. His skill as a television performer was now recognized and at the beginning of 1972 he and his Aunt Sybil jointly took part in a television programme entitled *An Evening with . . .* , in which they read poetry and pieces of prose which had particular meaning for them. As Reta told Freda in one of her letters, they made an attractively contrasting pair, and the programme was well received.

Plans were now underway to extend the College premises, exactly as stated in the 1967 press release, with H. T. Cadbury-Brown as architect in association with Sir Hugh Casson, and correspondence of the time shows Hugh always as the link man between College and planning authorities, College and planning lawyers, College and architects. The correspondence was profuse, because this further extension, which involved demolishing buildings in both Kensington Gore and Queen's Gate, hit the planning rocks hard. Supported by the Royal Fine Art Commission and many other eminent authorities as an excellent scheme, it was nevertheless rejected, and then again rejected on appeal because of the putative demolition involved. The project was accordingly abandoned.

(An extension was finally made to the Royal College of Art, but not until well into the 1980s. Then it was a different, less controversial building, and the commission went to John Miller, who was by now Professor of the Environmental Department. Cadbury-Brown made no attempt to conceal his bitter disappointment at this change of architect. Casson was ostensibly more sanguine, though he regretted – as architects always do – the months lost trying to get permission for the Cadbury-Brown scheme.)

During the 1970s, when the firm was at the peak of its popularity, Casson Conder built two successful civic buildings. After preparing a development plan for the Borough of Swindon – Hugh had by now acquired a considerable personal reputation for this type of work – they went on to build its Wyvern Theatre and Arts Centre, for which they also did a complete furnishing scheme. And in 1970 they won a competition to design Derby Assembly Rooms, which finally opened to a warm reception in 1978 and received an RIBA Award. All this was achieved despite the fact that Hugh made only brief visits to the office in Thurloe Place when he could spare the time.

The twenty-three years Hugh Casson spent as Head of Department at the Royal College of Art were happy and stimulating ones, made more so by the consultancies, the committees (he liked committee work which he regarded as a sort of art form), the broadcasting, the writing, the painting and the architectural commissions, which had taken up so much of his time elsewhere. The student unrest which beset the College during the early seventies, under the Rectorship of that reasonable and peace-loving man Lionel Esher, who took over from Robin Darwin in 1971, was largely manifest in other Departments. Casson's Department was small – varying between thirty and fifty students – and the relationships between them and the staff were generally close ones which tended to obviate major problems. David Lyall, who came to the College from a three-year course in Industrial Design at the Central School of Art & Design, remembered that 'one of the attractions of the Interior Design School was that there was no doctrinaire straitjacket or methodology to restrict the students' development. Considerable latitude was allowed not only in how projects might be tackled but in the nature of the projects themselves. In my final year, 1972–3, I worked on experimental structures and lightweight space-enclosing systems for travelling exhibitions, etc., and other students worked on the design of boats. The degree shows then also featured landscape design projects, work that veered towards textile design, circus tents, as well as more conventional interior-design projects. Every project was the product of an individual personality; there was no corporate image, no sense of the stamp of an atelier in the work. Yet curiously, and this may sound quaint, it was almost like being part of a large family, and this was very much due to the atmosphere created by Sir Hugh and Lady Casson. Sir Hugh was extremely interested in the students' individual development, not only while they were on the course, but long afterwards. He provided former students with encouragement and also with very direct help and introductions to enable them to secure commissions or appointments.'

Despite his liberal approach, Casson always said that the students in his Department had discipline, 'they were not free expressioning all the time', they had to know how to draw and to measure and to put things together. Such problems as did arise during the troubles were largely because the students *were* working on the many innovative and unusual projects David Lyall described. They were anxious to shrug off the straitjacket they felt they were forced into by the words Interior Design. Casson, anxious to placate them, agreed to change the Department's name to Environmental Design in 1972. The

College was apparently not best pleased at having this newly fashionable term hijacked by its most maverick of departments. But the deed was done.

Reta continued maintaining a calm presence at the centre of Hugh's furious whirl of activity, and she had increasingly proved herself as a figure of authority in the world of design, sitting on the Design Council and other establishment committees. She was far from being just an adjunct to Hugh. In the early seventies, towards the end of their joint period at the Royal College, she was in Japan for a month with a group which included Joanne Brogden, the Professor of Fashion, to help set up an exhibition in Tokyo of work by Royal College students and staff, past and present: everything from ceramics to fashion. This, held in an art gallery at the top of the Seibu department store, was remarkable because of the expertise, fervour and intense respect with which it was handled by the Japanese. It immediately followed an exhibition in the same gallery by Giacometti, giving an indication of the importance with which work emanating from the Royal College of Art was regarded. Shortly afterwards Reta went to Prague to take part in the judging of an international jewellery competition. In addition, family problems and demands continued to fall on her shoulders. Carola's marriage had finally collapsed in 1968 and Carola was living with Joshua in a house Reta had bought in Westbourne Park Villas in north Kensington. Nicky and Ian, whose marriage was a happy one, were living in one half of the house at this time, though eventually they moved into the house next door with their children, Caspar, born in 1972, and Rosie, born in 1974. Dinah, having done well at art school, had married writer Nicholas Wood in 1970 and was beginning her career as an interior designer. Her children, Emily and Matthew, were born in 1973 and 1976. Freda's property continued to demand Reta's attention, and in her letters to Malta she continued to sound tired and overworked.

Now, as he came towards the end of his time at the Royal College, Hugh instigated a new venture which was soon working well. Asked to consider the problem of restoring the old jail at Abingdon, a fine building dating from 1810, he decided to set up a school Project Office with this as its first job. The Office was to be run by Julian Bicknell, an architect with a reputation for making sympathetic modern restorations of old buildings, who was already teaching part-time. The new Project Office gave students a base from which they could get real experience of working on environmental schemes, and it served to formalize their hitherto rather casual involvement with work for Casson's own office. The Project Office flourished from the start. Sometimes there was almost too much work, according to Bicknell, and during the remainder of Casson's time at the College, as well as restoring Abingdon, the Office was responsible for designing two major exhibitions: One Hundred Years of the British Monarch at Bath, and the Bugatti Exhibition at the College. Bicknell said, 'Hugh was immensely supportive. At one point we over-ran the budget at Abingdon – by a large amount. There was no question of him blaming me and the Project Office. He just went to Abingdon, said it was entirely his fault and somehow smoothed them over into accepting the overspend because the result was going to be marvellous. He always shouldered responsibility. I learnt from him never to justify myself beyond the facts.'

In 1974, Hugh participated in a television series called *The Spirit of the Age*, in which a number of experts each surveyed one period of British architecture. Selected by the overall series director, John Drummond, these people were of a very high calibre: Alec Clifton-Taylor fronted the medieval period, for instance; John Julius Norwich the Palladian; and Roy Strong the Elizabethan. Hugh Casson, who had already demonstrated his skills in individual television programmes, was asked to take on the modern era, from the thirties onwards, both writing and presenting the one-hour broadcast. The programme's director, David Heycock, remembered him as 'an excellent performer in every way. Quick, easy, adaptable, never showing any impatience and always absolutely calm. And he was such excellent company when we travelled to locations. It fascinated me that apart from his great fund of architectural knowledge, he was well read in all the contemporary literature that I, aged thirty, was interested in at the time.'

Hugh scanned the modern period in architecture with aplomb, enlivening it with the personal anecdotes of which he kept an inexhaustible supply, and maintaining a well-balanced compromise between objective comment and personal opinion. A small, dapper figure, he had both *gravitas* and immense quiet authority; viewers learnt about the scope of architecture between the thirties and the seventies from the programme, and felt confidence in everything said by its presenter. When he stated so assuredly that Charles Holden's thirties underground stations were minor masterpieces, it rang true, though it may have been a surprising concept for viewers more used to accepting their everyday surroundings without proper consideration. When he agreed with many people's negative opinion of sixties architecture, but then went on to show certain good buildings of that period, it immediately became possible to view them in a new and favourable light. Once again he was helping to open the door a little further on a subject which had for too long been shut away from the general gaze.

Fellow architects naturally warmed to this likeable proselytizer, this gentle fighter of the battles many of them funked. Paradoxically, some were all too ready with the pejorative epithets 'butterfly' and 'lightweight', charges which he unfortunately invited at times by accepting commissions he would have been better to pass by. *Nanny Says*, the book he wrote with Joyce Grenfell and illustrated, was a charming stocking-filler, not meant to be taken seriously, but its appearance in 1972 was one of the things which frayed the serious thread of his writings and lectures. Rightly or wrongly, certain of his peers could not equate this popular and frivolous little volume with the work of a serious thinker. Despite having what the architect Julian Bicknell described as 'an encyclopaedic knowledge of great buildings', Hugh Casson never wrote a major academic work of the sort which is read by few but earns the awed respect of many. With a multiplicity of commitments and projects, a mind which was too quick to linger over deep reflection, and the apparent inability to sit in one place, alone and without distraction, for very long, he never allowed himself the time for that. This was something he came to regret.

Hugh Casson would probably not have chosen to retire from the Royal College of Art in 1975, when he was sixty-five. 'I hung on till my wrists were slapped and I was told to push off.' He had enjoyed his involvement with the unusual department he had created, and it had become increasingly healthy over the years, despite its unpopularity with certain other members of the College who, as John Miller said, 'thought it a maverick outfit, rather weird and mixing interiors with landscape architecture and furniture design, which had no place there'. Some of them also, whether they admitted it or not, resented the high public profile which their energetic colleague had fashioned for himself. His was a personality which was now well known way beyond the bounds of academe. He mixed with the great and the good. He served and was a friend of the Royal Family. And somehow he ran his Department at the College, if not with distinction, at least with verve and obvious competence. They weren't quite sure how all this had been achieved, particularly by someone who appeared to expend no great effort in the process. Their resentment was mixed with envy.

Hugh Casson never had an inflated sense of his own importance, but he was aware of his worth and the contribution he had made in many areas. By the mid 1970s he expected other people to acknowledge his distinction, at least tacitly. When he visited John Miller, who had now taken his place as Professor of Environmental Design, shortly after he had left the College, he noticed and commented upon all the alterations Miller had made in his old room. And when he had left the Department, a note was found pinned to the door. Beneath an unmistakable drawing of himself were written the words 'HC was here.'

Reta had retired from the College the year before, and there was work for Hugh at the Casson Conder office, so despite his reluctance to go, Casson was certainly not about to embark on an empty retirement. He was now free, should he wish, to slot back into his role as a full-time architect. Again, though, he swerved off in a completely different direction. In early 1976, Sir Thomas Monnington, President of the Royal Academy, died in office. Hugh Casson, a member of the Academy since 1962, and full Academician since 1970, was elected in his place, and immediately entered one of the busiest, most eventful periods of his life.

XI

The Royal Academy

Those who knew Hugh Casson well had thought it extremely unlikely that he would settle down with much devotion to the daily grind of architectural practice, something he had not really done since his days working with Kit Nicholson during the 1930s. And when the time came to leave the Royal College, he faced the future with only limited enthusiasm, and with qualms about how he was going to cope with a life which would be more prosaic and prescriptive than the one he had become used to. To make matters worse, he had a real fear of inactivity, of an unstructured day. 'I've always had a place to go to and something to do when I got there.' And he loved being at the centre of things, a person of consequence mingling with those of distinction in every field.

The Presidency of the Royal Academy, the job to which he was now elected by a large majority, might have been created for him, and it solved instantly the problem of what he would do – and enjoy doing – for the next few years. He would also continue to be senior partner at Casson Conder and make his flying visits to the office there, as well as keeping on much of the writing and committee work which had been an ever-present thread in his life. New demands would be made upon him because of his position. He would not be bored.

When Sidney Hutchison, who had replaced Humphrey Brooke as Secretary of the Royal Academy in 1968, telephoned

Buckingham Palace to notify the Queen that Hugh Casson had been elected, and to ask her consent as Patron, she expressed herself delighted. In view of her close connection with the man the Duke of Edinburgh later described as 'our architect and friend', this was probably more than a conventional response. She was not more delighted than her new President though, and he took up the job with vigour. He knew it was going to be fun, and it was. The gold medal and chain of office which George IV had presented to the Academy in 1820 looked well on him despite his small stature, and he took to wearing a Mao jacket for evening events which made a simpler background for its splendour than the traditional dinner jacket. The Royal Family was more in evidence than usual at the Royal Academy during Hugh Casson's time, sometimes making private visits as well as attending official functions. The Queen Mother in particular enjoyed luncheons there with the President, who provided the type of amusing company she patently enjoys. He would greet her, arms spread wide in welcome in the warm, loving gesture few commoners dare to assume in the presence of Royalty, certainly not those occupying such a formal and dignified office as Hugh did.

The Royal Academy is an independent, privately funded institution of up to eighty eminent artists and architects who are elected by their peers. Founded by such a group in 1768 through a direct act of George III, it aims to promote the creation, enjoyment and appreciation of the visual arts by means of exhibitions, education and debate, and its first President was the painter Sir Joshua Reynolds. For a hundred years this new and unique institution was housed variously at premises in Pall Mall, then at Somerset House, and lastly in the eastern portion of the new National Gallery in Trafalgar Square which, designed by William Wilkins, was opened by William IV in April 1837. It was not until 1866, prompted by the National Gallery's need to occupy more of its building, that the Government offered the Academy a 999-year lease of the splendid premises it occupies to this day at a peppercorn rent of £1 per annum: Burlington House, Piccadilly. Built around 1664, Burlington House was much improved subsequently by the Third Earl of Burlington, and by William Kent, who lived in it till his death in 1748 and who had, as Sidney Hutchison wrote, 'transformed a rather uninspiring house into a palatial, Italianate mansion'.

Notwithstanding its nominal rent, the Academy had, at its own expense, to make necessary alterations to the façade, raise the roof to include a further floor, and build additional premises to house galleries and schools in the garden on its north side. And it has, in addition to that initial capital outlay, always been responsible for the huge cost of upkeep all this entailed.

Despite his decade-long connection with the place, Hugh had not been deeply involved there at first. His commitments elsewhere precluded that, and in any case he shared up to a point the faint disdain with which, for a long period, the Academy was regarded by the more avant-garde and cosmopolitan members of the arts world. It had taken years to overcome completely the marks left by Sir Alfred Munnings, President from 1944–9. In addition to taking other reactionary stances, Munnings had made a virulent attack upon modern art in his speech at the Royal Academy Dinner in 1949, disparaging both Picasso and Matisse in particular. Its catastrophic effect spread wide, not least amongst Academicians themselves, for he had not spared them from his sweeping range of condemnations, saying, 'I find myself a President of a body of men who are what I call shilly-shallying.' It was another twenty years before some important modern artists could be persuaded that times had changed sufficiently for them to become members of the Royal Academy. Others never did. Casson, a liberal man even if he was no iconoclast, had shared these reservations about the Academy's right to be taken seriously in the world of modern

art, and this probably precluded his whole-hearted commitment to the place during the sixties.

But for some time now things had been improving. Over the
years, Humphrey Brooke, a dynamic and energetic figure who
had come from the Tate Gallery to be Secretary in 1952, influenced successive presidents to adopt a more adventurous
approach. By the time Casson took over, reform was underway.
His predecessor, Sir Thomas Monnington, had broken with
precedent by inviting women to the Royal Academy Dinner in
1967. But this was only one small indication that outdated
values and habits were to be rejected. More importantly, he
created an atmosphere which meant that innovative and criti-
cally acclaimed young artists such as Elisabeth Frink, Eduardo
Paolozzi, Peter Blake and Anthony Green were sufficiently
reassured to accept membership. After too many years in the
doldrums, numbers of visitors to the annual Summer Exhibition – the Academy's most effective public face – had started
to rise.

Nevertheless, Hugh, who during the past few years had
worked closely with Tom Monnington as a member of his
Policy Advisory Committee, and for just a few weeks before
Monnington's death as Treasurer (despite claiming in print
that he was completely innumerate), knew that all was far
from well. Not for the first time (or the last) in the Academy's
history it was in financial difficulties. Running costs of the
extensive premises it occupied on this prime Piccadilly site
were huge, and ever increasing as the buildings aged and
deteriorated. A great deal of the trouble stemmed, unfortunately, from the members' determination to maintain the
Academy's independence, resisting suggestions that government funding should be sought, and looking inward rather than
outward for their *modus vivendi*. Outsiders were bemused by
what appeared to be such an élitist and obdurate stance.

Hugh Casson was bound by no such niceties. Sidney Hutchison remembered the first Council Meeting of his Presidency, when the gravity of the financial situation was discussed at length. 'Hugh said very little for a while. He just listened to the requests from various members of the Council that independence should be maintained at all costs. Then eventually he said, "You know there is no independence in bankruptcy." '

Bankruptcy was not an option. Apart from anything else, the Academy had too many valuable and saleable assets for that to be likely. But members needed a sharp reminder that their position was serious and Hugh, numerate or not, was determined that the problem should be resolved. Moreover, he wanted the Council to go with him along the route he had chosen without confrontation or conflict. Amongst other things, this involved introducing more major exhibitions, seeking wide and adequate sponsorship, opening the whole of the Royal Academy premises to a broader public by various mainly commercial measures, and in general proclaiming its important presence to the world.

Here, just as he had done during the Festival of Britain, he achieved what he set out to do by gentle means, demonstrating once more the steely determination and deep intelligence which lay beneath a deceptively insouciant exterior. As Hutchison remembered, 'Hugh never steam-rollered anything, but he got his way by just patting people on the back, and using persuasion and charm. There was no pomp. It was obvious from the beginning that he was an approachable person.' Casson in his generous way attributed much of what was done – and there was plenty – to Monnington before him, and to Roger de Grey, who was a staunch supporter and adviser during the Casson years, as well as being Treasurer from April 1976 and his successor as President from 1984. De Grey was in no doubt at all that changes must be made, especially as the Academy overdraft stood at £500,000 by the autumn of 1977, and was still rising. He backed even Hugh Casson's most controversial innovations, which involved opening to the general public parts of the building which had hitherto been private, and imposing charges where up till now none had existed.

With the notion of independence cast out of the window, or at least not clung to like a velvet shackle, the job of getting the books to balance began with an immediate application for help to the Arts Council, and later to the same source for an annual subsidy. On neither occasion were replies forthcoming for a long time, but when they did come they were in the negative. Meanwhile, fortunately, other remedies were in hand. Some had been mooted for years, but had never hitherto been put into practice.

An early measure was the establishment of the Friends of the Royal Academy. Hugh Casson sometimes quipped that the RA Friends were his sworn enemies, but this was simply a flippant joke of the type which occasionally earned him an acrimonious response. He was in fact delighted at the success of this new institution. His only reservations were that by the time he retired, the Friends were flooding the place, crowding the exhibitions (to which they had free entry) together with *their* friends, reducing the private view of the Summer Exhibition, which had hitherto been regarded as a socially élite occasion, to something resembling a rout, taking over a handsome room on the ground floor as their lounge, accosting him in the entrance hall with their ideas, and generally imposing a demanding presence on Burlington House. Nevertheless, they had been a godsend. Established on 1 January 1977, their arrival was the first in a series of changes which would, eventually, return the Academy to financial health. With the main body of Friends paying an annual £10 for membership at the beginning, the institution was immediately popular and more than 8,000 people enrolled during the first few months. By the summer of 1999 there were nearly 80,000, and they continue to be amongst the Academy's most loyal supporters. Piers Rodgers, who joined the Academy as Secretary during Casson's time, remembered a letter from one devotee amongst the Friends, asking for an enrolment form for her husband. 'I'm giving it to him as a surprise for Christmas. He's expecting a lawnmower.'

Beginning with the Summer Exhibition of 1977, a 15 per cent commission on sales was introduced, markedly less than the 30–50 per cent which is charged by most commercial galleries, but still a new departure for the RA, and one which became a useful fund-raiser. And in that year too, fees began to be charged for students at the Royal Academy Schools. This had little effect on most of the students, who were able to obtain grants from their local authorities, but again it increased the amounts rolling into the RA coffers.

Hugh rarely visited the Schools himself, which considering his own long years of experience at the Royal College of Art seems strange. But it was almost as though he was wary in these professional quarters of being rebuffed as an amateur by students and staff, much as he had felt he was at the College. Explaining his absence, he said, 'The tradition of Royal Academicians dropping in and doing a couple of hours' teaching has gone, partly because painters have become more professionalized, with dealers and galleries and contracts, and they live miles away and teach where they live, so it is not a great temptation. So sadly I had very little contact with the Schools other than going to their exhibitions and presenting the prizes.' This was an excuse. He admitted at one point that it required quite a lot of courage to go down into a room full of students. It was something he rarely did.

Perhaps the most dramatic change to take place in these early years of Hugh's presidency of the Royal Academy was the hugely increased number of exhibitions which were held at Burlington House. From five in 1975, they leapt to around a dozen in the year following, with fifteen taking place in 1978,

and they spread out to occupy parts of the building hitherto
sacrosanct for other purposes. Sidney Hutchison had worked
at the Royal Academy since he was a young man in 1929, and
would continue to do so until his retirement from the post of
Secretary in 1982. As he pointed out in his *History of the Royal
Academy*, this almost overwhelming influx of exhibitions was
not an unequivocally beneficial development. More staff were
required. Little good showing space was left for the Academy's
permanent possessions, and with not an inch of space left
unoccupied, the building suffered under the strain. There were
more than a million visitors in 1980 which, apart from entrance
fees, was going to push up takings at both the restaurant and
the new and spacious shop.

Selina Fellows, another of those individuals whose abilities
Hugh had recognized long before they had been tested and
proved by others, was in charge of the shop from the start. She
had come to the Academy a few years previously, straight
from reading the History of Art and Architecture at university,
worked for a short while in the Friends' office, and then started
a mail-order catalogue of products which she had encouraged
(or persuaded) Royal Academicians to design. This too had
been Hugh's idea. It worked. People loved the glasses designed
by Gert Hermes, the cookery book containing Academicians'
recipes, the prints of drawings and paintings, many of them by
Hugh himself. Soon it became evident there was scope for more
retail activity than was provided by the catalogue and a small
counter in the octagonal entrance foyer. Gallery XI was transformed into a full-scale shop, designed by the architect Academician Leonard Manasseh, and it opened in 1981. Nor was
this all. The Royal Academy's various trading activities – the
shop, the mail-order catalogue, the restaurant and catering, and
a small framing company – were incorporated into a subsidiary
company, RA Enterprises, with both Reta and Selina Fellows
as directors and artist Anthony Green RA as chairman. Profits

from all these enterprises were healthy and contributed much to the Royal Academy's financial recovery. And in the shop particularly, such trophies as Elisabeth Frink T-shirts and products linked to the 1983–4 Genius of Venice exhibition (Reta and Selina had gone there to select the best available) were pounced upon by the increasing flow of visitors.

Hutchison, a careful man who along with certain Academicians had his reservations about this rush to embrace a wider public, said, 'The wear and tear on the Private Rooms of constantly changing exhibitions was considerable, especially as so many of the shows seemed to need structural installations. Built in the seventeenth century as apartments in a stately home, the Private Rooms had never been intended to accommodate large numbers of people tramping through them daily. And there was a lot of pressure on the staff.' Another innovation, cushion concerts which were held in Gallery III, met with Hutchison's more wholehearted approval. 'We'd had concerts before Hugh's time, of course. But the organization had been most awkward, with the installation of a platform, chairs and so on having to be done in a rush after the exhibition closed at six o'clock to get everything in place. These cushion concerts which were put on in conjunction with Sir Robert Meyer and were aimed at the young, mainly under twenty-five, precluded all that. The audience simply sat on cushions, provided by W. H. Smith.'

The Academy's activities had been vastly expanded, but not without cost and the accumulation of new problems. Nor, despite the drive for sponsorship of every exhibition which became endemic during these years, were the financial problems at an end. Some exhibitions were naturally more successful than others, and financial returns fluctuated accordingly. With the Arts Council's declared inability to help, the Royal Academy Trust was formed under the chairmanship of Lord Lever of Manchester and this was announced by Hugh Casson at the Royal Academy Dinner in May 1981. It captured the corporate imagination. By September 1982, two and a quarter million pounds had been raised, which included the promise of £250,000 from the Government to be used for much-needed repairs to Burlington House. By the time Casson retired in 1984, the amount realized by the Trust had gone up to something like four and a quarter million pounds.

Not that it was all worry. The presidency of the Royal Academy involves countless social occasions and encounters, many of them with people who are distinguished and important in their own fields. It also, during Hugh Casson's presidency, became a massive public-relations job. His easy, gregarious nature enabled him to take on this part of the role with equanimity, not to say huge enjoyment, and he did not neglect to ask old friends dating back to his student days, and members of his family, including his sister Rosemary, to some of the most interesting events which took place. When Cousin Angela, friend of his days at Ellesmere with Aunt Jo, was brought to an exhibition by her niece, Mariel Toynbee, she was too infirm to walk, but Hugh, telephoned by Mariel, organized a wheelchair. He also invited them to lunch, and though he was late and lunch was frugal – a sandwich, a yoghurt and an apple, which was what he always ate himself when he was alone – they were warmly welcomed. Similarly, the Casson daughters and their families were also made much of if they arrived, and there was never any question of Hugh being too busy to see them as a more pompous man might have been.

Free weekends for the Cassons were few and precious. In the winter, when they were not so likely to go to Needs Ore, these usually comprised hours of drawing, and then a walk around the Round Pond in Kensington Gardens. Both the Cassons, particularly Hugh, loved the house in Victoria Road where they had lived during the happiest and most productive years of their lives. It was in a beautiful area of London, close to both

Hyde Park and Kensington Gardens, within walking distance
of Kensington High Street, the Royal College and all the Kensington museums. But in 1980, they decided that the time had
come to move on. It is not easy to understand exactly why they
did so then, when demands on their time were so heavy, or
why, in July of that year, it was to a five-storey, large-roomed
white stucco house in Elgin Crescent in west London, which
would seem to have been no more suitable for elderly people
than the one in Victoria Road. But Reta, who was already
struggling with what she thought was arthritis (though it
turned out to be the polymyalgia which was also to afflict
Hugh in 1990), was finding their existing house difficult to

negotiate, particularly the staircase with its half-landings at every turn, and she was determined to go. Crossing the park is not a move Londoners traditionally favour, though in the Cassons' case it meant they were closer to their daughters, all of whom had long since gone to live on the north side, whose raffish quality they found more to their taste than the gentility of Kensington. Carola and Nicky were still in West London, now living next door to each other in Westbourne Park Villas, and Dinah, with her husband Nick Wood, lived nearby in Elgin Crescent.

Both Reta and Hugh contemplated the forthcoming move without much pleasure, and Hugh was particularly reluctant because he adored the house in Victoria Road. Getting him to move was, as Nicola said, like drawing a snail out of its shell, and Nicky's husband Ian Hessenberg recalled it as the only time he saw Hugh dig in his heels and become stubbornly resistant to what was happening. He finally gave in but left the rest of the family to get on with the move, taking little part in any of the arrangements. Reta, on whom the brunt of the preparation and packing had fallen (though she was helped by her daughters and friends), was exhausted and unwell by the time removal day arrived.

Like many an unsuspecting owner before him, Hugh discovered that the quality of Victorian speculative building could be pretty indifferent 'after our solid, owner-designed masterpiece'. As he went on to record on 23 July 1980 – in *Hugh Casson's Diary* which he published that year – when writing about the Elgin Crescent house: 'Wobbly balustrade, bulging plaster, damp scrofula round skirtings, picture glass in windows, broken sash-cords, none of it serious, all of it – one sees ahead – difficult to get done because too trivial. How one longs to be a handyman.'

This was rubbish. In fact he never had the slightest desire to become one and it was Reta and their daughters, particularly

Carola, who now turned to, organizing, painting, polishing, arranging furniture and bringing the new abode into some semblance of order. Hugh spent much time at the beginning sitting outside in his Mini – 'a tiny private bubble' in which he could write letters and notes away from the hubbub. With Royal Academy demands in addition to many other commitments, this was a judicious move. It was also a selfish one. It was certainly indicative of the way he behaved – with Reta's connivance – during all the long years of his married life. Ian Hessenberg found him quite incapable of changing an electric plug, and with rather different capabilities himself – he was a photographer, endowed with all the technical competence and ability to improvise which that profession demands – he was often on call to undertake household repairs. 'Sometimes it was a relatively big job he wanted done, sometimes quite trivial. But I always got a sweet thank-you note from him afterwards.'

Reta recovered from what must have been a traumatic move, and resumed her consort position with no apparent ill effects. She had become a little less shy but she was still no lover of the limelight, and would stand by Hugh's side on formal and grand occasions, frequently looking as unrelaxed as she felt. Wisely for both of them, he left her to cope as best she could, and her contribution at a more private level was unstinting. She headed a committee which chose well-designed goods for the Academy shop, and her contribution there was pertinent and valued. Unlike some wives of public men, she was also well able to converse knowledgeably with most of the luminaries she had to entertain at dinners and parties. She drew the line, though, at going to those City dinners where spouses are required to sit in the gallery above the hall where the main event is being held, watching the diners below as though in purdah. 'What an idea! I was always previously engaged for those sort of occasions.'

Banquets at the Mansion House were normally more con-
genial, though she was not amused on the occasion when she
was seated next to Evelyn Waugh. 'He was an unpleasant man
and by that time he was extremely deaf, but instead of having
a proper deaf aid, he used a horrid silver ear-trumpet. He had
his wife on the other side, and I thought he was pretty beastly
to her. Fortunately, Hugh was on *my* other side, so I'm afraid I
gave up on Waugh.'

Both Hugh and Reta were present at Hampton Court on the
night in July 1984 when Prince Charles made his infamous
Carbuncle speech which was damning in its condemnation of
modern British architecture. At dinner afterwards, they sat at
the small top table of eleven people which, in addition to the
Prince of Wales, included Charles Correa, the most distinguished Indian architect who had just received the RIBA Gold
Medal from the Prince, architect Norman Foster, and RIBA
President Michael Manser. The Princess of Wales, who was
then pregnant with Prince William, was not present because,
according to her husband, the baby always chose the evening
to make his presence felt with bouts of energetic kicking.

It was an awkward occasion, with Foster in particular ready
to engage the Prince in strong – though polite – verbal combat,
the remainder of the group both uneasy and embarrassed.
Casson balanced delicately on the fence. He was not going to
challenge the Prince's views, but nor was he going to join him
in attacking fellow architects. In retrospect, it seems that it was
his good-humoured presence and avoidance of an unequivocal
stance which helped to defuse the tension. It was also a
reminder of his undidactic – indeed, detached – views about
architecture generally. Reminiscing about the occasion in private a few years later, when there was no danger of lighting a
touch-paper which might result in an explosion, he took a
populist viewpoint, crediting the Prince with having stirred up
latent interest in the subject. 'The architects reacted to [the

speech] with hysterical, spinster-like cries of "How dare he?" and "Doesn't he realize how difficult it is to be an architect, with all the regulations and everything?" But most of the hysteria had, I think, a strong guilt backing to it. Architects know as well as anybody that most of what we see around us is not very good. The main result of all this was not just stirring up the architects into a state of agonized self-examination, but it meant that for the first time in this country people actually thought about architecture . . . I think the constructive result of Prince Charles's speech was to raise the point that architecture should be better, and could be better, and why isn't it better? I think that was a tremendous thing to do because it was not easy for anybody else to do it.'

Said in public, this opinion would have enraged the more polemical members of his profession, and confirmed the view of certain others that he was but a decorative butterfly in a hard world. But he spoke only in private. He did also have private correspondence with the Prince at the time, first of all suggesting a small dinner with a few architects at which the Prince could discuss his views with them (this took place), and offering some palliative comments: the Prince's response to the latter included the following remarks: 'But you are quite right really – we all expect too much of these poor old architects sometimes, and most of us don't understand the pressures under which they are working. However, you must admit there are some unnecessarily arrogant ones who need to be stood up to occasionally.' Hugh was plainly attempting to operate as a peacemaker even if he did not publicize the fact, and even if he did not succeed.

Hugh visited the Academy almost every day, buzzing into the courtyard in his yellow Mini (since immortalized, complete with its distinctive number-plate, in Leonard Rosoman's mural in the RA restaurant), and bounding up the entrance steps ready for whatever awaited him. Affairs of the day were conduc-

ted not from a grand office, but from a tiny cubby-hole of a
room overlooking a light-well. This was his secretary's; Hugh
did not even have a desk, but perched on a corner of hers. Meg
Carpenter, a tall well-built young woman, had been secretary
to Tom Monnington, whom she had liked, and at first she
was dubious about the arrival of this new President, most
particularly because, looming above him, she was conscious of
the ridiculous difference in size between them. He asked her
if she did shorthand. She did not. Like many other employees
at the Academy in those days, she lacked conventional qualifi-
cations although, like others, she made up for this by enthusiasm, loyalty and devotion to her job. Her doubts about Hugh
were soon swept away, however, under the onslaught of his
kindness and charm, and they worked together happily for the
next five years, with her inability to take shorthand proving
no problem since he wrote so many of his letters by hand.
Their relationship would have been considered unusual by
many people – though not in Hugh's eyes – and would definitely
have been queried in the climate of political correctness which
was soon to affect office life. He would hold her hand against
his face as he gave her instructions, put one hand on her knee
as he worked, rest his head on her shoulder when faced with a
problematic assignment, saying 'Do I have to?' She drove him
to some appointments – to talk to the girls at Wycombe Abbey,
because 'I can't face them alone' – and he always introduced
her to the interesting people with whom he was surrounded
both inside and outside the Academy building, rather than
leaving her to float unexplained in the background as
employers frequently do. She in her turn was both secretary
and nanny, flinging important papers into a large box she kept
under her desk (for there was no very efficient filing system
then) and dispensing the weak whisky with which he would
boost his flagging energies at the end of a phenomenally busy
day. His nails, she noted, were often grubby and needed cutting,

'just like a child', and he would take out his comb before someone arrived and ask her if he looked all right after he had combed his hair. Childlike or not, Hugh amazed Meg by the efficiency with which he tackled his job. 'He never talked about doing things, he just did them, one after the other, the minute they needed to be done, and he was very much respected by the artist members as well as the architects.' She was impressed too by the way in which he constantly increased the circle of his friends, without ever neglecting those from his past. George Devine was visited when he was ill in hospital, Gontran Goulden when he was recovering from an operation in a nursing home on the Isle of Wight. When Michael Pattrick, the architect who had headed the Architectural Association School and St Martin's School of Art, and who also had a cottage in the Needs Ore terrace, died in the spring of 1980, Hugh arrived at the house of his widow Jo Pattrick, offering genuine sympathy and comfort, within twenty minutes of receiving the news in his office at the Academy. The Pattricks had long been two of his closest friends, and his compassion swept away the demands of any official duties. Later, he spoke most movingly at Michael Pattrick's funeral. There were tears in his own eyes, and he reduced many of the congregation to tears with him.

Both he and Reta were now entering their seventies – Hugh's seventieth birthday had been celebrated with a huge party given by his family at the Academy – but with four years of his presidency still to go, their level of activity did not diminish. They had settled, albeit a little painfully, into the house in Elgin Crescent (which had been home to Pandit Nehru when he was a law student in London), and in addition to making two offices for themselves, they once again filled their home with lodgers, as they had the house in Victoria Road. Hugh thought this was a good way to live. 'We like having the house full of people.' It became a magnet to visitors too, as Victoria

Road had been, and even if they no longer gave dinner parties
(Mrs Aldridge had retired to a small house they bought for her in
Eastbourne and Reta felt no desire to demonstrate her abilities
as a cook), they were profligate with their offers of coffee and
drinks. Being in touch, seeing people, learning about new ideas
were important facets of their life still. Hugh was terrified of
being sidelined. As President of the Royal Academy, and with
his faculties still intact, there was no danger of that yet.

Hugh treated not just his secretary at the Academy, but every
member of the staff, from doormen to exhibition organizers, as
friends, and he came to regard Burlington House like a second
home. He didn't actually stand at the door welcoming people
in, but you felt he might well have done, because as he said
himself on more than one occasion, it was people who interested him, rather than ideas. He liked and fostered the Academy's relaxed domestic atmosphere. 'I'd never be surprised to
find a whole lot of walking sticks stuffed behind the front door,
with an aged retriever snoring at the foot of the stairs.'

Some people thought he went too far in this direction, but as
he pointed out, the Academy had a built-in and indestructible
dignity which was never affected by his moves to encourage a
broader spectrum of visitors, and he welcomed the sight of a
mother breastfeeding her baby in the restaurant.

His public profile was as high as it had been during the
Festival of Britain period, and the books he wrote and illustrated during and just after these Academy years, *Hugh
Casson's London, Hugh Casson's Cambridge, Hugh Casson's
Oxford* and *Hugh Casson's Diary*, were immediately recogniz-
able and relished by a healthy cross-section of the public. The
beautiful Casson water-colours on the jackets ensured them a
certain coffee-table status, but this was misleading. Those who
read the text of the books about cities, rather than just gloating
over the illustrations, learnt much about the subject. Despite
his busy life they were well researched (he was brilliant at

engaging secretaries and assistants on this task), allusive, and shared Casson's knowledge of buildings with his readers in the least taxing manner possible. Hugh responded to this new period of public recognition with a warmth which served to increase not only his own popularity but that of the Royal Academy too.

The *Diary* he published about his presidency, covering the year 1980, is an intimate, vivid and self-deprecating account of that time. He likened his task at the Royal Academy – the problems associated with getting exhibitions in and out quickly, tickets, posters, publicity, the gambles constantly being taken on success or failure – to running the London Palladium. This book, if anything, reveals the nature of his busy life: the meetings at the Royal Fine Art Commission, the British Rail Environmental Panel, the National Trust, the British Council, and as a Trustee of the Arthur Koestler Award,

Of all the subjects which Hugh drew, boats of every type –
including those with more than a touch of the fantastic –
were probably his favourite.

not to mention all those at the Royal Academy; there were visits to universities and polytechnics, trips to many places including Canada, Sardinia and the Greek Islands; there were weekends at Royal Lodge, Windsor as guest of the Queen Mother, parties at Buckingham Palace, family occasions like the weekend at Needs Ore when he introduced his five-year-old grandson Matthew to the delights of sailing, the writing which he did whilst on train journeys so that this time should not be wasted, the architectural work at Casson Conder. His humour is impregnable throughout. Sitting on a beach in Goa during a trip connected with the Aga Khan Awards (reading a local arts magazine dealing with the cultural influences upon India of foreign colonizers), he tells how he is 'approached by a smart young white-clad figure who trudges from a distance across the sands like a survivor from some disastrous desert expedition. He is carrying two bottles. He suggests I need a massage. "Ah", he says, "you very very old man . . . very tired . . . very much work" . . . he pinches my leg and my upper arm . . . "very very old," he says, shaking his head. I am nettled by this and, refusing his attentions, walk off into the surf, squaring my shoulders. But he has the last laugh as a comber knocks me off my feet. I remember a previous encounter with an itinerant masseur at Agra. When I refused his ministrations he offered, in sequence, his daughter or a copy of *The Reader's Digest*.'

Predictably, *Private Eye*, for which he was ever a popular target, produced a rather limp take-off of his style. Book buyers, though, delighted in this evocation of a life which was likely in many cases to have been so much more interesting, colourful and glamorous than their own.

Broadcasting, which Casson had done with increasing virtuosity for many years now, reached a new level of frequency in the year on which he based his *Diary*. He took part in innumerable television and radio programmes, apparently

finding it not in the least stressful to air his opinions on a
motley collection of subjects, ranging from Paul Hogarth's
drawings of architecture to a Constable painting of Salisbury
Cathedral. More substantially, he fronted a series of television
programmes entitled *Personal Pleasures*. He was now seventy,
and these six programmes were to represent the apogee of his
media career. The subjects he chose, in consultation with Anne
James the producer, were mostly quirky and offbeat, offering
him scope for ventures into the imagination and what James
described as lyrical descriptive passages. 'The series just
evolved,' she said afterwards. 'The subjects weren't pinned like
butterflies to a board, because Hugh was full of ideas, many of
them good.' She enjoyed working with him and he with her.
His *Diary* covers a large part of the period in which the films
were being made and he describes several of their working
trips: to Castle Drogo, built by Sir Edwin Lutyens for Julius
Drewe of the old Home and Colonial stores; to the Lake District, where they made a programme about Ruskin, whom
Hugh admired almost to the point of idolatry; and to the tiny
Watts Gallery and chapel near Godalming, which he had discovered as a child staying with his Aunt Jo, and which he
described as 'this angry, red-faced little building'.

Because he was so busy, Hugh occasionally became irritated
by the need to hang about waiting for the weather, the electricians, the continuity requirements, the intrusive public who
interrupted filming . . . Nevertheless, it was a world he enjoyed
inhabiting, and as he had done for David Heycock, he performed superbly and with professional expertise, dressing with
just slightly bohemian precision, a bright scarf knotted at his
neck, wandering through the buildings and landscapes he
chose, and capturing for the viewers all the enjoyment he was
manifestly experiencing himself. He had gained in confidence
since the *Spirit of the Age* film, and was completely at ease
with himself. There were no set scripts but he always brought

with him much of the material he intended to use (reading Mary Lutyens's study of her father on the train journey to Castle Drogo, for instance), and then learning by heart the essence of what he wanted to say.

Anne James described how, late one night, she realized they were short of some text for the next day's filming at the Russell Cotes Gallery and Museum at Bournemouth. 'I slipped a note under his hotel door, warning him we wanted more, and the next morning he appeared at breakfast having prepared exactly what was needed.' He thrived on working in this apparently perilous way. He says in the *Diary*, of a day when they were filming at the Watts Gallery: 'Fine and dry again today. I feel encouraged by progress and Anne J. has permitted more freedom of speech – not so much learning of notes. It has its risks: important adjectives are omitted, words are less apt, but it is looser and more relaxed.'

The whole series – the other subjects were Portmeirion and the Royal Academy – was relaxed indeed. It got a most enthusiastic reception from the critics, with Bill Grundy in the *Standard* perhaps best capturing the flavour of the presenter, if not of the six programmes. 'There is nothing I will not listen to Sir Hugh talking about. With his glittering eye, his walnut-crinkled face, and his scarlet socks, the man's a must. Oddly he also reminds me of a Chinese meal, but only because, like Cleopatra, he makes hungry where most he satisfies.'

Anne James remembered one particular thing Hugh said when walking alongside the sea during the Portmeirion programme: '"Everybody has a personal recipe for happiness, and mine I think has three ingredients. A daily tiny success, like catching a train or finding some shoes that fit you; a daily bit of reassurance; but above all a daily glimpse of a pretty wide stretch of water. One of the magical things about this place, indeed I suppose all places where mountains meet the sea, is that the light is constantly changing, morning, midday and evening, and the clouds scurry across the hills spreading stains of shade. Somebody once said of a woman he loved that she had a skin so translucent you could almost see to read by it. I think the same lovely compliment could be given to the light that comes off the water of this beautiful estuary."' His words, as so often, had a resonance with which many viewers could empathize.

These were Hugh Casson's *Personal Pleasures*. It is no coincidence that three of them – the Watts Gallery, Ruskin in the Lake District and the Russell Cotes Gallery – all told the story of eminent Victorians. And even Castle Drogo, finished in 1930, looked, as he said, 'as old as the hills'. The older he got himself, the further away from the influences of his architectural teachers and youthful friends, the more Hugh Casson's interest was directed towards the Victorian period: its people, its buildings and its art. When he talked and wrote about those closer to the present, there was just a slight slackening in the strength of his commitment. Nevertheless, he sustained his ability to comment authoritatively on all periods of architecture. Many critics and pundits settle into the camp with which they are happiest, quite often treating those of other persuasions with reserve or even contempt. Hugh never did. To the end of his working life – which came when he was well into his eighties – he was speaking and writing with enthusiasm about all periods of architecture, and would never have risked alienating critics or fellow architects who had deep feelings about one of them by showing intense bias in another direction. It was probably only those closest to him who realized the strength of his affinity with the Victorians.

There was no question of Hugh having relapsed into an involvement with the past which precluded his participation in the present, however. In that he was very much involved. In 1978 he had been approached to design the sets for the following year's production of Haydn's *La Fidelta Premiata* at Glyndebourne. He was at his busiest, but it didn't prevent him from relishing the task, which he described in the *Diary*. It was to be his last opera.

Hugh's drawings of the bears and kitchen maids in La Fidelta Premiata *at Glyndebourne.*

Taking place in Arcady, *La Fidelta Premiata* required a much more light-hearted and bucolic set than the previous two operas Hugh had designed, and it entailed a park, a lake, several gazebos and a distant stately home. As he explained in the *Diary* the following year, when *Fidelta* was again in the Glyndebourne repertoire, 'I treated it romantically – wet and freely drawn water-coloury backcloths (with a faint hint of Glyndebourne itself).' He went on in this same *Diary* entry to give credit to others: to Joyce Conwy Evans, who had by now left Casson Conder but who had worked with him on

L'Incoronazione de Poppea and who was on this occasion
entirely responsible for the *Fidelta* costumes (after Hugh had
courteously fended off Glyndebourne's other proffered con-
tenders for the task), and to the technical team – electricians
and milliners, hairdressers and carpenters – 'and the lavish
rehearsal time always allowed saves the amateur designer from
the worst mistakes, while good lighting rescues all'.

This was typically modest and generous, and it was
undoubtedly true, but it makes no acknowledgement of his
own great talent and of the immense amount of his time which
went into research, innumerable concept drawings and the
revisions which were essential for every production; the hours
Joyce Conwy Evans remembered they spent travelling backwards and forwards to Glyndebourne for rehearsals, particularly in the last two weeks before first night when adjustments
and alterations would be made; and the opinion of the *Fidelta*
scenery builders, who said Casson's were the best working
drawings they had ever had, with exact measurements and
specifications facilitating the precision of their work. (Working
drawings, as opposed to concept drawings, would have been
done by someone else, in this case Michael Cain, who generally
supported Hugh in his thespian enterprises, but they were done
from Hugh's designs and overseen by him.)

A concept drawing of his design for Scene 1, Act 1 of *Fidelta*
appears in the *Diary* and reveals the sheer beauty of his cre-
ations, what the *Guardian* described as 'Sir Hugh Casson's
exquisitely drafted landscape' and what the *Architectural
Review*, which may have been biased, called 'some of the most
beautiful [sets and costumes] ever seen at Glyndebourne.'

A casual note in the *Diary* relates: 'Do a dozen drawings as
first-night presents for the cast.' It demonstrates again the level
of activity in which – now aged seventy – he was still engaged.
Reta became worried at the intensity with which he was working at so many different projects, quite apart from his onerous

duties at the Royal Academy. 'He was so excited when he was asked to do another Glyndebourne design. He worked too long and too hard on it, I thought, considering he was doing all the other things at the same time.'

Hugh and Reta liked to escape to Needs Ore for the rare weekend, and this was the place where Hugh could most easily indulge his lifelong predilection for sketching boats of all sizes, from the ocean-going vessels which passed along the Solent at the end of his garden, to the small and often battered craft which lay about on the nearby shingle. These sketches filled his notebooks. Many were made during these weekends, but visits to foreign waters – in places like Turkey, India or Italy for instance – were never wasted. Anything which took to the water became a subject for his pen.

At Needs Ore, Reta would try to fend off the friendly overtures of their neighbours: 'We've come here for peace,' she would say, 'and we don't need dinner parties.' But generally Hugh paid no heed to her worries, darting along the row of

Drawings made on the Bosphorus during a trip to Turkey.

cottages to visit friends, enjoying an evening drink in one of the small back gardens, visiting his doctor occasionally when beset by minor ailments, and carrying on with his crowded schedule however tired or unwell he felt.

The fact of Hugh having made gifts for all the cast of *Fidelta* confirms how little he counted the cost of the time spent on drawings and paintings, because even if these were tossed off quickly, they would still for most artists have represented work and, potentially, money. For Hugh they were just the way he knew best to show warmth and gratitude. This may have occasionally been counter-productive. Rosie d'Avigdor Goldsmid had paid for none of the Casson drawings which lined her bedroom walls. She hadn't needed to. As she said so triumphantly, 'They were all gifts from Hugh.' It can also be surmised that, wealthy and adventurous enough to buy a collection of modern paintings which included works by Mark Rothko, Kenneth Noland and David Hockney, she probably calculated that Hugh's work was from a lesser stratum. Perhaps she would never have bought his paintings.

The 'fatal charm' which he bemoaned in his work brought him admiration from a huge public, however, which was soothed and flattered by its accessibility, its romanticizing of buildings and scenes with which they were familiar. His books, with their depiction of buildings he knew and loved, bore all the accuracy and understanding of the seeing architect, overlaid with the poetic grace of the artist. He saw life in close-up rather than from the position of a remote overseer, and he had, as someone once noted, a gift for inserting small domestic touches into a painting of a formal setting without in any way diminishing its decorum: the cat by the door, a couple reading, the pot of flowers on a window-sill, the child's bicycle propped against a wall, the overstuffed pigeon-holes of a writing table. Very personal, mildly idiosyncratic, it was this work which confirmed his popularity, so that when his

water-colours appeared in exhibitions and in the public spaces at Glyndebourne, modestly priced and charming, they were pounced upon by an increasing band of devotees. He was continually being asked to produce drawings – sometimes without payment – for advertisements, promotional booklets, programme covers for events like the Windsor Festival, exhibition leaflets and brochures. He rarely refused and years after they were first commissioned some of these drawings would suddenly loom unmistakably in an advertisement for a foreign-travel firm (with his evocative little sketches of Indian palaces, Kashmiri houseboats, Italian chapels), or on the stationery of the National Trust. His love of buildings sang out from almost all. He was, for instance, a trustee of the friends of St John's, Smith Square, and the water-colour he painted for the cover of a booklet he wrote about Queen Anne's Footstool, as that church is affectionately known, was a classic Casson: depicting a building that was sumptuously three-dimensional, just marginally more beautiful than in life, rich in the merest suggestion of detail, and delicately coloured.

Few of the buildings he *chose* to draw for his books were modern. Back in 1975, the Lion and Unicorn Press, which was associated with the Royal College of Art, had published in an edition of 100 copies a small book containing twenty-five of the drawings of London buildings he had been commissioned to make for publication in the *Illustrated London News*. There was a rather maudlin introduction by John Betjeman, but Casson's accompanying comments were telling.

'The quality [these buildings] have in common is character – the expression in brick and stone of a personal point of view. Not surprisingly, most of them were built in that self-confident, romantic and individualist period 1850–1920 when every building was expected to tell a story – and to point a moral as well.'

This was a period he had always liked and one to which he was increasingly drawn as he got older. He once said, 'Modern architecture can be exciting to look at but is seldom fun to draw,' and, apart from architectural renderings which were made for professional purposes, it was one type of drawing he did not do particularly well. The romantic miasma was absent, and even though he was aware of this and tried to remedy the lack by using a kind of washy, watery style as he did in his painting of the National Theatre which appears in this book, it somehow doesn't work.

Significantly, the architectural perspectivist he claimed to admire most was William Walcot, who was at work during the interwar years. 'He was Russian and ambidextrous, and he used glue, fish paste, spit, blood, anything to get his effects. His drawings aren't much seen nowadays, but they were fantastically exciting to me. They were mostly reconstructions of the Baths of Calacalla, with huge columns disappearing into gold dust, hair oil, or whatever he had on the desk at the moment.' This was not a man who would have been happy with Modernist buildings either.

Joyce Conwy Evans said that Hugh's art was an extension of himself, an extension of what he was, straight from the heart. Perhaps when it came to drawing modern buildings, his heart was not in it.

Casson, true to his thespian forebears, always enjoyed making a public appearance, and his skill as a speaker, honed over the years from Festival of Britain time onwards, served him well during his years at the Royal Academy. Not always completely audible without amplification – as Edward Montagu once commented, he didn't really project his low voice sufficiently and it was often necessary to strain to catch everything he said – his deficiency in this direction did not detract from his popularity. Able to adapt his content quite swiftly to match the mood of an audience, he cloaked serious messages in humour and affability, so that his listeners were left with a warm feeling on even the most solemn of occasions. Typical was the address he gave at the Memorial Meeting held for Dennis Serjeant, who had been the Academy's well-liked Surveyor for some years. Listeners laughed, cried a little, and were reminded of things about Serjeant they had almost forgotten. It is unlikely that they were unmoved. On a different level, his speeches at the Royal Academy dinners which take place just before the opening of the Summer Exhibition each year were models of propriety and pride. But they were funny too. The painter Flavia Irwin (Roger de Grey's widow) remembered that Hugh was often laughing at what he was about to say almost as soon as he got to his feet.

Casson's fund of private stories was much enhanced by one about Margaret Thatcher's attendance at an Academy dinner, where she arrived, regal and radiant, in a black taffeta dress. For a socialist voter he reacted with surprising sympathy to her confession that there had been little exposure to the arts in 'the primitive Methodist household where she was raised. She told me that they never went to the theatre or an art gallery or a concert, and she never hit the arts at all until she went to Oxford when she occasionally went to concerts with friends. That was her first brush with the creative arts and she was modest about this ... She said the same sort of thing in her speech. I was just getting my notes together to make mine and she suddenly said, "I hope you're not going to be funny. I find it a terrible waste of time and energy going to a dinner and listening to twelve familiar anecdotes about an Englishman, a Scotsman and an Irishman or something. It's really a waste of an evening. I like to learn something from after-dinner speeches, not just listen to amiable waffle." Fortunately, it was nearly the end of the evening, and I was feeling quite relaxed by then.'

Some would have crumpled under this formidable woman's exhortation. Hugh performed with his usual adept professionalism. He had never had lessons in public speaking – perhaps his projection would have been better if he had – but he knew just when to change the tone or rhythm of what he was saying, or bring in an unexpected or amusing comment to wake people up. 'I was speaking about two or three times a week during the Academy time. There are certain people you see in an audience, you can spot them clasping a handbag on their knees, with an expression of "Now show me" on their faces, and you worked on that lady. You were determined to get her attention and interest. It's funny how they stand out in an audience. It's as if they've been lit by an internal glow of potential disapproval, and I used to notice that.'

On the occasion when Thatcher made her daunting remarks just as Hugh was about to begin his speech, nobody seems to remember whether she laughed at it or not, but it is unlikely that Casson trotted out the type of Englishman, Welshman joke she so detested. Such banalities were not his style either. He obviously had a soft spot for his Conservative Prime Minister too, despite his dislike of her politics. But then she was, some think, an attractive woman, a breed to which he invariably responded with enthusiasm. Norman Rosenthal, who became Exhibitions Secretary during Hugh's time, believed Thatcher was supportive of the Academy because she knew it was not a drain on the public purse.

Hugh's last Royal Academy Dinner before his retirement in

1984 was another fraught event. This time the principal guests
were the Prince and Princess of Wales, whose presence was
obviously an acknowledgement of the affection they, particularly the Prince, felt for Hugh Casson. The main speaker, at
Casson's own invitation, was Laurie Lee, who was an old friend
from the days when Lee had worked on the Festival of Britain
and who Casson knew was an amusing speaker. Or could be.
On this occasion, Laurie Lee, beset by nerves, had unfortunately primed himself with a few drinks before the occasion
began, enjoyed the Academy's excellent wines during the
dinner, and had eaten nothing. Casson spotted the ominous
signs of imminent disaster, and warned the Princess of Wales,
who sat next to Laurie Lee, to keep an eye on him and if he
began to ramble on to tell him to sit down. This was not Casson
at his most sensitive, especially as Diana, still relatively
unused to formal and what seemed to her very highbrow
occasions, had already confessed to him her own nervousness
at sitting next to a poet. However, all went well at first. Laurie
Lee started in great form and was greeted with responsive
laughter by the other diners, many of whom knew him well.
Unfortunately, in a haze of bibulous euphoria, he then became
over-confident, flung down his manuscript and started to
extemporise. He seemed unstoppable. What he was saying
made increasingly little sense and his audience was torn
between laughter and embarrassment, between consternation
that this should be happening in the heartland of the establishment, and delight at being witnesses to such an uproarious
episode. Eventually Diana, who was trying to suppress her own
laughter, kicked Lee's shin, pulled at his jacket and managed
to halt the flow of the speaker's rambling discourse. He sat
down, left after a short while, and the evening resumed its
traditional and stately course. Belatedly aware of his blunder,
Lee then crossed the road to Green Park and lay in a heap on
the grass, reduced to a state of misery and self-loathing.

Some might have resented this marring of a great occasion with its Royal guests and, for Hugh, such strong personal significance. But as another Academician pointed out, Hugh knew Laurie Lee well enough to have been aware of the risks involved in inviting him to speak, and this time the risk did not pay off. Afterwards, he simply felt terribly sorry for his friend, blamed himself a little, and generally played down the event as of little consequence. But, in all its grandeur, all its laughter, all its demonstration of human frailty, it became a vivid memory for those who were present.

It was during his Royal Academy years that Hugh Casson most clearly demonstrated this propensity for taking risks which some of his colleagues found unnerving, and they were generally of more importance than the one which resulted in the Laurie Lee débâcle. But because his own quiet confidence had grown and was now at its zenith, they were risks which Hugh barely acknowledged. To him, the new routes he opened up were manifestly going in the right direction.

One such risk which he took during the early years was to appoint Norman Rosenthal as Exhibitions Secretary. He did this against the earnest advice of many who might have been considered to know what they were talking about. He'll cause problems, they advised.

Rosenthal had first come into Hugh Casson's line of vision in January 1977, when he had an article published in the *Spectator* entitled 'The Future of the Royal Academy'. It was not particularly well written, but its message was cogent and it was a message which Casson, not long in the job, was delighted to have expounded, for it coincided with his own views. The Academy, it said, 'is operating to everyone's detriment far below its maximum capacity'. This was a sympathetic article, certainly not in the Brian Sewell genre of scathing dismissal, but it went on to say:

the aims of the founders can only be carried out if the annual Summer Exhibition is not only improved upon but supplemented by a carefully planned programme of contemporary art, from this country and from abroad. The increasing internationalism of the language of art, though it allows any number of local and personal differences, is something that is denied only at the risk of burying critical faculties in the sand. If successful, such a programme could slowly win back to the RA the support of many significant artists who for their own legitimate reasons have turned their backs in this century on what was meant to be their own platform.

This was the nub of it, and when Rosenthal went on to demand public funding for the RA, Casson knew that here was a supporter, well known in the art world, who had intelligent and constructive ideas about the direction in which the Academy should be going. He circulated a copy of the article to all Academicians, and wrote Rosenthal one of his famous congratulatory letters. Further, he privately decided that this extravagant and quixotic personality would be better inside than outside the organization. Rosenthal, with characteristic hyperbole, describes the morning he received Hugh's letter as one of the happiest in his life, and when Casson made him Exhibitions Secretary later that year, his loyalty was ensured and his admiration unequivocal.

The people who had questioned Rosenthal's appointment were proved wrong. An experienced exhibition organizer since his student days, and someone who, as Casson has said, 'has enormous enthusiasms, and they're so strong he almost explodes with excitement about them', he led the expansion of the RA exhibition programme to encompass all the internationalism and imagination it had tended to lack and which, though it sometimes drew critical fire (the worst of it at the time of the *Sensation* exhibition in 1997, long after Hugh's retirement), eventually put the place right back on the map as an important and world-class art institution. Rosenthal said, 'It was a deeply provincial place when Hugh arrived. He really reinvented the Royal Academy, and he and Roger de Grey encouraged me to do what I've done. I couldn't have done it without their support.' Hugh, in particular, was instrumental in fending off certain personal criticisms of Rosenthal's methods, and occasional residual demands that he should be dismissed.

XII

The Academy
in the Ascendant

The exhibitions which from now on began to fill the Academy galleries were both eclectic and exciting. They did not all take place in Casson's time but, apart from *Light Fantastic*, a particularly unusual one focusing on lasers and holography which Anton Furst, who had been one of Casson's students at the Royal College of Art, mounted at his old Professor's instigation (with great rod-like laser beams crossing the courtyard), they resulted directly from Rosenthal's appointment. Beginning with *A New Spirit of Painting* in 1981, they included a masterly series documenting the art of the twentieth century (the first was *German Art in the Twentieth Century* in 1985), and such popular exhibitions as *The Genius of Venice* (1983–4) and *New Architecture: Foster, Rogers, Stirling* (1986). These and many others were sufficiently distinguished to travel to galleries elsewhere in the world, notably Europe and the United States. The series documenting the art of the twentieth century raised some problems when it came to mounting the British Exhibition. Casson said, 'Some of the Academicians were pretty keen they weren't forgotten. This caused pursing of lips in the Council Chamber because they thought if it's the Royal Academy's view of British twentieth-century painting, the Royal Academy had already stated its view by electing those deemed by it to be the best of the time. But we were going back to 1900, and some Academicians had fallen out of favour in the intervening years, or didn't look part of the mainstream. So the small group of experts who made the selections – some of them outsiders to maintain objectivity – had fairly delicate moments with that exhibition.'

One of the exhibitions to take place during the later part of Casson's presidency was *The Great Japan Exhibition*, from October 1981 to February 1982. Showing art of the Edo period it was, at a cost of three million pounds, the most expensive the Academy had ever organized, though a third of this sum was met by the Japanese. It was brilliantly successful with both the critics and the public, and resulted in the Cassons being invited on a generous trip to Tokyo by the Japan Foundation. They had both been to Japan before, Reta when she had helped to organize the Royal College of Art exhibition in the early seventies, and together just a year or two previously. The latter trip had also been connected with an exhibition, this time at Mitzukoshi, a Tokyo department store. It had comprised exhibits from seven of Britain's greatest stately homes, as well as fifty pictures which the store had bought from the previous year's Royal Academy Summer Exhibition and which were the reason for the Cassons' presence. The organization was superb, the hospitality warm, and there were lavish gifts from their hosts. But both Cassons were disconcerted by the cavalier and ill-mannered behaviour of certain stately-home owners despite the importance of the trip as, at the very least, a promotion of their properties. Reta remembered, 'I was really surprised by them. These were frightfully grand people. All well-known names. At one dinner Mitzukoshi had given us all presents and one of these gentlemen first of all opened the present, which it is bad manners to do in Japan, and then seeing the watch inside said, "I have one of these already. Could I go and change it in the store?" It was awful. We cringed with embarrassment.'

On this second joint trip in 1983 as guests of the Japan

The Cassons at a tea ceremony in Japan.

Foundation, they were again treated with immense generosity and kindness. Staying at first at the British Embassy in Tokyo, they were taken in the Embassy Rolls Royce by Sir Hugh and Lady Cortazzi to see the temples of Kyoto, and to Nara, a journey much enhanced by the fact that the Ambassador spoke fluent Japanese. An interpreter then accompanied them on a ten-day trip during which they were able to explore Japan's south islands, which they had never seen. It was only marred by the fact that Hugh, his xenophobia surfacing, did not much care for the traditional Japanese hotels where they sometimes stayed, despite their aesthetic simplicity which might have been expected to appeal to his architectural sensibility. He found no pleasure in sleeping on a futon, or in the Japanese habit of washing before immersing oneself in water, and was much happier on those occasions when they were staying in a Western-style hotel. A stickler for simple, nursery-type food and with a complete lack of interest in trying anything that was more ambitious or different, he hated Japanese food too, and they would search out Chinese restaurants, as this was a cuisine he found supportable. He was, though, very happy to renew a friendship he had struck up with Princess

Chichibu, the aunt of the present Emperor, who had travelled to London to open The Great Japan Exhibition. He and Reta visited the Princess at her house in Tokyo, and went on a shopping expedition with her and her ladies-in-waiting, enjoying the reverence with which their high-born companion was greeted everywhere. They now had connections with two royal families, to Hugh's satisfaction, and he maintained a correspondence with the sweet-mannered Princess Chichibu for many years.

Hugh Casson's knowledge of Japanese art was limited, though he enjoyed and learnt from The Great Japan Exhibition as he did from others which came to the Academy. He stoutly disclaimed any expert knowledge about art generally, and judged at the highest, academic level, this was correct. But he had a keen layman's interest, probably far exceeding that of most of the visitors who crowded the Academy galleries. And his personal taste was quite precisely defined. 'I like rather understated painting, people like Gwen John. I don't like being hit in the face by paintings and violent things. I always think of them in my own room, and consider whether I would really like having them there longer than about twenty minutes. So my vote when it came to selecting paintings for specialist exhibitions at the Academy was so amateur as to be worthless. I was, after all, only an architect.' Rosenthal, a heavyweight himself and one who suffered fools with no pleasure or patience at all, had an astute perception of Hugh Casson's capabilities. 'He was *not* a lightweight as some have suggested. He just had no pretentions. He knew exactly who he was. Most people (including myself) know less than they like to claim. He knew more than he claimed. He was playful and it amused him to feign ignorance, and that could sometimes lead him into trouble. And of course he was a consummate actor. Hugh loved the ephemeral, which can also be profound.' Another reason for Hugh's constant proclamation of his amateur status regarding art history was, I think, to guard himself against being caught out in ignorance. He had read far too widely for his knowledge to be lacking in depth, as he claimed, but he would not risk the occasional gap being revealed at an inauspicious moment.

Rosenthal was sometimes in trouble too, particularly in the early years of his employment, for travelling widely and expensively. But even if he had not asked for permission first his trips were always in the Academy's interests, and it was not long before he was accepted as a most successful if slightly eccentric member of the staff. He is also an endearing soul who, in the years before be married and had children of his own, amused Hugh by carrying his sister's baby on one arm as he prowled the galleries of the building to inspect exhibits as they were being hung.

Another Casson appointee of what some considered wobbly provenance was Piers Rodgers, who took over as Secretary after Sidney Hutchison's retirement on 1 April 1982. Eton and Oxford educated, his first-class degree was in Modern Languages, and he'd been a merchant banker before working for Unesco in Paris as Director of the International Council on Monuments and Sites. Rodgers applied for the Secretary's job when he saw it advertised because he wanted to return to London, he'd studied art history, and the Academy appealed to his undoubtedly establishment propensities, as well as presenting a challenge. 'After all, an artists' institution which is shunned by most distinguished artists isn't going to go far, and that's how it had been for some time.' Despite his being a little behind the times in this assessment, and unknown in the art world, Casson again chanced his arm in appointing him to this prestigious post. Rodgers said, just before leaving the Academy some fifteen years later in 1997, 'He told me afterwards he was hoping to make the Academy more academic, and indeed we did institute a new rigour. We began to ensure more effort was put into explanatory texts, so that scholars were stretched as they hadn't been before. The education department was started, which he favoured.'

Piers Rodgers conceded that the physical demands of the exhibition programme may have got a little out of hand in Casson's time, but pointed out that it did give an impression of total activity which served to enhance the Academy's resurgent reputation. As a one-time banker, he understood the thought processes of those who were being constantly invoked to sponsor or underwrite exhibitions. Or, as Casson so cogently put it, 'He was pretty well informed where money lay. He could hear the distant chink of a gold bag being laid down.' Rodgers himself believed that they got far bigger commitments by asking people to underwrite exhibitions than with outright sponsorship. Sometimes, he pointed out, the underwriters got off scot-free, and were able to enjoy the publicity without any cost in real terms, but when talking to them about sharing risks he was talking a language they understood, so it worked.

Piers Rodgers particularly remembered Casson's aptitude in chairing meetings either at or concerned with the Academy. 'He didn't always find it necessary to express an opinion, which was refreshing and saved time.' Similarly, he wasted little time on bureaucracy, or on dictating letters. Instead, he unleashed on his staff a flow of handwritten but pertinent notes, some of them with such headings as GRIPE or DEPARTMENT OF WATER UNDER BRIDGES, and some of them five-pagers on up to a dozen different topics. Many were thank-you notes. As Rodgers remembered, Hugh *always* thanked people for their efforts.

As an architect President, Hugh Casson showed himself sensitive in other ways, proving a responsive listener to the ideas and wishes of artist RAs as well as to those of the relatively few architects. 'Not all architects are so aware of those outside their own profession,' Piers Rodgers pointed out. 'But then curiously, Hugh himself showed work as an artist, not an architect, in the Summer Exhibitions.' This was not so remarkable. Passionate and dedicated water-colourist that he was, Casson was not going to miss any opportunity to show the results, and the Summer Exhibition was a splendid one. But he did not neglect the interests of fellow architects. During his time in office, and despite the fact that he chose not to show in it himself, the architecture room at the Summer Exhibition, hitherto shunted off into a cramped side area, became gradually larger and more prominent. This coincided with the growing public interest in architecture and was possibly a perceptive reaction to changing taste on Casson's part rather than a bequest to his profession. Nevertheless it was well received by the architects.

His contribution to the work at Casson Conder was, by the middle of his time at the Academy, beginning to wane. There simply was not the time for him to make his regular visits to Thurloe Place, certainly not in the evening as had been his wont in the past. His partners would hold meetings with him at the Academy, and there were particular jobs, usually those which he had personally brought in, where he would take the lead or make specific interventions, but not in the dynamic way in which he had in the past. There was one job, however, which came into the 'gentry work' category, with which he was quite emphatically involved. It was one which would demonstrate clearly that no architect's working life is without controversy and elements of spite, even Hugh Casson's.

This was the interior restoration and redecoration of Sutton Place, near Guildford in Surrey, which, after years in the penny-pinching ownership of Paul Getty, had been purchased in 1980 by another wealthy and reclusive American, Stanley Seager. Seager had philanthropic proclivities. He established the Sutton Place Heritage Trust under the executive trusteeship of Roger Chubb, and he appointed the great landscape architect Geoffrey Jellicoe to transform the gardens. That part of the project went well. It was the improvements he asked Hugh

Casson to make inside the building which caused an outcry from, amongst others, the Society for the Protection of Ancient Buildings, the Ancient Monument Society, the Victorian Society, Mayford and Woking District History Society and, finally, Woking Council. There were rumours of extensive interior alterations to this Grade I Tudor mansion, although as Stuart Taylor of Casson Conder has pointed out, Sutton Place had already been much altered by previous owners, including Paul Getty.

What the Casson Conder 'alterations' actually amounted to were the removal (into storage) of a Victorian stained-glass window, and the painting of some panelling (which had been bleached by Getty) in rather strong colours: peach, dark grey and black, to be exact. At one point the project became the subject of an enforcement notice, but after the appeal (Michael Howard, later to be Conservative Home Secretary, was the QC acting for the Trust), this was lifted and the work went ahead. In May 1983, *The Times* published a histrionic article lambasting the project and sneering at Seager's plans to display his considerable collection of modern art there – including a triptych by Francis Bacon – as well as having concerts and visiting exhibitions in the great hall. Casson suffered with stoicism the abuse which was hurled at him, only pointing out in his placatory way that none of the works was irreversible.

There was a season or two of dinner concerts in what was still a beautiful house. But Seager eventually sold up (to another rich American, who subsequently embarked on his own cycle of restoration) and moved on. He had gathered about him such distinguished trustees as Henry Moore, the Viscount Norwich, Sir Roy Strong and Dame Margot Fonteyn, intending Sutton Place to become a centre for the performing and visual arts. He was surprised and hurt at the venom with which his generosity and vision had been received.

The writer from *The Times* (in his other role as *Private Eye*'s

Piloti) had subjected Hugh to more personal criticism when
the Ismaili Centre, a commission given to Casson Conder by
the Aga Khan, was opened some months earlier at the end of
1982. An enigmatic building, handsomely clad in polished
granite, with such windows as there are made of bevelled glass,
it is set on a cramped site opposite the Victoria and Albert
Museum. At the junction of several roads, nudging an expensive residential area and in the shadow of three great museums,
it was eyed with critical attention by every Londoner who
passed it by. There was resentment expressed by some that
this golden site, once intended for the National Theatre, should
have gone to adherents of what they considered an alien creed.
One neighbour had construction times curtailed because she
couldn't stand the noise. And Piloti, ever ready to be offensive,
described it as the worst building of 1982, adding, 'It is well
known that Sir Hugh has not actually designed any of his firm's
buildings for years: his job, assisted by his celebrated charm, is
to get jobs.' Historically he was wrong. From now on, though,
his description of Hugh's contribution to Casson Conder would
be largely accurate.

Subscribing to the Islamic tradition of an architecture whose
plainness conceals riches within, this glinting, finely detailed
box of a building with its neighbourly champfered edges and
rooftop garden is now regarded with a certain amount of affection, even by those who remember that it is a relative new-
comer to South Kensington. Piloti's comments, bordering on
racist in their venom, were disregarded at the time, and are
now forgotten. But for Neville Conder, an introspective man,
apart from being the partner who ran the Ismaili Centre job –
and who was largely its designer – they rankled. Hugh was too
busy to experience more than passing spasms of irritation. But
the Sutton Place affair, coming less than a year later, was an
unnerving reminder that no one, however popular and careful
to avoid controversy, is immune from attack.

The criticism and insult to which Hugh was sometimes subjected in the outside world did not, on the whole, follow him through the Academy's handsome portals. There, in the last few supremely successful years of his presidency, he could wallow in affection born of his sunny nature and his considerable achievements. He was, almost without exception, supported and encouraged by the staff, from the junior to the most senior, such as Norman Rosenthal and Piers Rodgers whom he had personally appointed.

In 1983, the American Associates of the Royal Academy Trust (AARAT) was established, with Griselda Hamilton-Baillie (later Mrs William Kerr), who had helped to set up the British Friends of the Royal Academy, as its main organizer. She had worked at the Royal Academy since 1971, becoming Press Officer in 1974. Only twenty-one when she started, with no degree and no public-relations training – in fact, as she said, 'nothing to recommend me but a willingness to put my nose to the grindstone' – she developed into a powerful and original woman with many ideas which she remembered Casson giving her every encouragement to implement. The idea of Friends of the Royal Academy had been around for some time, but it was she who had finally got that scheme going. 'Sir Hugh gave me a completely free but utterly supportive hand. I don't remember him interfering except to improve my script time and time again, and I never remember him putting up any obstacle that he was not prepared to jump over with me.' With the Friends well launched, she took on the running of the RA Appeal in 1979, because she had found no one else willing to do or capable of doing the job. 'We launched the Appeal with the most beautiful appeal brochure I have ever seen because Sir Hugh illustrated it and wrote a wonderful preface about the RA.' By 1982 Griselda had become instrumental in launching AARAT.

'I knew I had to face raising funds for the Appeal in the US from people like Paul Getty, Armand Hammer and Paul

One of Casson's famous thank-you notes –
this time to Kitty Ockenden of AARAT.

Mellon. It happened that I was asked at the eleventh hour to curate an exhibition of *The Treasures of the Royal Academy* which would travel around eight major cities in the States. The curator who should have done it had been revealed as an alcoholic and sacked.' It must have required a strong nerve to entrust an inexperienced and professionally unqualified girl with this important operation. But the decision was taken and sanctioned by the President. 'It was a fourteen-month, eight-venue tour, which meant I had to go out to a new place in the US every ten weeks for fourteen months right in the middle of running a new appeal. I don't know how we did it but off I went, dragging my luggage behind me, taking buses to airports and staying in cheap hotels. At the first venue, Sir Hugh and Lady Casson were there, and it was hair-raising as all I knew about the RA was picked up from Sir Hugh, or Sidney Hutchison's history. But Sir Hugh encouraged me, introduced me to countless immensely rich ladies in Palm Beach who wondered who on earth I was but accepted me because I was attached to him – people like Jane Wrightsman, Carolyn Lynch, Anne Armstrong and Georgia O'Keefe, who were all entranced by him. It was this tour which gave me the opportunity to meet lots of people, and get AARAT going.' And this she did. But plainly she could not continue to run what was obviously going to be an important institution from an office in London, and she soon found and appointed an American, Kitty Ockenden, as its Executive Director. In Ockenden's hands it grew and flourished, becoming, as Griselda Hamilton-Baillie affirmed, 'among the best fundraising bodies world-wide'. She herself went on to launch the Corporate Membership scheme in 1988, with Margaret Thatcher as Patron, and left the RA on her marriage in 1990.

Hugh Casson always appreciated the contribution which AARAT members were making, and he was particularly adept at demonstrating the gratitude which was felt towards them by the Academy's powers that be. Although he was on the verge of retiring when Kitty Ockenden took over in 1984, she stipulated that she wanted Hugh to continue acting as a liaison between the Academy and AARAT, for she had been quick to spot his potential in the fundraising field. Americans loved the warmth and conviviality which emanated from this patently distinguished Englishman. Unlike so many of his compatriots, with their stiff little bows and frosty smiles, he embraced them all with genuine pleasure, drawing them into the circle of his friends and loved ones. Not to put too fine a point on it, these generous and wealthy Americans – they included Mrs Henry Ford II, Alfred Taubman, John Hay Whitney, Mrs Henry J. Heinz II – demonstrated their affection for the Academy in the way which had come to mean most for that financially stressed British institution: they donated hard cash.

Hamilton-Baillie described him in action: 'He charmed, literally charmed, the great and the good on to the first Appeal Committee, and then on to the first list of Trustees, not through carefully composed letters, but through his magnetic, witty, endearingly light touch under which lay a great depth of wisdom, compassion and understanding. It was this which gave them the confidence to accept his invitation to become involved in what they knew would be a time-consuming, absorbing, aggravating and probably costly *pro bono* activity. He illustrated the appeal literature, wrote all that was memorable about it, spent countless hours, in both Britain and the USA, being charming to prospective donors who were inevitably won over. He made fundraising seem effortless but everyone knows what incredibly hard work it is.'

The Secretary, Piers Rodgers, had by now become an accepted member of the Academy's team. He always cut an elegant and distinctive figure, and apart from his intellectual contribution he had a regal manner, quite different from Hugh's, which nevertheless appealed to Friends and important sponsors of the Academy, even if, amongst colleagues, he was known to be lax over tackling his more mundane duties like answering letters. Whilst he was still Secretary and Roger de Grey (who Hugh had always intended and hoped would succeed him) had just become President – though Hugh Casson was still much in evidence – contact was made with two people who were to be amongst the Royal Academy's most generous benefactors, Jill and Arthur Sackler. It was May 1985, and the two men were on one of the visits – de Grey's first – which RA Presidents were by now making to the United States in order to maintain contact with AARAT members, when it first became apparent that the Sacklers might be prepared to make a major contribution towards the cost of a new gallery, which it was planned would replace the old Diploma Galleries on the top floor of Burlington House. A party of the members, together with de Grey and Rodgers, was due to visit the Chagall show which had come from the Royal Academy and was on at the Philadelphia Museum of Art. 'We were going by bus from New York,' Ockenden related, 'and Jill and Arthur Sackler just got on the bus. I mentioned to Piers and Roger that they might do well to talk to them, and they all got on very well. Arthur Sackler, a great benefactor in the worlds of both medicine and art, had already met Hugh Casson at the Edinburgh Festival and liked him enormously, and I think it was on that trip that he first expressed an interest in being involved with the new gallery.'

The prospects looked good. A period of negotiation began. At one point the Academy side was warned by the Sackler attorney, who was apparently perturbed by the unlikely-looking space he was being shown right at the top of the Academy building, 'You know Dr Sackler is not interested in a loft conversion.' But Sackler liked the ideas coming from architect Norman Foster's office, he was on excellent terms with both Casson and Roger de Grey, another charming man, and events culminated in a lunch party for the Sacklers at the Academy in London.

This time, Casson was present, and for him, Piers Rodgers and Roger de Grey it was an important occasion; all were aware that their plans for an extension must not be jeopardized by any failure of performance on their own part. As the meal drew to a close, Dr Sackler at last announced, 'I'll give you—dollars.' There was a split-second of silence before Hugh said in his cheerful way, 'Oh go on, Arthur, make it pounds.' Such a rejoinder from anyone else could have sounded crude. Coming from Casson, it broke the tension, Sackler responded in the most positive way possible, and the Royal Academy's fine Sackler Gallery, designed by Foster Associates with the Sacklers as major benefactors, was the result. It was opened by the Queen in 1991.

Quite apart from the Sacklers' personal gift, AARAT, which is completely separate from the Friends of the Royal Academy in Britain, has benefited the Academy to the tune of many millions of dollars. Art collector Dee Nixon, who has been an Associate almost from AARAT's inception, remembers what a dreary, down-at-heel place the Academy had seemed in the seventies. The improvements which have made it the sumptuously welcoming place it is now cannot all be attributed to AARAT money – many others, including the British Friends of the Royal Academy, have played an important part – but the new library, the Friends' room, the new picture-storage room, and the American Associates' Gallery all can. Kitty Ockenden ascribed much of AARAT's success in its early years directly to Hugh. 'He would come over with Margaret to attend our functions and give speeches on the Academy's behalf, and he worked incredibly hard. He just liked people so much and he knew everybody, people like Brook Astor and Dru Heinz, who all appeared out of the woodwork when he was there.' As Dee Nixon said, at an Academy dinner in London, years after Hugh had retired, 'Hugh was so wonderfully un-academic. He didn't frighten us by a constant display of learning.'

Casson's persuasiveness almost certainly attracted several members of the Royal Family to this vital cause too, with Prince Philip the first President of AARAT, succeeded by Prince Charles, and dinners in Washington and London attended by the Prince and Princess of Wales in the mid-eighties. By 1996, when he was eighty-six, Casson's energetic contribution was over. There were no more fundraising journeys to the United States, few appearances even at Burlington House in London. But in that year, AARAT, in recognition of his work and Reta's steadfast support, set up the Hugh and Margaret Casson Fund, its purpose to assist in the research and development of new Royal Academy exhibitions, enabling recipients to travel to the United States.

AARAT was a brilliant concept. Watching these rich and cultivated Americans revelling in the Royal Academy's seductive splendour when they come on one of their well-organized visits to London, it is too easy to take their generosity for granted. They do after all enjoy tax concessions associated with their gifts. But why not express their benevolence in their own country? Paul Myer from Cincinnati, who was present on one such occasion with an AARAT party, was in expansive mood when the question was put to him: 'Well, we have plenty. And you know we would rather give to this great place than to a rival institution in the next State back home.' It was never necessary to spell out such subtleties to Hugh Casson. He always had his finger on the pulse of affairs and he understood the ways of people.

In 1996, quite apart from the Hugh and Margaret Casson Fund established by AARAT, the Royal Academy showed its own gratitude to Hugh for this extra work he had undertaken on its behalf long after his presidency had ended. The then President, architect Sir Philip Dowson, had the nice idea of presenting him with a replica of the Michelangelo *Tondo*, the Academy's most treasured possession, which hangs in the entrance to the Sackler Gallery. The presentation was marked by the type of event Hugh liked best: an elegant lunch in the Private Rooms at which the Queen Mother, Reta and several of his closer Academician friends were present.

XIII

The Perfect Courtier

The client–architect relationship is a notoriously difficult one, never more so than when it centres on residential projects. Architects can become arrogant and overly convinced of their design invincibility when faced with what they come to regard as intractable clients, forgetting that it is the client's money they are involving in pursuance of their grand schemes. And some clients get so emotionally involved with what is being done to their property that they consider it the architect's single concern: even late on a Sunday evening, when he's still deep in a weekend stupor and neither equipped nor eager to enter into long detailed discussions on the telephone. Tales of architect inadequacies or client transgressions on the residential front are legion, and the number of such connections which end in recrimination, anger or even a law suit is high.

It says much for the understanding and intelligence demonstrated on both sides (plus an intrinsic compatibility) that Hugh Casson was able to serve the Queen and the Duke of Edinburgh in an architectural capacity for over thirty years. There was no falling out, no stomping off in the direction of another architect, and certainly no griping about difficult clients from him: just a steady working relationship which reflected trust on their part and an eagerness to satisfy their needs and predilections on his. As Hugh once said to a young architectural student on his staff, who was querying the suitability of a modest fabric Hugh was proposing to take along to show to the Queen at Windsor: 'I know what Queenie likes.'

This was an unusually flippant remark from Hugh, certainly to a junior member of his staff. He relished his Royal connection. And it worked so well, not only because his professional advice was informed, sensible and geared to their tastes, but because his discretion was total and unquestioning. Others might regale dinner-party guests with tales of Royal encounters. Hugh never did that. Close acquaintances often had no idea he was engaged on Royal work, and Pamela Robinson, who worked in the Casson Conder office for years and was his assistant during the redecoration of guest suites at Windsor and of the Royal train, said he never chatted about his meetings with his Royal clients, even when he had been staying with them for the weekend. On their side, they responded to his wit and to his friendly manner which maintained that difficult balance between relaxed charm and the type of incautious intimacies they so plainly resent. Hugh amused them, he treated them like human beings, he served them, but he never made the mistake of encroaching on Royal territory. He was the perfect courtier.

The relationship began when he was asked to produce some designs for the interior of the new Royal Yacht in 1951. The ship was being built at John Brown's, the famous yard in Glasgow where John Brown himself, bowler-hatted and affable, supervised the design and construction of many notable vessels. *Britannia* came to be regarded as a fine and handsome ship and her demise as a Royal Yacht in 1998 was mourned by many who had seen her in foreign as well as British waters over the years. But during her building, the interior threatened to make an incongruous contrast with her grand marine exterior. John Brown had asked another Glasgow firm, McInnes Gardner, to design the Royal apartments and reception rooms. These designs, when produced, demonstrated a total misunderstanding of the role which the new ship was to play in her world travels. They were dull, richly formal, and altogether too ornate for the young, hard-working Royal couple.

Reflecting on these events years later, Hugh said, 'Prince Philip didn't like them. He thought they had a transatlantic-liner sort of décor. Being a naval officer, he wanted something simpler. He went to Gordon Russell, who ran the Council of Industrial Design (later to become the Design Council), and asked him to recommend someone who could make a better job of it, because there were tender feelings involved. Gordon was good enough to recommend me. Because of the problems I'd coped with at the Festival of Britain, I suppose . . .'

Splendid, unexpected opportunities had been a recurring factor in Hugh Casson's life, and he had invariably seized upon them with gusto. This was the best of all, and the one which certainly gave him the most pleasure. He loved ships, witness the teenage years spent mooching around the docks at South-ampton. His parents' next-door neighbour then had been the Captain of the *Queen Mary* who, appreciating the boy's inter-est, had presented him with a pass which gave him access to many of the ships which docked there, including the *Mauret-ania*, the *Aquitania* and the *Berengaria*. He also, like most of his generation, revered and respected the Royal Family. He simmered with excitement at the idea of visiting Prince Philip to talk over this most prestigious of design commissions. There was something about working for a young and beautiful queen with her dashing naval officer husband which appealed to the romantic side of his nature too. 'I saw Prince Philip. He was extremely good-looking, and very decisive. Rather nervous – although perhaps that's not quite the word. There was a lot of banter, a sort of relationship of banter so that every remark was a faint joke which is a sign of nervousness as a rule. I was terribly nervous too.'

Fortunately, the two men established an immediate rapport.

Casson then went up to Glasgow to see *Britannia*'s hull and to meet McInnes Gardner, who had relinquished the task of producing design concepts for her interior with relief. They were happy to act in an executive capacity for Hugh's designs. 'Philip wanted everything to be in the spirit of the present age. He started off being very dominant because he had this vision which the Queen respected. There was the occasional family argument, but I was experienced in this sort of situation and knew how to lighten the tone.'

At the end of 1996, not long before she was decommissioned, *Britannia's* interior – unlike that of *Canberra* – looked much as Casson had left it over forty years before. It had been designed in a period of austerity – long before Habitat's influential arrival on the British design scene – shortly after the Festival of Britain, when stirrings of life became manifest amongst both designers and their patrons, and there had been a tight control on costs. All these factors remained obvious so many years later. When the decommissioning was announced, Prince Philip said that *Britannia* had been special as far as he and the Queen were concerned because, unlike in their other homes, they were involved from the beginning, instructing their architect, organizing the design and furnishings, and equipping her. In that sense, she was their own.

In contrast to their other homes, and partly as a result of Prince Philip's inclinations, the designs which they evolved with Hugh Casson were simple, almost austere. There were white walls with grey carpets throughout (Philip chose white because he decided that when it needed repainting there would be no need to hunt around for a match), with a gold line around the cornice in the public rooms. Hugh had visited the previous Royal Yacht, the *Victoria and Albert*, at Portsmouth, where she lay in a mudbank 'so thick they were growing tomatoes around her'. He enjoyed going through everything on board and selecting pieces of furniture and pictures which he recommended should be used again on *Britannia*. 'We kept virtually all the pictures because they were a good collection, wonderful oil paintings which depicted scenes like Edward VII greeting the Shah of Persia, and the King of Norway arriving for a State visit in 1911. I recommended they used all the Hepplewhite dining chairs too, and a large glass-fronted bookcase, and a gimbal table designed by Prince Albert.'

These sound alien to the spirit of the age Philip had specified. Nevertheless, as anyone who went on *Britannia* during her years of Royal service will confirm, the public spaces were refreshingly unpompous in their simplicity, quite bereft of the ornamentation which distinguishes most Royal palaces. And *Britannia was* a Royal palace. In the private rooms, the suites belonging to the Queen, the Duke and the Royal household, restraint was total. The treatment given to the necessarily small spaces was reasonably modern for the times, but in a cautious sort of way. The Queen's suite had the comfort level which would have been expected by a prosperous housewife of the 1950s, no more, whilst the Duke's was almost spartan, with an Anglepoise lamp on the desk, the simple cone-shaped wall-lamps which featured in all architects' drawings of the period, and linoleum in the bathroom. And so it all remained, apart from minor replacements to carpets and upholstery. In succeeding years there was the addition, in the Duke's suite, of a print of a charming painting of the Queen which he had seen and acquired in New Zealand. Sycamore writing-desks and dressing-tables with Bakelite handles – fashionable in the fifties – were designed by Hugh's long-time ally in these matters, John Wright; simple chandeliers in the public rooms by Jim Cadbury-Brown; a fireplace by Christopher Ironside; fabrics by Eduardo Paolozzi and Roger Nicholson. The plain fitted carpet originally laid in the reception rooms was enhanced in 1979 by fine Persian rugs, one a gift from the Emir of Abu Dhabi and two more from the ruler of Qatar during the

Queen's tour of the Gulf States, but these remained the only items which could be deemed opulent. Other gifts flowed in during all the years *Britannia* was afloat, but these were of a far simpler nature. As the Keeper and Steward, Royal Cabins, wrote to Hugh at one point: 'We have now completed Prince Philip's Pacific cruise which has left us with a further supply of artefacts to be placed in the dining room – Portobello Road has nothing on us.' Somehow, the understated interiors enabled all the acquisitions to be accommodated without stressful effect, and Prince Philip in particular enjoyed overseeing their arrangement.

That was all in the future. Back in the summer of 1952, Casson dispatched his initial ideas, many of them depicted in his own water-colours, to Buckingham Palace. The Royal Family was by now on holiday in Scotland, and Casson received a summons to Balmoral – complete with his dinner jacket – to talk about the schemes. This was the first of many such visits, none of them quite devoid of the tensions which ordinary middle-class people feel in the presence of royalty.

On 6 September Casson arrived at Aberdeen on the night train from London, to be met by a large black Austin car, and swept off, sleepy and nervous, for the seventy-minute journey to Balmoral and for this first experience as a Royal guest. Speeding through the forests and rocks of the Dee Valley, the car eventually drove through barren-looking hills, swung left over a bridge, past a saluting policeman who stood amongst the shrubs lining the drive, and pulled up under the clock tower of the castle. The lawn was still wet with dew and the shadows were long as the tweed-suited figure of Lord Plunkett, equerry to the Queen and a courtier Hugh would get to know well over the years, appeared on the front step, and footmen in blue battle dress came to unload the luggage.

Describing this visit later, Hugh talked of trembling knees, of moments of indecision about whether there was time to bathe before dinner (his hosts always seemed to cut it extremely fine yet still arrive punctually), and he was beset by a terror of entering the drawing room after the Queen despite his dashes along the scarlet-carpeted corridors. He also agonized about whether he should join in the singing while being driven to a picnic by the Queen when she, Princess Margaret and Lord Porchester started singing the choruses from *Guys and Dolls* with assumed American accents. 'I compromised on low, respectful humming.'

He survived what must have been an ordeal, albeit an exciting one. The singing episode happened when the Royal party – which included Lord Westmorland, Lord Porchester and the Queen's secretary, Martin Charteris – was heading for a picnic by a stream, where they were joined by the Queen Mother, who had telephoned to ask if she could bring along her own large house party which included the American Ambassador. 'That means saucers,' said the Queen. 'Don't pander,' said Princess Margaret. A slight argument ended in a decision to take saucers, if not use them, and the picnic outside a small stone cottage perched on a bank above the river was fun, apart from the intrusion of several rather fierce horses which the Queen and one or two braver men (not Hugh) eventually shooed away.

The purpose for which Casson had come to Balmoral took up comparatively little of his time there, and he was made welcome as a guest to the point where, as he later related, he became, after one enjoyable and intimate dinner, dangerously confident. He got on particularly well with Princess Margaret, not yet married and also a guest, discussing art, architecture and the theatre with her and noting how pretty she looked at dinner in her black lace dress with its pink underslip. But he was too intelligent and socially accomplished to let fleeting moments of bravura lead to disaster, and he continued to behave with the discretion of a courtier. He surveyed his bedroom with a professional eye on retiring, noting the cream-painted walls, stripped-pine woodwork, the pretty carpet with its fine tartan pattern, the large brass bed and the Landseer engravings which hung on the wall, one of them depicting Queen Victoria sketching at Loch Laggan. The large adjacent bathroom did not contain a WC and Hugh had to ask several footmen before he located one along the passage. On his way there after breakfast on the first morning he received a smart blow on the shin from Princess Anne, tearing at full speed on her tricycle down the corridor.

On this first visit, all Hugh's water-colours, plans and fabric samples were spread out in one room for the Queen and Prince Philip to inspect. They approved almost everything he showed them, suggested one or two alterations, asked to see more samples, and told him to proceed with the work. 'They were extremely easy people,' he said later. 'She was very young, of course, interested and excited about everything and not worried by the load of her responsibility. I don't think it had hit her yet.' Prince Charles and Princess Anne were much in evidence on this and other visits Hugh made to Royal palaces, and a short description he wrote after this visit to Balmoral shows the Queen and Prince Philip in a different light from the cool and detached parents they are often claimed to be. Casson first encountered the Queen on this occasion dressed in a blue woollen frock and sitting on a fireside stool in her private sitting room while Prince Charles 'cut' her hair with white plastic scissors, 'and Princess Anne bounced reflectively on the sofa'.

When it was over and Hugh had said goodbye to the Queen, who was taking the children up to meet the shoot at which their father and other members of the party were engaged, he was given a brace of pheasants, labelled 'From the Queen' in large letters, which he admitted to having displayed with pride at Aberdeen station, and went home pleased with how things had gone. Reta was fascinated to hear the details of this unaccustomed visit, but grateful that her husband had been bidden to Balmoral alone. It didn't occur to her then that she would not always be spared.

There was another occasion connected with *Britannia* which even the most blasé of architects would have found thrilling. And Hugh was not blasé and never would be. The Queen, accompanied by Prince Philip, went on a tour of the Commonwealth in 1954, during which period *Britannia* was finished. With Prince Charles and Princess Anne on board, the ship sailed out to Tobruk so that the Royal couple could join her for the last part of their journey home. They had not been long underway when Casson received a telegram saying how much they were enjoying everything he had done, and asking him to join them off the Isle of Wight for the remainder of the voyage into the Port of London. Hugh accepted, elated and relieved at this clearest possible indication that they were pleased with the ship.

Arrangements for the visit were made by the Admiralty, but Casson did not know until he arrived at Waterloo station for the jouney to Southampton, and saw the commotion and flashing of light bulbs from the other end of the train, that Winston Churchill was to be another guest on board, complete with his entourage. Arriving at Southampton, the two parties were driven out to the Needles on twin motor torpedo boats, and went roaring abreast down Southampton Water. 'Thank God it was a calm and sunny day. The Commander of my boat didn't quite know who I was and what the hell I was doing looking rather silly in civilian clothes and a snap-brim felt hat. But by the time we were off Cowes, we were a bit matier and had tea on the bridge. When we reached the Needles at the western end of the Isle of Wight where *Britannia* was due about half an hour later, the Solent was thick with ships. The Queen was going to review the fleet, so they were all at anchor like in some old-fashioned print.'

Casson now joined the Churchill party in their vessel, and they sat, he and Churchill, making difficult conversation – 'he was very friendly but terribly deaf' – until suddenly there was a distant roar of aircraft which got louder as the planes swooped overhead, and then *Britannia* came into view.

As she approached them she slowed and lowered an accommodation ladder. The job of hauling Churchill on board was a tricky one, for he was both heavy and cumbersome, and Casson, never short of imagination, had a sudden fearful picture of him being dropped into the sea. But all went well, and he followed Churchill on board to watch the Queen reviewing the fleet. Clearly, he was overwhelmed with the drama of events, and with his own presence alongside not only the Queen but one of the most legendary British prime ministers of all time. By now he was familiar with several members of the Royal entourage who, as ever, eased the path of unwary commoners.

Casson found the voyage into the Port of London dreamlike in its splendour, despite the fact that at one point he was closeted with the Queen, both of them on their knees, inspecting the underside of her writing desk where some alterations were to be made. Minor changes and adjustments were necessary, and these were discussed with both the Queen and the Duke of Edinburgh, who seized the opportunity presented by having their architect on board. There was time though for a series of those elegant occasions with which Hugh was already becoming familiar. The first was a small dinner, only sixteen at table (the menu – sole fillets and mussel sauce, roast lamb, orange bombe), with Winston Churchill on one side of the Queen, Hugh Casson on the other. There had been the usual frenzy to get ready in the small amount of time allotted to changing for dinner. 'No bath. I couldn't find my socks, and had just dispatched the attendant valet to borrow some, when I found my own tucked into the toes of my shoes by Reta.' She did his packing, as she did so many other things for him.

At the film show after dinner, Casson was placed in the front row of armchairs, along with the Royal couple and Winston Churchill, whilst the remainder of the guests and a sprinkling of ship's officers were 'pushed back in the ninepennies'. This distribution impressed him no end, though his confidence was far from impregnable, his amazement at the singular height to which he had ascended considerable. 'My glow of pride was pierced by a nagging suspicion that I'd be found out.' The evening ended with him sitting on the main stairs between his clients, discussing suggestions for improvements, including giving a more domestic feel to the sun lounge, which turned out to be the room they were using most often. (By the time *Britannia* was decommissioned, this place had become so homely it would have appeared familiar to many of Her Majesty's subjects, with garden lounge chairs covered in a large floral pattern which one of *Britannia*'s crew described as 'very B & Q'.)

As the handsome ship progressed into London next day, excitement mounted, the Royal children raced about the decks or telephoned each other on the ship's telephone, and Casson watched it all – the cheering, flag-waving crowds on the banks of the Thames and the boats which escorted and followed them – crossing continually from port to starboard for fear of missing something. They passed under Tower Bridge with its Welcome Home banner and, the difficult task of mooring without tugs accomplished ('The Navy does not use tugs,' according to Admiral Abel-Smith who was in charge), the Queen Mother and Princess Margaret came aboard, Churchill, who had not been much in evidence for most of the day, disembarked, and the whole extraordinary experience drew to a close. Hugh's pleasure at being drawn forward by the Queen with the words 'I think you know my mother and sister' was intensified by their admiration of his work. 'I'm so glad you have got plenty

of gold. Very important,' said the Queen Mother. After lunch
the Royal party went ashore, and it was all over. Hugh Casson
was driven home to Victoria Road along with Admiral Abel-
Smith, by now in civilian clothes and a bowler hat, who had
been knighted by the Queen before she left the ship.

'It was deeply moving, and yet I felt completely detached
and dreamlike,' Casson wrote of the voyage a few days later.

He had already been asked to redesign Prince Philip's library
and office in Buckingham Palace, and these rooms again were
to be in the contemporary style which the Prince favoured.
He knew exactly what he wanted, to the gratification of his
architect, who afterwards insisted that the Duke had designed
most of it himself. Tim Rendle, the young architect who did
a survey of the apartments in preparation for the changes,
described them as being grand and elaborate rooms into which
they were now inserting a large and complicated modern desk
arrangement. 'Hugh took the brief, but I did the drawings.
That was how he worked with young assistants. What he was
terribly good at when things got tricky was whisking into
action himself: for instance if something was late. I once saw
him dictate a specification straight off, just standing beside the
secretary's desk. When people got into scrapes due to their
youthfulness, he was able to walk into a tricky meeting with
the client and change things on the spot. He used his wit and
humour, and they didn't know what had hit them.'

Such remedies were never required during the Buckingham
Palace job, however. Rendle was himself an able practitioner
and a very good designer (though, a typical Casson-type aide,
he did not go on to make a big reputation after he quit Casson
Conder), and the Royal connection survived without untoward
incident.

Until now, the jobs undertaken for the Royal Family had
been straightforward and contained within a limited timescale. The one for which he was next called upon enjoyed no

such boundaries. Nevertheless, it was the saga of Sandringham
which drew Hugh Casson inexorably into the Royal network.
It started in early February 1958, when he was invited to spend
two nights there to discuss the plans for this huge and unwieldy
mansion. It was grossly inefficient to run and its services
needed modernizing: central heating was by no means comprehensive, with servants' quarters, for instance, heated by electric fires.

A note to Hugh's friend Rosie d'Avigdor Goldsmid
during one of the periods when he was involved in
advising the Queen about Sandringham.

By now Casson was comparatively experienced at handling such visits. He was on affable terms with many members of the Court, particularly such intimates as Patrick Plunkett, for his friendly, humorous and relaxed style matched theirs, and he was also known to some of the servants as a visitor who they would be seeing from time to time. He relied on them to nudge him gently in the right direction when necessary, providing a black tie when, unbeknown to him, there had been a death on the outer fringes of the Royal circle, rescuing him when he was lost in a labyrinth of corridors and in danger of being late for a meeting with the Queen. He arrived on this occasion aware of the routine: the greeting from a pack of barking dogs, the games of Scrabble, the films after dinner, the meals, light and delicious, when he was often seated next to the Queen, drives with the Queen at the wheel of a Land Rover. But he was aware too of the pitfalls which lay in wait for the over-confident or insensitive guest in Royal households. As ever, he was beset by the imperative to bathe before dinner. The bath was always run and waiting for him when he shot back after pre-prandial drinks. But the time allowed never seemed sufficient, and he sometimes resorted to stirring the water with a bar of soap and dampening the towels.

Sandringham, which appeared when Casson arrived with Patrick Plunkett as a romantic, Hanseatic silhouette of chimneys and cupolas under a full moon, was later described by him as 'warm and for all its unpredictability of levels, its hideous quirks of shape and decoration, its fabulous load of ivories and china plates, of animal heads and oriental armour, not uncosy nor pompous'. The Queen had a sentimental fondness for the place too, particularly as it was there that her father, King George VI, had died. Nevertheless, she said after a quick walk around the main house with her architect, 'How *could* anyone have made anything quite so ugly?' – a not unexpected reaction to this heavy Victorian pile from a woman barely out of her

Sandringham, with corgis.

twenties. Hugh always had a penchant for anything Victorian
though, and it stood him in good stead now. With Mr Mannington, the Sandringham Superintendent who was devoted to
the house and its contents, he was able to take a guided tour
on the second morning of this visit without flinching. Other
architects of his generation, imbued with the Modernist
principles of the time, might well have done so at the sight of
certain areas in the nether regions where servants sat over
coal fires, their stockings drip-drying over basins, and at the
kitchens which were twenty feet high. He was insistent afterwards that even the servants' rooms were not uncomfortable,
however, and he obviously assuaged the fears of Mr Mannington, who was at first on the defensive, and, fearing their
destruction, was anxious to prove that every room in the house
was invaluable. 'We don't use this one much,' he admitted of
a room shaped like a small railway tunnel, 'but of course at
Christmas it's absolutely filled with Christmas presents.'

Nevertheless, when Hugh was summoned to Prince Philip's

study before lunch – where the furnishings included an easel and palette, and a few still-life studies were propped on a window-sill – the talk was of change: of improvement, of drastic reconstruction and even of total abandonment. Casson's opinion was sought, and the whole subject was discussed and argued about on this and other occasions, with the costs entailed for each option always a major consideration. He was eventually commissioned to undertake a rough survey for demolishing some parts and linking the dysfunctional areas which would remain in an effective way. Ronald Green went up to Sandringham to undertake this task – though in a more workaday and less intimate manner than Hugh had done before him. It was twenty years later, though, when the nettle was finally grasped and Sandringham modernized to any great extent.

Though Hugh served the Royal Family by working on other Royal buildings in the meantime, major architectural performances were rarely required. He was never to follow in the footsteps of such distinguished Royal architects as John Nash or James Wyatville. Much of the work, particularly at Windsor where other architects were employed on projects connected with the main fabric of the building, involved little more than presenting a carefully chosen array of furniture, fabrics and paint colours to the Queen from which she made her own selection. This was no empty courtesy. The Royal client had strong views about what she did or did not like in her homes. She wrote in one letter: 'The chair model to my mind looked better when Anne tipped it upside down, for then the seat was longer than the back which is what makes it look rather uncomfortable.' And of a carpet: 'Philip took one look at it and said it looked like a dog's mess.' Generally though, as he had told the architectural student working in his office, Casson knew what the Queen wanted, and she was decisive in endorsing his selection – or, on certain occasions, otherwise.

Over a period of many years, the Duke of Edinburgh was a largely unsung proselytizer for design. The support he gave to the Design Council and to Paul Reilly, who was its director from 1960–77 when the impact it made on public perception was at its highest, was staunch. This support was not merely of the figurehead variety. He produced creative ideas – the Duke of Edinburgh's Award for Elegance resulted from one – talked to people, arranged small dinners where designers could meet industrialists, travelled the country to visit projects where design was an important factor, and generally expressed immense enthusiasm for modern design, not a concept the British have ever found it easy to comprehend or encompass. His interest embraced every aspect, and he had strong views which he developed over the years. He is, however, far too intelligent to think he could introduce hard-edged modern design of the type propounded by supporters of the Modern Movement into any of the Royal palaces. 'Hugh's architecture', he said, many years later, 'was advanced as opposed to modern. He was perfectly prepared to discuss things with us, though of course he had his own likes and dislikes. He had a thing about strong colour, I remember. And of course he could make a sketch to illustrate what he meant as he was talking to you. He had a generally all-embracing taste, and he loved curiosities.'

Combining these interesting little idiosyncrasies with the manners of a perfect diplomat ensured that Hugh suited the Royal couple. As he spoke about Casson in the late nineties, forty-five years after their first meeting, the Duke was sitting in the library Casson designed for him at Buckingham Palace. As is the habit of the Queen and the Duke, nothing has been altered. The room is today much as it was in the fifties. Simple modern bookcases line the walls. They are topped by a decorative plinth which conceals wall-washing lighting and is the only concession to the room's beautiful gilded ceiling. Seats which are grouped around a low table where the Duke receives visitors were modern in their day, and the Duke chose them himself. Next door in his study, the ceiling has been lowered – a favourite fifties practice – and the large hardwood desk/storage arrangement which Casson designed is fairly dominant. Prince Philip said that in retrospect he should have asked for something more versatile and flexible. Nevertheless, he was still using it and it has taken its place as a piece of period furniture amongst others.

At Windsor, from the 1950s onwards, Casson, with Reta's assistance, refurbished a number of guest rooms and suites, one of them, at the Queen's request, realized in contemporary – i.e., 1950s – style. There was special bedroom furniture designed by Neville Ward, chairs by Gordon Russell, wallpaper by Edward Bawden. It was all very restrained, nothing wild, nothing plastic, nothing which would have interested the design magazines. And the modern paintings which Anthony Blunt had viewed with such disdain were by important but safe artists such as Barbara Hepworth. 'These were from her series of drawings of surgeons' hands,' Reta Casson remembered later, 'but we didn't even consider more controversial work by Francis Bacon, for instance.' (When Paul Reilly, then Director of the Design Council, was invited with his wife to dine and stay the night at Windsor in the late 1970s, they were allotted this suite of contemporary rooms in the Edward III tower, presumably because it was thought these were appropriate for people with their interests.)

The refurbishments had been set in motion by another weekend visit to a Royal home. This time it was to Windsor, in December, and Reta, initially terrified, and in a panic about what clothes to take, was invited too. The young chauffeur who arrived in a Daimler to collect them from Victoria Road drove so fast that they arrived too early. The lodge keeper at Windsor had to be extracted from his house by the hooting of the horn, so that the gates could be opened, and then, after the

Sketches of Casson's ideas for various apartments at Windsor.

drive up a dark tree-lined avenue, suddenly the black silhouette of Windsor Castle reared up ahead, a few lighted windows adding to its theatrical appearance. A sentry presented arms as they passed beneath an archway into the upper courtyard and drew up at the Sovereign's Entrance. The chauffeur rang the bell. Minutes passed. The silence was absolute. Reta shivered in her seat and Hugh began to feel uneasy. Then came the sound of distant running feet on stone. Lights clicked on. The door opened, and the Cassons emerged from the car as the Queen, two corgis at her heels, was seen running downstairs within, buttoning her jacket as she came. She greeted them warmly on the doorstep, apologizing for the wait: 'I wasn't expecting you quite so soon.'

It was an inauspicious start, especially for Reta who was feeling sick with nerves. But the Queen made them welcome with the warmth of a middle-class hostess greeting guests after a tedious drive, showed them their suite, which included a beautifully comfortable sitting room as well as two bedrooms and a bathroom, and went off 'to find Philip who is somewhere with the children', leaving them with the maid and valet who had been allotted to them, and the luggage.

The children, Prince Charles and Princess Anne, appeared quite frequently during this weekend and there was no sign of nurses, governesses or any other attendants, though they were presumably on duty. Reta's tenseness was a little assuaged by the children's presence, and Casson relished such intimacies. This weekend was the most intimate of all so far. He and Reta were the only guests, without even the usual array of courtiers being present, and they dined alone with the Royal couple on both evenings, at a table set by the fire. Both Cassons had stomach upsets during the first night, perhaps due to nerves as much as to the strength of the Royal drinks, which others have always reported as packing a powerful punch. The food, as Hugh was now coming to recognize, was delicious, but light and digestible. Conversation was elegantly directed towards the guests' presumed interests: art, architecture, music, and the new Festival Hall which was judged by the Queen as 'exciting but a bit too disintegrated inside – ceilings, walls, floors, stairs disappear into space or mirrors, and reduce your confidence'. They discussed the Graham Sutherland portrait of Winston Churchill, which the Queen thought portrayed an uncharacteristic pose, and wondered 'what sort of job will Graham Sutherland make of Mummy?'

Both the Queen and the Duke were gay, even flippant, and the Cassons relaxed, Reta relieved to realize that the clothes over which she had agonized were perfectly appropriate. Hugh noted that the Queen was better informed about pictures than her husband, although his knowledge was stronger when it came to industrial design and architecture. A tour of the pictures and State rooms, led by their hostess in a black tulle dress with a tiny grey mink cape, was fascinating for them both, with the Queen demonstrating a sure knowledge about the history of her possessions, and able to give pertinent reasons as to why some were favourites. The great rooms were empty and only dimly lit, and the party of four was headed by the corgis, their toe-nails clicking over parquet, stone and marble. In the Waterloo Chamber, the flags and balloons of the previous evening's staff Christmas ball still littered the floor, and the pictures were not back in position, their places on the walls occupied by panels designed many years ago by pupils at a local art school when, as the Queen said, 'we used to do pantomimes. How thankful I am too for those pantomimes. They taught me so much about speaking in public.'

Both then, and the next day in church, 'the Queen and Prince Philip, Moggie and me', Hugh was constantly aware of the singularity of the situation in which they found themselves. There was puzzled nudging in the congregation who could not identify the Royal guests. Conversation at lunch was about the rooms they were to refurbish and about tactfully Casson-oriented subjects, with the Queen describing how Annigoni was getting fifteen sittings for the portrait he was making of her, which was boring as he didn't talk and worked very slowly. She dreaded the result, sure he would record every pore and mole. At tea in front of the fire in the Queen's sitting room, Charles and Anne complained that the lateness (it was five p.m.) meant they would miss *Muffin the Mule*; their parents, after first telling them to be quiet and eat up, or so Casson related, then relented and switched on the television. 'This kept us all quiet until it was over, and afterwards Prince Philip went off to organize a treasure hunt for them. The clues had to be drawn as they couldn't read.'

On Monday morning when the Queen and Prince Philip had departed, leaving the Cassons to complete a survey of the guest suites they were going to rearrange, and with all the strain over, Hugh and Reta revelled in the euphoria of a taxing but enjoyable experience having been accomplished without any perceivable calamity. Hugh said, 'We felt reasonably satisfied with our performance despite the usual tendency on my part to talk too much and on Moggie's not to talk enough. Our hosts' verdict of course we shall never know.'

His evident awe at the company he was keeping seems mildly surprising now, particularly to people of equal sophistication and distinction who are apt to rub shoulders with Royalty spasmodically, even if in less intimate circumstances. This was the fifties though, when the Royal Family was at the height of its popularity and when the barrier between 'them and us' was almost palpable. Hugh retained the Edwardian values and standards of his parents. While his mother was alive he would send her an account of every visit he made to a Royal palace, and sometimes these narratives were passed on to other members of the family.

In addition to Reta, two women who had been his students

Above: A drawing by Hugh Casson of the Shot Tower, which was the only existing building to remain on the Festival site.

Left: The Shot Tower with the boathouse and barge dock which Casson designed for the display of small craft.

Right: The competition for a vertical feature was won by the young architects Philip Powell and Hildago Moya with this poised and elegant structure which came to be called the Skylon.

Piccadilly, showing treatment of Bond Street entrance. — K.C.

Above: Casson's Coronation decorations for Westminster City Council included this one across Piccadilly at the entrance to Bond Street.

Left: Hugh and Carola (aged twelve) on their way to watch the Coronation from seats in Hyde Park.

Top: Casson's design for the Queen's study on
the Royal Yacht *Britannia*.
Bottom: The Duke of Edinburgh's study.

In 1953, Hugh Casson was asked to design stage sets for the
opera *Alceste* at Glyndebourne.

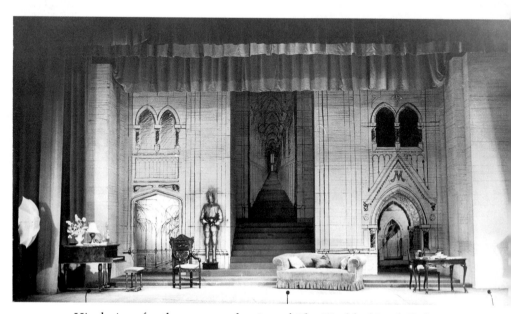

His designs for the 1959 production of *The World of Paul Slickey*
by John Osborne were well received. The play was not and came off
after a few days.

Casson's interiors for the P&O liner *Canberra*, which sailed
on its maiden voyage in 1961, included this sculptural spiral staircase
which rose through three decks.

Casson Conder did the master plan for the Arts Faculties on Sidgwick Avenue in
Cambridge, and designed most of the buildings, including the one housing faculties of
Modern and Medieval Languages, English and Moral Science.

A view of the Royal College of Art building from the internal courtyard.

The rough, bush-hammered surface of Casson's design
for the Elephant and Rhinoceros Pavilion at London Zoo evokes
images of the animals within.

The animals are housed in linked circular pavilions with daylight coming from the tall
lantern lights which give the building its idiosyncratic shape.

Hugh wearing the Presidential Medal of
the Royal Academy of Arts.

Reta at home in the 1980s.

Hugh and Reta in Venice during one of their summer holidays with
Queen Elizabeth the Queen Mother during the early 1990s.

at the Royal College helped Hugh with the rooms at Windsor: the first was Joyce Conwy Evans (who, at his request, made the garland which was to deck Sir Joshua Reynolds's statue in the courtyard at the Royal Academy during the Summer Exhibition from Hugh's time onwards), and then in later years Pamela Robinson took over. These two very different women adored Hugh (though they were not very keen on each other), and were content to act as his assistants even when much of the work they did for him involved quite trivial tasks. Never venturing beyond the 'Sir Hugh' stage of intimacy, they bathed in the afterglow of his reputation, without ever demanding, or getting, much personal credit. They were, as the exuberant Conwy Evans said years later, 'just fabulously happy to be part of his world'. She and Robinson, spinsters both, played an important part in it. Nevertheless, in 1975, shortly after working with Hugh on the internal refurbishments of the Albert Hall (paint colours, finishes, interiors of boxes, lighting, new seats, etc.), Conwy Evans departed to work on her own. Pamela Robinson stayed on until her retirement in 1991, during the latter years working in the main Casson Conder office at Thurloe Place.

The contribution which these two contrasting personalities made to the work at Windsor was ongoing and substantial. Conwy Evans painted some of the descriptive images of interiors which were submitted to the Queen for approval, and Pamela Robinson, quiet and reserved, spent hours at Windsor, taking photographs, making surveys and painstakingly drawing architectural details in the rooms which were to be redecorated. By the early eighties she was helping Hugh transform Queen Victoria's Audience Chamber, a High Gothic extravaganza, into a more comfortable and relaxed sitting room, which was initially intended for Prince Andrew. In January 1985, though, the Queen wrote to Hugh: 'The Audience room was a great success over the Christmas period and much admired by the people who came to criticize it. Also it became a haven of peace and quiet for the Gloucesters.'

All these projects involved Pamela Robinson in scouring fabric showrooms for suitable designs, selecting wall coverings, negotiating special editions and colourways to meet the exacting Royal requirements and to further the general aim of making the rooms lighter, paler and prettier. 'Sir Hugh would tell me what he wanted, having formed his own ideas about what was to be done. Then I'd produce a whole selection of samples for him. Often his initial idea would be represented by one of his own water-colours.' She would then translate the water-colour into tangible fabrics and appropriate paint colours, preparing working drawings when necessary. It was Hugh, however, who took the Royal instructions and gave his advice, often at informal and friendly occasions when the Queen and Prince Philip plainly took pleasure in his company quite as much as in his expertise. Pamela Robinson never got near them, except on one memorable Friday afternoon when she was at Windsor discussing some problem with Casson and the Castle Superintendent. 'There was a tiny hush. Then about eight corgis came slithering all over the floor, and suddenly the Queen was in the room. Sir Hugh introduced me as "my colleague" which pleased me enormously, but I think it was to raise the level of my importance in the Queen's eyes.'

Pamela Robinson was precise and diligent in her work, and unlikely to make errors of taste or performance. Nor was she demanding in her expectation of reward or recognition. In fact she was the perfect assistant for these sensitive projects and Casson was lucky to have entrapped her. Meg Carpenter noted the flirtatious technique he used when discussing the Royal projects with this paragon of designers, and the gentle pleasure it evinced.

The hours Pamela Robinson spent working on Windsor and other Royal projects were properly charged to the Royal account. Hugh's hours never were. He seemed content to be rewarded with their hospitality. Both the Queen and the Duke were profligate in their letters thanking him for his help after each and every job. When *Britannia* was finished, Prince Philip wrote: 'I can't tell you how grateful we are to you for all your help and hard work, and for delivering us from the horrors of marine decorative architects.' It is doubtful if, despite their awareness of costs – and anger when the press accused them of extravagance – he or the Queen knew then, or ever, the extent of Casson's munificence.

Though this omission of charges to the Royal household was noted and queried by the other partners at Casson Conder, it was accepted without serious objection as just another of Hugh's outside activities. Looked at objectively, though, there appears to be substantial disparity between the writing, speaking, broadcasting and travelling he did, which, quite apart from the fact that they often attracted a considerable remuneration, were valuable in terms of public relations, and the Royal work, secretive, rarely spoken of even in the office, which was not. The failure to charge for his time was particularly bizarre in the light of Hugh's often-repeated dictum: 'You've got to make a charge however small, because otherwise people don't think you're actually doing any work.'

His partners were indeed generous in their support of this engagement with the Royal Family, which stretched over many years and took up no mean portion of their senior partner's time. Ronald Green described Casson Conder in retrospect as 'a social experiment rather than an office, with Hugh being what you might call a non-chargeable overhead' and he was only half joking. But like the other partners, he seemed mesmerized by Hugh's success and charm. Such a relaxed attitude to cash flow – though with different personalities involved – saw the downfall of certain architects' offices from the 1980s onwards when the outside world had become altogether tougher and more competitive. But by then Hugh had retired and Casson Conder survived.

In January 1973 there was another call to Sandringham where, as Hugh recalled afterwards, little had changed. He described how the front door opened directly into the large family sitting room (he had surreptitiously combed his hair before getting out of the car which had brought him from King's Lynn station), and his fellow guests included Princess Margaret and the Duchess of Gloucester. The problems, centring on the large unmanageable building with its huge complement of staff, remained the same, except that they had been exacerbated over the years.

There was dry rot in the roof and the central heating needed replacing. To rationalize, reduce or abandon? The arguments had not changed and they now became heated, with the Queen and Hugh sitting on the floor surrounded by dogs, mulling over Hugh's rough sketch ideas, and Prince Philip looming above them from a sofa to make his contributions. A tour with Mr Mannington the Steward, son of the previous Steward, and the new Agent, Julian Loyd, found everything much as it had been in the 1950s, with few floors in the different wings at the same level, and some not even interconnecting. All the servants' rooms now had wash handbasins though, and only one was shared. Discussions became even more argumentative, so that the Queen drifted off, leaving Casson to thrash over the difficulties with Prince Philip and Patrick Plunkett. Philip was exasperated by this intractable problem and by what he saw, according to Hugh, as the impenetrable conservatism of all women. Eventually he too departed to take Prince Edward, who had had tonsillitis, for a day at the beach.

Talking or writing of these Royal encounters afterwards, Hugh invariably reviewed them, as he did all events, in visual terms. This was particularly true of the clothes. A considered and mildly offbeat dresser himself, with a great fondness for

Nehru jackets which obviated the necessity for a tie, he could describe in detail everything that was worn by the Queen, the Queen Mother, Princess Margaret, even Prince Philip and the children, in the most graphic and exact terms. Few men outside the fashion industry are competent to name fabrics and subtle shade differences with any confidence. Casson was, and he had strong opinions about outfits which were particularly flattering (or otherwise) to their wearer, as his daughters well remember. Ironically, one of the few gaffes he made in the Royal presence was on the subject of dress, and it was on this particular visit to Sandringham.

At dinner, Princess Anne was wearing a white silk shirt and a dress tartan skirt with a black velvet belt. Afterwards, chatting to her as they sat on a sofa, Hugh asked her if this was a dress MacDonald tartan. 'Are you serious?' intervened her mother (ivory silk embroidered with sparklers). He admitted he didn't know one tartan from another. 'Not even the Royal one?' she queried. He apologized abjectly. 'Presumably you know the family name is Stuart?' was the spirited response.

More freehand plans were drawn up for Sandringham, demonstrating several solutions. Hugh did them himself, for it was in these initial stages of a project that he was always most active. He was then asked to investigate the approximate costs of his various tentative proposals, and a survey of the whole building by Clutton's was commissioned. By March, Casson, acutely aware of the complexities involved whichever solution was adopted, had opted out of the primary position, stating that in his opinion it would be more satisfactory if a good local architect was employed, though he would be pleased to act as consultant. He was immediately asked to suggest a suitable candidate. His powers of patronage were intact.

The man on whom Hugh Casson bestowed what could have been viewed as either a plum job or a millstone was David Roberts, who was then a tutor at the School of Architecture at

Cambridge. In the event, as both men suspected, it turned out to be a millstone, albeit a fairly light one.

The Queen liked Roberts, who was a pleasant, civilized man, moderately eccentric (he would write on each cigarette packet the number of cigarettes already smoked) and a good architect. A one-time Cambridge student said, 'His was plain architecture in a gently modern style, but when you looked closer there was evidence of much care and thought.' He remembered Roberts's frequent imprecations to those who rushed in late for a lecture: 'There is nothing so uncivilized as a man running.'

This was an architect with whom, because of both his personality and style of architecture, the Queen and the Duke could work. But every difficulty – and there were many – was referred back to Hugh. He had written to Roberts after his appointment: 'As you know, my role in all this is as midwife. I do not wish to come between architect and client now the scheme is launched except by invitation from either side. So please neglect me as much as you like.'

The scheme was in fact not launched. The arguments went on for many more weeks, with Roberts becoming ever more disconsolate, and it was May 1974 before plans were announced to the press (Hugh was unable to be present), and August 1976 before David Roberts wrote to Hugh saying: 'I thought you might like to know that on Friday 13 August the builder actually finished the work at Sandringham and indeed the whole place could be used tomorrow if it was necessary. However, Julian [Julian Loyd, the Agent] and his staff have quite a lot to do inside the house before it can be used to the full.' There was more about the slowness of the contract, the costs (which had been cut to the extent that problems would, in his opinion, occur in the future), and also about how much he had enjoyed the commission.

Hugh knew most of this already. He had been informed and consulted over many months by the Queen and Prince Philip, by members of their staff such as Julian Loyd and Sir Rennie Maudsley, the Keeper of the Privy Purse, by Freeman Fox, the engineers who had had a long involvement with Sandringham (and had worked with Casson on the Festival of Britain), as well as by Roberts himself. He had given advice about the architect's fees to the architect, and about multifarious other details to the Queen. He was where he liked to be, at the centre of things, but without too much tedious, detailed responsibility.

At one point, the Queen wrote to him 'I hope Sandringham doesn't break us,' for there is no doubt this was a hugely expensive enterprise. One wing had been pulled down, new areas had been constructed, and the main house much updated. Everyone, not least David Roberts, was aware that it had been a compromise. Back in the fifties, when first invited to look at Sandringham, Casson, uncharacteristically radical, had suggested pulling the whole place down and building anew. What a glorious act of patronage and a real contribution to architectural history that would have been. But it did not happen. Invited for a shooting weekend during January 1978 (though they didn't participate in the sport), he and Reta agreed that the new arrangements were nevertheless a considerable improvement. As usual when they stayed with the Queen, Reta breakfasted in bed while Hugh went downstairs to join the predominantly male company, which included Prince Philip. On this occasion there was high-pressure talk about holography, fish-farming, Marxism, family planning, and the future of the Government.

Hugh worked on designs for the Royal train over a number of years, and numerous letters on the subject were exchanged between him and his clients. Often, especially when they were travelling, letters from both the Queen and the Prince included creditable drawings of their requirements. Prince Philip's explanation of a curtain heading he had seen and liked was

samples will he collected Monday 24ᵗʰ anyway unless instructed to the Company

particularly graphic and well drawn. It was work done on the train during the eighties with which Pamela Robinson was involved, and this centred on the dining room which was now to double up as a meeting room because Prince Charles was likely to be using it for this purpose. Royal advisers were ever mindful of security. After the shocking death of Lord Mountbatten, who had been blown up and killed by the IRA in 1979, security arrangements were reviewed with some urgency, and it was decided that those charged with making substantial alterations to the train must treat as a prime objective the task of forestalling hazards of this nature. Casson's brief was to work with BR engineers at Derby on detailed design and materials, and in this he was aided by Robinson. She remembers that an important task was to make heavily engineered tables look as light and elegant as possible. She would travel backwards and forwards to Derby with Hugh – he writing, sketching, making notes and reading throughout their journeys – and he gave her precise and detailed written instructions of his requirements. As at Windsor, the ideas were his; she slogged away, helping him to execute them, ever the faithful and compliant employee.

Not all of Hugh Casson's meetings with members of the Royal Family were connected with work. As the years went by and they came to rely on both his professional acumen and his discreet and affable personality, he and Reta would often be invited to purely social occasions. In 1971, for instance, they

went to Prince Philip's fiftieth birthday party at Buckingham
Palace, which was a relatively small affair, with about eighty
dinner guests seated at small tables, and others arriving later
to dance. They found old friends amongst the crowd: Joan and
Solly Zuckerman, and Patrick Plunkett who was, as so often
during Hugh's Royal episodes, a comforting and knowing presence, reassuring them as they arrived that the Mrs Heywood-
Lonsdale who was to be on their table collected pictures, that
the Princess of Hesse was English and managed the Benjamin
Britten household at Aldeburgh, and that Lord Brabourne had
a house near the Sainsburys' which would give them a conversational meeting point. 'Very carefully chosen,' said Plunket,
moving off to comfort others alarmed at the hint of so many
foreign Royal relatives.

Hugh loved moments of intimacy with his hosts. On this
occasion, the reception of guests over, 'Her Majesty was perceived swimming purposefully through the throng, fetching
up – hooray – with us. What do I think of the room . . . just
finished . . . tried to do it herself . . . is it OK? . . . sorry about
the curtains. (The room is the throne room, bright scarlet
watered-silk paper, mostly concealed by pictures, gold-and-
white ceiling, red-velvet throne, curtains port wine and beige
Elizabethan.) I agreed the curtains were dingy and should go but
Her Majesty couldn't imagine where as they were in excellent
condition.' He would find a better fabric, he promised. (The
discarded curtains would presumably be hung in a less prominent part of this conscientiously thrifty household than the
throne room.) As he and Reta departed in the early hours, after
an evening spent with some of the Royal couple's courtiers and
friends, many of whom had become close acquaintances of
their own, Hugh glowed with the delicious improbability of it
all. 'Don't forget my curtains,' cried the Queen, after she had
bidden them good night.

Both Hugh and Reta were on the guest lists for other Royal

occasions: the marriage of Charles and Diana, the dance at Buckingham Palace to celebrate Charles's fortieth birthday, a reception at Buckingham Palace before Princess Anne's first wedding, a dance at Windsor, a reception on *Britannia*, a concert arranged by Prince Charles to celebrate the ninetieth birthday of Queen Elizabeth, the Queen Mother . . .

Neither of the Cassons ever worked for the Queen Mother, but their friendship with her became close, probably because they were less than ten years behind her in age; but also because Hugh was just the type of warm, witty and affectionate man she plainly favoured. By the end of the 1970s they were spending weekends as her guests at Royal Lodge, Windsor. Other guests would include John Betjeman, Roy Strong and his wife Julia Trevelyan Oman, who had been one of their first students at the Royal College of Art. These were cosy, gossipy occasions with generous-sized drinks, huge nursery-style teas (to which several Eton boys were usually invited), visits to Frogmore and readings by Betjeman or John Gielgud after dinner. Hugh prided himself after these weekends on what he saw as the extra warm and personal attentions he received from his hostess. But then so, according to his published diary, did Roy Strong. Here was a woman with a gift, which went well on into old age, of making everyone feel specially wanted and loved, and these were cultural weekends for those of her friends to whom they would appeal.

The Queen would call in with guests of her own, and there would be discussions about her visit to the Gulf States, Prince Edward's education at the time he was struggling with A-levels, and – in 1980 – Prince Andrew's pottery, which the Queen had asked Hugh to look at and which he thought (as he surely would) 'not half bad'. By this time, though, Andrew was learning to fly, and pottery seemed irrelevant. 'Her Majesty is touchingly diffident about her children's abilities,' Hugh wrote.

On such a weekend in 1979, the whole party trooped off to

see the memorial to that kind friend of so many Royal guests, Patrick Plunkett, who had died the previous year. The Queen Mother had been much involved in the making of this memorial for, as she wrote to Hugh at one point, 'he was someone I have known and loved since I held him in my arms soon after he was born'. Working from Hugh's initial sketch, this graceful little stuccoed brick building was designed by Stuart Taylor, the Casson Conder partner who specialized in classical and conservationist work. 'The idea was to get a classical effect without employing classical details which would make it just a pastiche.' Taylor remembered the job starting with a trek through the Savill Gardens accompanied by the Queen Mother, the Duke of Grafton and Hugh, to identify the site which had been chosen for the memorial. 'She was so easy to talk to, and she knew exactly where the memorial was to be.'

By the late eighties and on into the nineties, the Cassons were spending summer holidays with the Queen Mother and a close coterie of friends. There were wonderfully romantic voyages on *Britannia*, and an apocryphal story that Hugh once arrived on the quay at Venice, ready to join the ship, with some of his minor possessions bulging out of a plastic shopping bag. His identity was immediately questioned by a disbelieving crew member. At this stage in his life, retired now from his last major post as President of the Royal Academy, he certainly had a rather dishevelled appearance, not helped by thinning and wispy hair, which the man would have found disconcerting. Reta's appearance, though, was unfailingly elegant and dignified. They were eventually allowed aboard.

On other such visits, to Brittany, the Haute Savoie and Perugia, the whole Royal entourage would sometimes pay calls on noble house owners whose property came within range of their itinerary. After each of these expeditions, which

A page from
Hugh Casson's
Venice sketchbook

seem reminiscent of eighteenth-century grand tours in their lordly progression, often with lectures and guided visits to galleries, Hugh would make a diary of the holiday, crammed with his own delicate water-colours, vivid evocations which he would present to Queen Elizabeth. Again, he was using his gifts to express friendship and gratitude as he did throughout his life with such a variety of people.

Hugh and Reta were invited to summer weekends at Sandringham with the Queen Mother, often going on afterwards to spend a few days at Euston Hall, the home of fellow guests, the Duke and Duchess of Grafton. One year, the Queen Mother wrote afterwards: 'It was such a pleasure having you both at Sandringham. I do so like things to be the same: same flower show, same warbling by David McKenna, same visit to Sybil at Houghton, same guests, and *specially* same you and Lady Casson.' In 1992, when they could not go because Hugh had had a heart-bypass operation, he received a cheery and friendly card signed by the Queen Mother and all her guests, wishing him well.

It is easy to emphasize the importance of Casson's Royal connection. It ran like a thread through the major part of his working life and beyond, and it was something he loved and nurtured. But there was room for this and much more in his life. It never impeded his attainments in other fields and it was not given precedence over the core activities: architecture, art and design.

I have the honour to remain Your Majesty's humble
and obedient servant,

XIV

An Addiction to
Committees and Commissions

For a man who was an immensely busy practitioner of more than one profession, and who was not of a patient disposition, Hugh Casson sat on an astonishing number of committees, councils and commissions, rising to be chairman (or president) of some, and remaining with many for year after year of meetings and minutes. This was not merely because they were there, that he was constantly being approached, and because he found it almost impossible to say no. Though he did. The real reason was that he was quite addicted to the whole business of being a committee man. He performed his duties with skill, making contributions which were usually creative and constructive, and sometimes very original. He was by all accounts an excellent chairman, eliciting anything of worth from other members of a committee, but dispatching bores or verbose incompetents with the kindest of put-downs. He did not suffer – had no time for – meetings which dragged on unnecessarily, and under his chairmanship the type of committee people who liked to settle in for the afternoon, enjoying tea at half-time, found themselves out on the street with all business completed in as much time as was absolutely essential, watching Hugh hurry off to his next appointment.

He got some feeling of achievement from his membership of these assemblies, extra confirmation if more was needed that he was wanted and effective and in the thick of things.

His almost obsessive appetite for people, and yet more people, was assuaged by his regular encounters with fellow committee members. Not all of them became his friends, but they were often people of reasonable distinction in their own fields, and they served to confirm the often-repeated adage that 'Hugh knows everyone'. Some of them he had known from his earliest days as an architect, or even as a student.

These involvements began early in his professional life. Almost immediately after completing his Festival of Britain work, in July 1951, Hugh, was elected a member of the Royal Institute of British Architects Council. In those days, the Council was an illustrious body comprising some of the most respected practitioners in British architecture and Hugh was properly numbered amongst them.

Meetings were held monthly but they rarely lasted more than two hours, often less, so that even members with busy practices to run were able to be present. Throughout the 1950s Hugh Casson rarely missed a meeting; he didn't speak a great deal, because prolix and irrelevant contributions were anathema to him, but when he did, it was to effect. In October 1952, he drew to his colleagues' attention the fact that there was no representative from the RIBA on the Arts Council, and furthermore that the Council had no proper section relating to architecture. This omission was speedily rectified and by 6 July the following year, the President was able to report that Leslie Martin had been appointed as architect member of the Arts Council Advisory Panel on Art.

Hugh was not so successful when, commenting on the illuminated address that the RIBA had presented to the Royal Society of Art on the occasion of its bicentenary, he suggested that an architectural drawing would be more appropriate on such occasions 'rather than an illuminated address on the quality of which some members might have varying opinions'. (This was Casson in art-connoisseur mode.) The Secretary, one C. D. Spragg, slapped down this veiled criticism with the rejoinder that an illuminated address was exactly what the RSA had asked for, though the RIBA President added that Hugh's point would be borne in mind in future.

Reading those dusty minutes years later when fewer distinguished architects serve on the RIBA Council, it is possible to admire the busy and successful architects who did so in those days, especially one with as restless and mercurial a temperament as Hugh, and to wonder if their interest was held even for the normal two-hour sessions. A strong feeling of obligation to their profession and its well-being must have pulled them in.

Once there, most people made forthright and trenchant contributions to discussions about government-imposed restrictions on building operations which were likely to affect architects' livelihoods (this was the early fifties). The President reported on a less than fruitful meeting with the Minister of Works, who had no plans for helping architects in this connection but instead had suggested young men should 'look for more employment in the overseas parts of the Empire, particularly the Colonies'. He apparently gave no consideration to women. They discussed the gift to the RIBA from the National Art Collections Fund of Christopher Wren drawings of St Stephen Walbrook Church. They pondered the question of whether ex-servicemen should be required to undergo the extra year of architectural education now being imposed on all students, a subject about which the Labour MP James Callaghan (one day to be Prime Minister) had written an impassioned letter to *The Times*. Hugh thought it unjust that the new regulation was to be introduced with retrospective effect, drawing in those already embarked on a course, and that it should be deferred. The inclusion of an additional number of students without the fuller qualification could not, he thought, injure the profession to any great degree. Others agreed, but they were defeated, and those already in the middle of their architectural education, even including the many ex-servicemen, had to endure that extra year.

There was another minor furore over the question of a proposed book of house plans to be put out by the RIBA. Predictably, many architects, particularly those in small provincial practices which often consisted of no more than one man working in a back bedroom, were against this, claiming it would encroach on their small supply of work. There were discussions about salaried architects working on the staff of contracting firms, about the exigencies of the planning process (this one, which Hugh had commented on in that 1930s Astragal column, still goes on to this day), about the problems of petrol rationing (it was now February 1957) and about cooperation with the newly formed Civic Trust.

Most of these matters were neatly and concisely dealt with, unlike the long-drawn-out debates which go on at the RIBA nowadays, often resulting in Council meetings of two days' duration. By July 1959 Hugh was a Vice President, which he remained until 1961. He continued as a member of Council off and on (there is a limit to the number of consecutive periods any member can serve) until 1971, much of the time he was at the Royal College of Art. With meetings now longer, he appears not to have attended quite so regularly, and his main additional duty was chairing the Awards Committee which selected the Royal Gold Medallist each year. He convinced Council, before finally quitting, that the medal could when appropriate be awarded to a group or pair of architects, rather than just a sole practitioner.

Years earlier, incidentally, Hugh was elected President of the Architectural Association, that élite architectural institution which, with its school, is revered and honoured all over the world – especially by its own members. Hugh, whose rush to qualify had prevented him from formally attending the AA

School, though he'd lurked around its lecture rooms often enough, was pleased and flattered by this honour, and his Presidential address in October 1953, if lacking the earnest contemplation of the profession which tends to typify such speeches, gave the attendant members the amusing evening they had probably expected from him: and, with its light-hearted analysis of varying types of architects, its literary quo-tations and its fun, must have taken hours to compile. Typically, it avoided controversial comment, or indeed any commitment to a doctrinaire line of thought. It must have been a good evening, but not one where the audience learnt anything new, or felt themselves roused to either disagreement or anger.

In November 1957, the Victorian Society was founded at the house in Stafford Terrace which had belonged to the illustrator and cartoonist Linley Sambourne and been kept exactly as it had been at the turn of the century. One of its stated intentions was to protect the Victorian buildings which were currently under threat from developers. Not every architect was drawn to Victorian architecture at this time, and students at many schools were educated to regard it with disdain. Hugh, who as we have seen took a different view entirely and had for several years made it quite clear that he was a proponent of the Vic-torians, was amongst the founding members that November day, along with his journalistic colleagues John Betjeman, J. M. Richards and Osbert Lancaster. They tried to persuade those of a didactically Modernist persuasion to take another look at the ornate edifices they so despised. They certainly gave the fledgeling society a terrific boost at its inception and it went from strength to strength. (Hugh Casson undertook a lecture tour of Canada on its behalf in 1975.) But Hugh, unlike some others who advocated the conservation of old buildings, was never a fundamentalist. As a founder member of the Victorian Society he was occasionally in trouble for arguing on the other, more Modernist, side in his even-handed and rational way.

In January 1958 Hugh had accepted an extra-mural activity on behalf of the RIBA, becoming its representative on the Council of the National Trust. He felt perfectly at home here amongst the great and the good, where the occasional controversies about modern architecture which raged in the outside world had no place. After the RIBA term came to an end, he was elected to the National Trust Council in his own right in 1971 and he remained until the statutory retiring age of seventy-five. Martin Drury, who became the National Trust's Director General, remembered Hugh as a regular attender at meetings, where he spoke rarely but wittily, often taking a different and interesting view. 'And of course he did all those water-colours for us. I remember driving up to Calke Abbey once, being aware of a shabby car parked on the drive and a rather dishevelled little figure scrabbling about in the hedgerow nearby. I stopped the car to see what was going on. It was Hugh in working clothes, setting up his drawing board, all alone and keen to get on with his work. But an even stronger memory is of the Council Meeting in 1985 when he was about to retire and we thanked him very warmly for his past services, etc. He made such an amusing and gracious speech in reply, saying how nice we'd been about him, and claiming that others bidding him farewell on similar occasions had taken a far less enthusiastic line, rather akin to the exhortation which used to appear on the lid of fish-paste jars: Prick with a pin and push off.'

Michael Cain, Hugh's erstwhile partner, had a memory of those National Trust years too. Hugh had been asked to design the Trust's Witley Common Information Centre in Surrey. Because he was on the Council, it would not have been proper for Hugh to undertake the work himself, and in any case it was Michael Cain who normally designed buildings of this type for Casson Conder. Cain's typically sympathetic touch resulted in a sturdy and very appropriate wood-fronted building which sat felicitously on its wooded site. At the opening ceremony, as Cain wryly commented, this building was described as 'designed by a partner of Sir Hugh Casson, who so unfortunately cannot be here today'. But there was no bitterness in Cain's comment, and he went on to say that of course when it came to *Private Eye*, it was Hugh who picked up the nastiness.

Because Hugh's life was so all-encompassing, many people recurred. Sherban Cantacuzino is an architect who worked alongside him in several capacities. They first met when Cantacuzino was assistant editor and then executive editor of the *Architectural Review* during a period when Hugh (along with Nikolaus Pevsner, amongst others) was a member of the Editorial Board as well as being an occasional contributor; he remained on the board until it was dissolved in 1972. Cantacuzino remembered Hugh writing a trenchant and knowledgeable foreword to an *AR* issue about the *QE2*, because by that time, having worked on the interiors of both *Britannia* and *Canberra*, he had come to be regarded as a big-ships expert. Both Hugh and Reta were also frequently consulted by Cantacuzino about interior-design matters in their roles as tutors at the Royal College of Art – who was doing what, whose work the *AR* should show – because he edited the ID section of the magazine. They responded with a fund of advice and ideas and they gradually became his friends.

But Cantacuzino was best able to observe the strength of Hugh's influence on the world of architecture when he himself was appointed Secretary of the Royal Fine Art Commission in 1979. Hugh had been a member of the Commission since 1960 – he was to go on until 1985, one of its longest serving members – and he was a regular attender at the meetings, which were convened to discuss the merits of proposed new buildings at their design stage. Here though, he was no silent attender, but was an enthusiastic contributor to every discussion, with strong views which did not always correspond with those of fellow architects on the Commission. His verbal contributions in no way inhibited his ever-active pen either, and Cantacuzino remembers that he was always doodling whilst others talked, often drawing his own – different – ideas for schemes as they were presented. 'Though this had actually been forbidden to members of the Commission by Colin Anderson, a one-time Chairman,' said Cantacuzino. 'We talked and we discussed ideas but without actually making images of how schemes should be altered or adapted if they were to gain our approval. But Hugh found it terribly difficult not to draw what he had in mind.'

Drawings aside, Cantacuzino has a clear memory of opinions Casson held on some of the Commission's most vexatious submissions: of his negative reaction to the design of the first building Peter (now Lord) Palumbo proposed to erect at Number One Poultry in the City of London, a tall, sleek, curtain-walled tower by that great Modernist Mies van der Rohe. 'Hugh was strongly against it on both planning and architectural grounds, and though the Commission was divided in its views, we eventually came out against it. Palumbo's publicity machine was particularly unpopular.' The tower was never built.

Casson did, on the other hand, support Richard Rogers' design for the Lloyd's Building, a much more radical and innovative project with its voluptuous exterior presentation of the services and its strong, demanding presence on Lime Street, again in the City. But there was no paradox in this apparent diversity of viewpoints. Number One Poultry was a true Modernist design, a representation of a hard-edged and ageing style to which Hugh had only ever been half-heartedly committed, whilst Lloyd's, with its soft, Baroque silhouette, appealed to both the romantic and the artist in him.

'Hugh was always a contributor when we were discussing who should be invited to join the Commission,' Cantacuzino remembers, 'and made excellent recommendations which we often took up. Wendy Taylor, who came on when the late Liz Frink decided to retire, was Hugh's very successful suggestion. But although he almost always came to the main Commission meetings – remarkably, considering he was President of the Royal Academy at the time I remember best – he was unfortunately rarely able to get to important follow-up meetings when projects were gone into in depth with the architect concerned. And certainly he hardly ever managed to make visits to sites out of London. He was just too busy to spare that amount of time.'

Casson's selection skills came into operation at one point to Cantacuzino's own benefit. He patently enjoyed exercising his influence when there were important jobs to be filled, and because of the respect in which he was held, and also because of his successful track record as a selector, his people nearly always succeeded in securing the post in question. On this occasion, after doing architectural work for the Aga Khan, including his private stud in Ireland and the Islamic Centre at South Kensington, he was asked by him to help establish the first Aga Khan's Award for Architecture. The steering committee included such other luminaries as Charles Correa, the great Bombay architect (who was to be recipient of the Royal Gold Medal for Architecture at the time of the Prince of Wales's condemnatory speech in 1984), Oleg Grabar from Harvard and William Porter from MIT. Casson proposed Sherban Cantacuzino, a man who, as well as being qualified as an architect, was both perceptive and broadly informed, as a member of the first jury to assess buildings for the Award. Cantacuzino said, 'We did a three-year cycle and I ended up as Chairman. It was hugely enjoyable and one learnt so much.' Casson, of course, was omnipresent, enjoying the travel to agreeable places which membership of the steering committee involved, looking at fine architecture, dispensing advice and meeting interesting people. During the first year – 1980 – alone, he went to Geneva, Cala al Volpe on the Costa Smeralda in Sardinia, India and Pakistan, always travelling in comfort, always staying at luxury hotels. He was in his element, particularly as these trips were extremely demanding of his intellect and energy; coincidentally, they provided colourful material for his Royal Academy Diary of that year. Had they been bereft of purpose, he would have been bored and restless.

Cantacuzino remembered the occasion just after the first Award ceremony when both steering committee and jury were at the Pakistan capital, Islamabad, then a new city: 'an incomplete new town,' as Hugh described it in his Diary, 'with its air of desperate optimism, its empty stretching boulevards and isolated pockets of housing making great demands on the imagination. We know that it is sensible, far-sighted, logical (why on a flat featureless plain try to escape from the rational grid), but every building is the same age and will die at the same time, and the fact that most people are doing the same job (government service) makes it basically an army camp.'

After touring the town, the whole party assembled for a seminar on new towns, during which Hugh pleaded for more of the passion and the courage that had fired those who set up Islamabad in the first place to enable them now to go ahead and complete the job, 'to take the jump in the dark' that was necessary.

There was humour in his approach too. Cantacuzino remembered him on this occasion admonishing them with gentle wit. 'You must remember architects are artists, and artists are difficult people to deal with. Lenin and Queen Victoria agreed on that, and if those two agreed on something, it has to be taken seriously.'

Cantacuzino held Casson in high regard. 'He was a very serious man and I always found his advice about so many things at the RFAC – new commissioners, buildings, art – was almost without exception first class. He was so articulate too, with a marvellous use of words and a quick wit. I remember he and Reta coming to dinner at my home when we served the first course on some curious little plates, each decorated by a drawing of a penny farthing bicycle. Hugh couldn't keep his hands off them. He immediately took a felt tip from his pocket and drew a figure on his penny farthing.'

A less sumptuously endowed concern with which Hugh Casson was associated for many years was the Arthur Koestler Award. He'd first become aware of Koestler in about 1937 when, already well known and widely read in England, Koestler was imprisoned in Seville because of his intervention in the Spanish Civil War, and was under sentence of death. A petition was organized by what might be described as the literary and artistic establishment in Britain pleading for his release, and Hugh was one of the signatories. Koestler always believed that this petition was instrumental in the Spanish government's decision to set him free. But he was to be deprived of his liberty on several occasions after that: in Vichy France, when he spent time in a concentration camp, and on his final arrival in England when he was interned as an alien in Pentonville. Koestler knew about life inside.

He and Hugh did not meet until about 1946, when a great friend of Koestler's who was a London neighbour of the Cassons brought them together at dinner parties. Hugh found him alarming, this compact, chain-smoking intellectual who he thought had a face like a lizard. Koestler had for Casson the same unmistakably alien aura as those clever and politically sophisticated Europeans in the MARS Group who – disingenuously, I cannot help surmising – Casson had claimed to regard with such suspicion. Koestler came from Hungary, and Casson judged him to be a natural Central European, the type he could, with his own chauvinist tendencies, imagine glimpsing through a haze of cigarette smoke at a café table, plotting.

*A thank-you note for Pamela Robinson after she had
worked long and hard on mounting one of the
Koestler Award exhibitions.*

He felt Koestler must have been difficult to live with too
because he had such an imperious attitude to women. 'You get
the impression that was the way of mid-Europeans, which of
course some women find attractive and sexy. Anyway he was
a very impressive man, a powerful personality. When he stood
in a room, people skirted him like the Inchcape Rock.'

Koestler was another brilliantly successful person of whom
Hugh claimed to be frightened, mesmerized by his powerful
brain and the impatience with which he regarded more pedestrian conversationalists. This can be judged as just one more
example of the hyperbole in which Hugh sometimes indulged.
He was not an intellectual himself, and he knew it, but he was
formidably well read and deeply knowledgeable about his own
subject. Despite Casson's declared misgivings, it is difficult to
believe Koestler was not attracted, even impressed, by his
nimble mind.

Koestler was a vociferous advocate of social reform. Under-
standably, in view of his own history, he took a particular

interest in prison inmates, and was convinced they needed to acquire the self-respect that comes from the stimulation of doing something creative. By 1960 he had decided to donate the royalties from his Spanish books to establish an annual prisoners' award scheme. With prizes given each year for any creative work which was considered to be of a high standard, this aimed at improving the morale and self-esteem of those in English prisons.

Hugh, at Koestler's invitation, became a member of the Arthur Koestler Award Trust in 1960, which he went on to chair for many years, turning up without fail to judge the miscellaneous collection of work submitted by inmates of many prisons. He believed implicitly in the value of this task in which the Home Office cooperated, and he drew in friends such as the painters Mary Fedden and Julian Trevelyan, and the designer Jo Pattrick, to serve on the various judging committees – one for each of the subjects, painting, craftwork, poetry, which were involved. Bryant & May donated matches for those prisoners who enjoyed creating elaborate models out of spent matches: huge square-rigged ships, caravans, railway engines, the Houses of Parliament.

During the year, after a preliminary selection had been made, they would all travel to the particular prison – usually Portsmouth in Hugh's time – where the works had been laid out for them to make their final selections. The whole cycle would culminate in a London exhibition of the winning entries, where there was an opening attended by any well-known and well-intentioned persons the organizers could pull in. Even after both she and Hugh had retired from Casson Conder, he continued to enlist his erstwhile assistant Pamela Robinson to help with the design of these exhibitions which, in later years, were always held at Whiteleys in Bayswater. The quality of the prisoners' work varied. As Hugh said, 'Some of it was interesting. Some of it was fairly obvious stuff, copies of photographs of their girlfriends, a favourite puppy, rose-covered cottages. And there was a certain amount of wishful thinking, of page-three girls, but really not too much.' Jo Pattrick remembered the sense of being overwhelmed by the great number of entries which awaited them when they arrived to do their judging. But Hugh weighed in immediately, an expert and confident assessor, dispatching the impossible and welcoming the better efforts. In a way, quality was not the point. Encouraged to concentrate on creative activity, the prisoners were being led into a new environment, one which might even widen their options and interests when it came to facing life outside again.

Several of the better exhibitors during Casson's time as Chairman were able to develop their talents whilst in prison, one or two of them even selling their work when they were released. One, an ex-sailor living in Newcastle, painted battleships and prided himself on the accuracy of every piece of rigging and armament. The Cassons bought three of these paintings, large, splendid depictions of First World War battleships, which they hung in their London home. The very disturbed work, generally in the form of paintings, which sometimes featured at the exhibitions raised deep, unanswerable questions and was visibly troubling to the many magistrates who attended the opening ceremony each year. Hugh, who knew something of the prison environment, having lectured at places like Winchester Jail and Pentonville just before the Second World War, was depressed by these less comfortable manifestations of the prisoners' creativity, but convinced that the Award, well supported by prison staff, had a positive and therapeutic effect. It was one of the reasons he continued his involvement with it for so long. In 1981 the Koestler Award scheme was a popular and well-established feature of prison life, and in Casson's wake, David Astor became its chairman, followed by Stephen Tumim, one-time Inspector of Her

Majesty's Prisons, himself a great collector of art and a renowned reformer.

Immediately after the Festival of Britain, Casson had been appointed a Royal Designer for Industry, an honour bestowed on relatively few designers by the Royal Society of Arts. It requires little of its recipients – except presumably a sustained high standard of work – and for some the responsibility of being its Master, a post which lasts two years. Hugh became Master in the years 1969–71, while he was at the Royal College of Art. There were no arduous duties to perform. (It was only when the fashion designer Jean Muir became Master in 1993 that she decided the post's responsibilities should include promoting and eulogizing the work of the Society.) Hugh's only tasks were to preside over a meeting each year when the latest batch of RDIs was selected, a duty he greatly enjoyed, and the presentation of the Society's Annual Address in April 1970. He began the address with one of his now ritual apologies. This time it was for having no personal design philosophy. Instead he proposed entertaining them with descriptions – from different writers – of buildings, places and events which he had himself recently visited or attended. It was an ingenious device which enabled him to quote such diverse writers as Daisy Ashford, Ruskin, W. H. Auden and his old friend Robert Byron, in an enjoyable array of fine prose pieces. This method of presentation was not chosen as an easy option. He simply thought it would be more interesting for his listeners than a self-indulgent exposition of his own opinions. And he scoured his library to achieve exactly the right balance of participant writers.

Diversity was always Hugh's forte. In amongst his membership of major committees of national status he slotted others of a lesser profile which he served with equal devotion. One such was the Solent Protection Society, aimed at guarding a

stretch of water to which he had a great and sentimental attachment. It was here that he'd first learnt to sail in his father's modest twenty-foot boat, about which he'd been so supercilious as a boy. It was close to this stretch of water that he'd spent school holidays, drawing the ships which docked in Southampton, and it was here that he spent holidays in the Needs Ore cottage which looked directly across the Solent to the Isle of Wight. In the early sixties, when the idea of building a nuclear power station at Newtown, the island's old capital, was mooted, Hugh wrote an impassioned plea for rejection of this crass idea in the *Observer*, a plea which culminated in the suggestion that the whole area should be designated a National Water Park. The power station never got built, and the Solent never became a National Water Park. But a Solent Protection Society was formed of which Hugh became first Chairman and then President, holding the latter role well into the 1990s. This was a cause in which he was passionately interested and he served it with his usual dedication, travelling to Southampton for meetings. The Solent, perhaps partly due to the Society's work, remains relatively unspoilt.

Most of his committee work was in London though, with

meetings of the Royal Mint Committee on which he sat from
1972–92 often being held at Buckingham Palace because its
Chairman was the Duke of Edinburgh, another busy man.
Guarding the quality of the Royal coinage was, like guarding
the environment of the Solent, a task Casson regarded as
both important and interesting. He was involved in other
areas of aesthetic concern too, serving (often simultaneously)
on the GLC's Historic Buildings Committee, the Post Office
Design Advisory Committee, BR's Environmental Panel
and, of course, as a Trustee of those great national insti-
tutions, the National Portrait Gallery and the Natural History
Museum.

He became involved with the National Gallery, however,
on a different basis. Hugh relished any selection process,
whether it was to pick out the winner of an art competition
for disabled children, which he did with gentleness and sensitivity, or the architect for a major and important building. It
was in the latter capacity that, in June 1981, during his time as
President of the Royal Academy, he was appointed as one of
the 'advisers' to Michael Heseltine, then Environment Secretary, in choosing an architect/developer team for the National
Gallery extension. A potentially splendid job for some aspiring
architect, this was a project which was nevertheless fraught
with problems, not least because the gallery area was to be
combined with, indeed partly financed by, floors of commercial
office accommodation. Hugh had some problems of his own.
Casson Conder had been approached by an interested developer
with whom they intended to enter the competition, but with
Hugh's involvement (about which he had not warned his
partners) they were obviously precluded. They were not
pleased. He was, in addition, the only architect amongst the
'advisers', and though no one is privy to what exactly happened
in the meetings where entries were sifted, it is obvious from
formal correspondence between Noel Annan, Chairman of

the group, and the others, that Hugh had to fight hard for his corner.

As so often happens when a new building is proposed in this country, disagreements threatened to inhibit the achievement of a first-class result. Seven finalists were selected – including Richard Rogers – whose entries were exhibited for public comment, and these were reduced (at Casson's suggestion) to three. The final three did not include the Rogers scheme (despite or perhaps because of the well-known intervention of the then RIBA President Owen Luder – 'That is the work of a man who has said "That is what I think the answer is and sod you"'). Public participation was a popular element in judging major architectural competitions in the eighties, and a questionnaire which visitors to the exhibition of the final seven were invited to complete had shown confusing results. The Rogers scheme was the most popular; it was also the most unpopular.

As the *Observer* commented at the time, there should have been a stronger architectural presence among the advisers, and it seems in retrospect that this would certainly have given weight to the final choice. As it was, Casson obviously needed to battle for the scheme which he believed to be the best. It finally won the day though, and Ahrends Burton and Koralek were announced as the winning architects, with the unsatisfactory qualification that there would have to be considerable alterations to their winning design. It was never built, of course. The whole project was abandoned after the Prince of Wales made his disparaging speech at Hampton Court, likening it to a carbuncle, and (with Hugh's participation ended) a totally different method of selection was later established, a different architect – the American Robert Venturi – chosen, and the Sainsbury wing, no longer linked with commercial space but funded by the Sainsbury family, finally completed in the early nineties.

The care of an historic city is likely to be burdensome and

worrying. Often, those charged with such work as part of their civic duties appoint an architect as consultant and adviser if for no other reason than to act – as Hugh liked to put it 'as a lightning conductor who can be blamed when something is done which the local residents don't like'. A good adviser is far more responsible and constructive than that though, and Casson, with his wide knowledge of historic architecture, his love of committee work, easy manner and addiction to having a finger in every pie, was a natural choice. For years during the seventies and eighties he advised the local authorities at Chichester, Bath and Salisbury, sometimes, in his lightning-conductor role, drawing wrath upon his own head for unpopular decisions – mainly in the form of emotional and inflammatory local newspaper articles – but invariably approaching the work with commitment and a genuine desire to achieve the best possible decisions.

Chichester, a small cathedral city, is an example of how historic towns have been best cared for and preserved since the era when these things became important. Beautifully pedestrianized in its centre, with a ring road to ward off excessive traffic, car parks hidden away behind the town's ancient buildings, Georgian houses properly restored, it has allowed no high-rise intruders. Hugh always disclaimed particular responsibility, but the files reveal him as giving active support to an intelligent and well-intentioned council, as well as submitting ideas for many improvements such as lighting the medieval market cross at its centre, and choosing high-quality materials for the pedestrianization. He was also robust in his defence of the local authority during his period as adviser, writing to one venomous critic: 'It is important not to get too excited about words like "office blocks" and "supermarkets". The buildings proposed are small and low and in my view easily acceptable in scale.' (Since his time, an unsightly scattering of large-scale retail centres – Sainsbury, Tesco, Halford *et al.* –

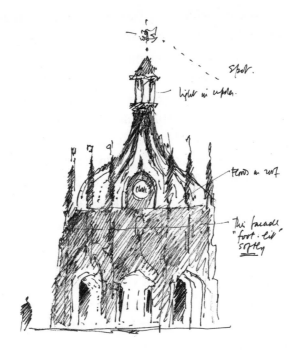

*The medieval market cross at Chichester,
with ideas for its lighting.*

have been allowed to encircle the town and suck trade from its centre. It is unlikely he would have been able to fight off this commercial onslaught had he still been involved.)

Although he acted in an advisory capacity to several other cities, most notably Bristol, Brighton and Salisbury, it was at Bath that Hugh Casson suffered the full weight of the criticism and even abuse so often attendant on this kind of role. The Chichester gripers were as nothing compared with the critics

– not all of them resident in the city – who gathered around Bath, most particularly in the early seventies when the conservation movement was gathering its full strident momentum.

All started well. In 1964 the President of the RIBA, Donald Gibson, had recommended that the city of Bath should appoint an advisory group, under the chairmanship of a distinguished consultant, with whom they could discuss all matters of architectural policy for the city, and on 21 December Mr Jered Dixon, the Town Clerk, wrote to Hugh, at Gibson's suggestion, asking him if he would consider taking on the job of Chairman. Hugh never seriously considered turning them down. The rejection of such an interesting and prestigious appointment would have been quite out of character. He stalled for a very short while, telling them of his other advisory posts and saying, 'I don't want to disperse my energies so widely that they become cursory or superficial and I particularly don't want to become a front man behind whom civic consciousness can ride easy.' He also stipulated that this should be a one-person advisory job: no committee, no group, just himself, or issues could become clouded and time wasted. By January 1965, the job was his at a fee of £1,000 per annum (the RIBA had advised him to push it up from £500 per annum, the figure he had at first accepted), and his duties were to be one day a month in Bath, looking through planning applications before they went in front of the Planning Committee, visiting sites and propounding his views on sensitive and important projects. In addition he would assist in the preparation of a Code of Practice for the guidance of the Committee and developers on broad architectural principles to be followed in all future developments; and he would always be available to officers such as the City Architect and Planner for consultation by telephone and letter. It was a bargain for them really, and his appointment was greeted by the *Bath and Wiltshire Evening Chronicle* as 'one of the best pieces of news that Bath has had for a long time'.

The next nine or ten years reveal Hugh Casson at his steel-iest, even thick-skinned. Despite doing his job most conscientiously, employing all his critical ability and creative skills, taking part in placatory meetings with such bodies as the Bath Group of Architects and the Bath Preservation Trust, he was increasingly a target of unpleasant comment and innuendo. He had been prepared for trouble in this architecturally favoured city which was loved and watched over by a far broader spectrum of interests than its own inhabitants. Even so, he was shocked by the emotion which was a concomitant part of some of the attacks; and by the extent to which they were often inaccurate and ill-informed. From the start, his approach to the job had been both rational and reasonable, with emotion, as far as possible, kept to a minimum.

For instance, he defended a proposed scheme for the Bath and Portland Group Headquarters, which was in effect a modern building very close to Bath Abbey. As he wrote at the time (1966), he did not support the retention of what he considered second-class existing buildings on the site, and said, 'I would not insist on or even recommend the adoption of a period or neo-Georgian style. The important qualities to preserve are colour, texture and an elegant robustness of design capable of good neighbourly relations with the Abbey.' Not everyone agreed. There was a passionate personal letter on the subject from Lady Menuhin, wife of Sir Yehudi, who knew Hugh quite well and who – amongst many others – decried the proposal. (It was built.)

In 1967 Hugh questioned the design of some old people's housing in the light of current research into the subject, which seemed to have been ignored. In the same year he remonstrated with the Town Clerk about alterations to street furnishing which were being made without consulting him or the Planning Committee. In 1968 he criticized a proposed new sports centre as being much too large for its site; he made detailed comments about proposals for a local hospital and for new buildings at Bath University, and about alterations to city-centre department stores, in all these cases making explicit and well-thought-out recommendations as to how they could be improved. Sometimes his advice was accepted and acted upon, sometimes not.

There were several moves to unseat him. In 1966 Casson Conder had been appointed to make extensive alterations to Pulteney Weir as part of a flood-protection scheme for the city of Bath, and they worked on the design of this in association with the Bristol Avon River Authority. There were sour comments about this seemingly nepotistic appointment from certain local architects. One of them, the Chairman of the Bath Group of Architects (who had already expressed their displeasure at the wave of outside architectural firms moving in on their territory), wrote to him direct, complaining that the appointment was contrary to the basic principles of Clause I of the RIBA Code of Conduct; he was gently rebuffed with long, courteous letters from Hugh, explaining (correctly) that the Code had not been contravened.

In 1967 the Chairman of the Bath Spa Committee (which was having problems over obtaining permission to alter and extend Bath Spa) questioned whether Casson was an essential adviser, and whether the city should go on retaining him. And in November 1969, the Bath Group of Architects mounted another attack, suggesting to the Town Clerk that Casson's presence was leading to a stultification of designs, and that he should be replaced by a panel of architects. The then City Architect, Howard Stutchbury, who was under constant fire himself, stoutly defended Casson, pointing out that his employment was both financially and practically more efficacious than that of a group of architectural advisers would be.

Hugh hung on through it all, steadily dispensing advice and maintaining excellent relations with most architects working in Bath and with members of the Council's staff. He had a friendly lunchtime meeting with the Bath Preservation Trust in May 1971, in which, amongst other things, he outlined the policy he and the City Architect were following.

Good architecture, he told them, only came from good architects, who were always allowed great freedom of movement. When architects who were in the Council's view not so good were employed, they – rightly or wrongly – plumped for inoffensiveness, even dullness and the minimum number of materials. There was, contrary to an impression which had got about, no rule about sash windows and mansard roofs being obligatory or providing a quick way through the regulations. And neither he nor the City Architect supported an insistence on 'stone everywhere'. On the contrary, they constantly pressed, not often successfully, for precast concrete, stucco, paint, etc., and he was glad to know that they had the Trust's support in this view. He went on to claim that much of what had gone up, dull as it might be, was probably less offensive than it would have been without them.

The Trust made it clear at this meeting that they thought he was being used as an alibi by the Council and that what he said was not always done. They wanted him to be tougher in condemning bad design. Although he questioned their first belief, Hugh privately felt there might be something in it and rather agreed with the second, conceding that fears of becoming an aesthetic dictator had probably made him over-tolerant. He promised to watch this. The meeting ended in agreement that it had been helpful to both sides, but with a final plea from the Trust for tougher resistance to poor architecture in future.

Hugh's very reasonableness and desire to avoid confrontation appear to have been catching up with him by now, though it is doubtful whether an abrasive and arrogant architect would have achieved any more than he did during a period when Bath was under considerable pressure from developers.

The question of policing architecture successfully is a large one which has defeated many individuals and many corporate groups. It seems almost impossible to resolve.

But the conservationists now had Bath targeted. In April 1972, there were two articles about Bath in *The Times*. One, by Adam Fergusson, headed ACRES OF GEORGIAN RUBBLE, really roused their ire, claiming as it did that 'If no town in Britain has so many statutorily protected buildings as Bath, none today has so large an acreage of Georgian rubble either, dispersed in great swathes across the city's face.' (He went on to write a damning book on the subject which was also given wide publicity.) *The Times* correspondence columns carried letters during the ensuing weeks from those eager to endorse and cap his claims of negligence on the part of both the local authority and its advisers. Hugh wrote at least two letters in their defence, but at this time his light, friendly style was ill judged and in danger of appearing flippant. His comment in one letter that 'Anybody rash enough to argue in your columns about planning and architecture has to stand well back to avoid being cut by flying adjectives and it is easy to forget the cause while enjoying the fun of the fray,' provoked the irate response from one correspondent that 'Those residents of Bath who care for the city are hardly in a mood to enjoy "the fun of the fray" as Sir Hugh Casson puts it.' James Lees Milne, who wrote the other (less emotional) article in *The Times*, revealed in his diary, *A Mingled Measure*, that Tony Snowdon, who had taken the photographs of what was claimed to be the destruction wrought in Bath, had described Stutchbury, the City Architect, as a fiend and Casson as having no taste whatever. Fortunately, Casson, who was on his customarily friendly terms with Lord Snowdon, had no knowledge of this at the time.

Exactly a year later, in April 1973, there was a debate on conservation in the House of Lords, during which Lord Kennet made the ludicrous suggestion that all Bath planning applications should be sent straight to the Department of Environment for consideration, without having previously worked out who there would deal with them and why the resultant decisions would be any better than those made by Bath Council. Lord (Kenneth) Clark commented on Casson being a member of the Royal Fine Arts Commission at the same time as being adviser to Bath. Hugh was incensed by both these lordly criticisms, and wrote firm letters in response. From Clark he received a reply which only made matters worse, saying as it did that 'since the informed public believes the Fine Art Commission to be a completely disinterested body concerned with preserving the highest standards, it is questionable if members of that Commission should be committed to large-scale plans for redevelopment. If you think of analogies in other branches of public life, e.g. members of the Treasury being advisers to private investment companies, you will see what I mean.' Hugh contented himself with a sharp letter in response, in which he recounted the terms and history of his long (and hardly overpaid) service to Bath. The apology when it came was gracious but less than fulsome.

The next attack came from his old employer, the *Architectural Review*, which in an issue devoted to Bath was also extravagantly critical of developments in the city, invoking facts about policy and demolition statistics which were often inaccurate, accompanied by photographs which tended to be so angled as to mislead. Hugh was swift to point out all of this in a letter to the editor, though, as ever, he did not duck his own responsibilities, saying, 'I can't escape such responsibilities as I have – nor do I wish to – for such mistakes as have been made.'

In August 1973, on hearing that Howard Stutchbury was quitting the post of City Architect, Hugh offered to stand down as consultant (an offer he had also made at the time of a previous changeover), but was asked to stay on at least until a new appointment was made. This took a year, and in August

1974 when he made the same offer to the man who was finally appointed, Roy Worskett, it was accepted.

I have recounted the saga of Bath in some detail because it reflects the downside of many prestigious appointments, and also the public stoicism with which Hugh – despite being privately hurt – was always prepared to accept criticism. It was not his nature to be dictatorial in Bath or anywhere else, and sometimes his own preferred method of improvement by persuasion and suggestion failed in the face of overwhelming pressure for development and profit. For once, he was not sorry to come to the end of a job which had been interesting but almost impossible to fulfil with perceived success.

The Final Years of
Public Life

After retirement from his presidency of the Royal Academy in 1985, Hugh returned to full-time practice, or at least as full-time as he had ever been. For some years he maintained a constant involvement with Academy affairs too, frequently travelling to the United States on goodwill missions on its behalf, or entertaining American patrons in London; and it was almost certainly due to his advocacy that Feliks Topolski was made a Royal Academician only six months before his death in 1989, a late honour which pleased this enthusiast for the English establishment enormously. Speaking at his friend's memorial service Hugh said, 'I remember his drawings with such envy because they used to crackle and sparkle with enormous electrical energy.'

Neville Conder always maintained that the practice lost its way in design terms during the period that Hugh was caught up in the final whirlwind years at the Royal Academy, with certain newer members of the firm creating a destructive and debilitating tension. 'This put us in danger of producing some unworthy buildings and it gave Hugh a new role as saviour of buildings going wrong. I had to accept that I did not have the stature and authority in the office of the more distant Sir Hugh Casson and that go-it-alone partners might regard a suggestion by me as a reason for *not* changing something. I would call his attention to drawing boards where that authority and sensibility were required. Sometimes it was too late. But our British Aerospace building on the west side of Charing Cross station forecourt [completed in 1985] is an example of where his intervention was crucial. Despite an excellent plan, the external treatment was originally banal, but Hugh with sketch after sketch transformed it, so there is base, middle, top in interesting vertical progression and an ingenious exploitation of special views from the corners.'

This anecdote is indicative of Neville Conder's position, one for which he always claimed he was best suited as number-two man in the practice. But a slight bitterness at lack of recognition for his very important contribution was inevitable. Hugh had always done his best to make it clear when Neville should be credited with certain jobs, but it wasn't enough. The public, led by the media, persisted in attributing all Casson Conder achievements to Hugh. When Conder went to receive a belated CBE from the Prince of Wales in March 1986, the Prince told him he had always wanted to meet the other half of the Casson Conder Partnership. Neville replied that he was glad His Royal Highness realized there *was* another half.

It is also apparent that Hugh Casson had always kept a certain distance between himself and the rest of the staff at Casson Conder, just as he had done with the students at the Royal College of Art. Pamela Robinson, despite having worked with him for years, first as a student in the Interior Design Department at the College and then as a most able and reliable assistant on the Royal projects, never called him anything other than Sir Hugh and was certainly never invited to do so, even if he did adopt a flirtatious manner when working with her. This reserve, partly generational in source, was also because he maintained an innate sense of his own position and dignity. It was accompanied by unstinting friendliness and charm, but the friendliness never advanced beyond a certain point. All this imposed a palpable barrier between him and most of his staff.

After his retirement from the Academy, there began to be a just perceptibly 'lost' quality to his life, according to Pamela Robinson, and he clung to this last 'job' as senior partner at Casson Conder for several more years. She remembered him sitting at her drawing table while they discussed a project, clutching a bag of rolls he had brought in for his lunch, and scattering crumbs all over her drawings, averse as he had always been to working alone. When, in May 1987, he finally retired from the partnership which still bore his name, it was with regret that his career as an architect had finally ended. The firm had handled over thirty jobs during his time there, many of them very large ones. One journalist summed them up thus: 'If you look at Casson Conder's work it certainly bears the mark of restrained tailor-made excellence rather than striving for effects.' Hugh liked that. Despite his other interests he had given unsparingly of his great energy and talent. As Michael Cain said, 'He always set things up before heading off in a different direction.' But it was those other directions which had helped to ensure the flow of jobs – until now.

His only office in the future would be at home, and for the next few years that was at the Elgin Crescent house, and it was one which, as if driven by habit, he occupied on a daily basis. The telephone continued to ring, the invitations to arrive, and a part-time secretary helped to deal with the preparation of manuscripts and with his post, which continued to be voluminous. This was partly due to his own inability to leave a letter unanswered, which meant that he sometimes found himself badgered by people quite unknown to him, who were at best bores and at worst oddballs, with whom he became stickily entangled. He continued painting every day and for long periods of time. He did so partly to keep up with the demand for his work, but also because this was a deeply ingrained habit. He

A thank-you letter for a birthday present from a friend.

drew incessantly: on scraps of paper, on paper table napkins, on the throwaway literature which comes through the door, and of course on every single letter he wrote.

His powers as a writer and artist had not waned; indeed, with more time at his disposal, his water-colours seemed to have taken on a new vigour, a fact which did not escape the eyes of those who commissioned him for commercial purposes. The public life began to be a little less demanding, with, as he had noted in the small booklet accompanying an exhibition of his life's work which was held at the RIBA's Heinz Gallery in 1986, committees and consultancies dropping away as age limits were reached. However, by the standards of so many people happy to retire at sixty-five or earlier, his life remained an active one, the engagements diary full.

Hugh put a bold face on this new existence, explaining that 'One of the pleasures of retirement from professional practice as an architect is that you're spared the endless meetings and arguments with buildings, putting on boots and wading round sites in November in the damp Midlands which was never very interesting to me because I was really a drawing-board man rather than a site-inspection man. And I like being able to work at home and do water-colours of buildings other than my own.'

The Cassons never lived in the austere, uncluttered style which is favoured by many architects and which their lay friends are inclined to find rebarbative. The house in Elgin Crescent was, like their previous homes had been, a warm, colourful place, the walls closely hung with paintings, the furniture a mixed bag from several periods, including a great teak bed designed by the architect Ernest Gimson, who won such renown as a designer and maker of Arts and Crafts furniture at the turn of the century; this had been left to them by Reta's uncle Frank, the architect. Every surface bore its share of art books, of unhung paintings, of random beautiful objects and bowls of flowers.

Few of the paintings were exceptionally valuable in money terms, though many of them were good. Some had been bought at students' shows at the Royal College of Art, or the Royal Academy Schools, when the Cassons had been able to pick out good work by people at the beginning of their artistic lives before the West End galleries sent their prices soaring. They bought Edward Lear travel pictures in the days before they became too expensive, because Hugh had always admired his work; paintings by Philip Sutton, who made a large, very beautiful portrait of Dinah; and they inherited a Ruskin drawing from Reta's uncle.

In addition, there were the works bought at the Arthur Koestler Foundation exhibitions. Hugh found that some of the works by long-term prisoners, who had been unaffected by reading the opinions of art critics, had an innocence and originality which were very moving and exciting. He rejected the idea of having purely altruistic motives in buying, though. 'We bought out of mercy to make ourselves feel good, help the fellow along, sort of business, but most pieces we bought because we'd have have bought them anywhere. They were that good.'

There are also many paintings done by friends of greater or lesser celebrity. They included the first art purchase Hugh ever made, a Prunella Clough drawing which he found in Heals art gallery back in the thirties and coveted for its wonderful use of perspective, a David Hockney etching ('the prize pupil at the RCA, but he was picked up I think in his second year by the galleries, and by the time he was in his third year when normally we would be buying things, he'd got far beyond my pocket'), and Feliks Topolski's portrait of Reta made just after she was married. There are numberless small water-colours by Hugh himself, often recording trips abroad to Greece, China, India and the United States, as well as family outings like walks on the beach near their Needs Ore cottage. There is nothing of the new, controversial art of any period. It did not appeal to either Hugh or Reta, and they saw no reason to buy it either for effect or as an investment.

An honour which escaped Hugh Casson, and which he must now have realized would never be his, was elevation to the peerage. Although a man who had contributed in so many ways to the public good, and who had been a well-known, frequent and articulate proselytizer on behalf of his profession, he never really considered this a possibility. Avowedly unclubbable, he would nevertheless have enjoyed taking his place in what has always been considered the greatest club of all, at the very hub of the establishment, assured of an ongoing connection with the many people of distinction who were his friends. Amongst the honours with which he *was* rewarded for his labours, he was made an Honorary Associate of the American Institute of Architects, an Honorary Doctor of the Royal Canadian Academy of Arts, and an Honorary Doctor of several universities. In 1978 he was made a KCVO, and in 1985 a Companion of Honour. Although it was not something he ever talked about, Reta, perhaps fearing for the emptiness of his life in old age, had hopes for this final accolade of a peerage. But despite his

Variations on this thank-you note were sent to all the many
people who congratulated Casson when he became a
Companion of Honour in 1985.

socialist leanings, he was largely apolitical, his fiery days were over, and in any case it was at that time rare for an architect to be given the job of representing his profession and environmental interests in the Lords. In the late 1990s, with the need for more working life peers, both Sir Richard Rogers and Sir Norman Foster were so rewarded.

Nicky and Dinah now each had two children, and with the presence of growing grandchildren family occasions were even more important. Loved when they were tiny, the grandchildren became increasingly interesting to Hugh as they grew older. Carola and Nicky, overawed and overshadowed by their father's high public profile, according to Roger Zogolovich, Carola's second husband, were never great careerists, but he took a conscientious interest in all the achievements (and inevitable problems) of their lives and they in their turn became increasingly caring and supportive as their parents aged. Dinah had followed more closely along Hugh and Reta's route through life. She looked back at Cranborne Chase as a school which did not encourage academic aspirations, and after completing her training as a designer had taught at several art schools, including the Royal College (though after her father's time), where for a short period she ran his own old department. By the time her parents reached old age, she had formed a successful interior-design practice, which was a source of pride to them both.

Roger Zogolovich was now a loved and accepted son-in-law, though his arrival in the family circle might have caused problems amongst less sanguine people. He'd met Carola in 1975 when she was Carola Ritchie, still using her first husband's name, and not long afterwards had gone with her to Hugh's farewell party at the RCA without realizing she was his daughter. His comment to the woman standing beside him on that occasion, as they watched slides of Hugh's architecture being projected – that it was a load of crap – produced raised eyebrows.

Nicky then revealed herself as Hugh's second daughter. But these were the words of a brash young architect, not long emerged from the Architectural Association school, and bold with the new-found confidence and excitement of setting up in a practice – CZWG – whose architecture was eclectic, irreverent, and already causing interest amongst the critics.

Zogolovich came of a generation which did not rate Casson Conder's architecture very highly, and he was no exception. In his opinion, 'Hugh wasn't any good at producing buildings the way he visualized them.' But he respected Casson's architectural achievements in a much broader way. 'His legacy was his influence on English towns and architecture from 1950 until well into the seventies. He was always demonstrating a good-mannered relationship between buildings, and he, along with Betjeman and one or two others, was a lone voice in trying to restrain the ravages of redevelopment. He had a real understanding of the history of English towns. The public likes to categorize in simple words and so it sees an architect only as someone who makes buildings. But he or she can practise something much broader, be influential in a much more important way. And that was Hugh.'

Unlike Ian Hessenberg, Roger was always mystified by the constant stream of little notes which emanated from his father-in-law. Though he learned to live with them as he became absorbed into the family, he suspected they were a substitute for something which was lacking in Hugh's emotional disposition. For his part, he was a source of interest to Hugh who, ever alert to the mores and inventions of the younger generation, often sought his advice about the network of emerging architectural stars and thinkers. From its beginnings, CZWG had a strong commercial leaning (Zogolovitch himself eventually turned away from architecture to take up the potentially creative activity of building development) which Hugh, with a client list which had been largely establishment based, found intriguing. His own generation would have been sacked from the profession if they'd had any truck with development, a restriction which was not lifted by RIBA until 1986. This new son-in-law – he called him that almost from the start, though Carola and Roger lived together but did not marry until 1987 – brought the world of young design talent, which might have slipped away from Hugh in his old age, securely into the centre of his own family.

The house in Elgin Crescent had never been a complete success and in 1988 the Cassons moved again. This time it was to that common resort of elderly city dwellers (by now Hugh was nearing eighty years old) – a flat. In their case they bought a flat in a mansion block in Hereford Road W2, found for them by their daughters, and somewhat deeper into the purlieus of cosmopolitan west London than before. Again, Reta was the motivator, the administrator and the activist. She it was who opened up the solid Edwardian rooms to make the more gener-

Despite this drawing of the Cassons in a state of total relaxation at Hereford Road, they rarely succumbed to tiredness, and in the early years there maintained busy, active lives.

ous, interlinked spaces they liked. Hugh never interfered with her arrangements. She was an excellent designer. Now in her mid-seventies, she worked on the flat to make it suitable for their lives as older people who still maintained a busy life, and it had the comfortable quality, the timeless detailing of all Casson homes. But the Edwardian block in which they were housed lacked outstanding architectural quality, unlike the homes of many distinguished architects, and seeing Hugh here in his later years, it was impossible not to wonder whether he was irked by his prosaic surroundings. Or whether, as was his wont and as it certainly appeared, he had resolutely and good-naturedly adapted to the place in which he found himself. Whatever his feelings, he continued with his glamorous social life, Windsor weekends and summer holidays with the Queen Mother – whom he always called Queen Elizabeth – being the most glamorous events of all. There was also frequent contact with old friends like the Jackson-Stops, with whom the

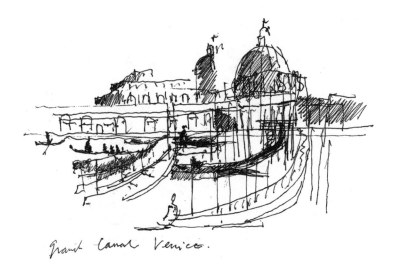

Grand Canal Venice.

Hugh made this drawing of Venice during a holiday visit with the Queen Mother only two or three years before his death.

Cassons spent several holidays including a Mediterranean cruise. Jean Jackson-Stops remembered how kind Hugh was during her husband's final illness. 'Other people were embarrassed to visit him, but not Hugh.'

He continued to leap at any suggestion of work and one project undertaken in his later years gave him special pleasure. This was a commission from the wine shipper Eldridge Pope to record the various châteaux and the environs from which their wines were imported. Delicate, appealing portraits, these were destined to embellish labels for the company's different bottles, and they involved Hugh in enjoyable trips through the beautiful French and German wine areas over a period of several years: the Rhineland, the Auvergne, the Lot, the Camargue – wonderful places and fine buildings made even more enchanting by the bonus of work. Reta always went with

One of the labels, showing the Château Cissac, which Hugh designed for wine shippers Eldridge Pope & Co.

him, and on later visits his daughter Nicky and her husband Ian Hessenberg went along too, so that they could drive the older couple and generally relieve them of strain. Hugh always spent some time making a water-colour of each château to present to the owner before moving on.

It was in August 1990, on the last of these trips to the vineyards around Toulouse and Montpelier, that Hugh was taken ill with what at first seemed to be influenza. In old-trouper fashion he struggled on with the drawings he had been sent to make, until after three days he had to admit he felt too ill and was in too much pain to continue. The Hessenbergs made arrangements for him to fly home.

The influenza proved to be the onset of the polymyalgia which had troubled Reta for some time, and which had indeed been a significant factor in her decision to move from the house in Victoria Road. One symptom of this illness is painful joints, and, after a week spent in hospital, it involved Hugh in taking steroids for the rest of his life. He was eighty now, but as he insisted a few months later, 'I feel terribly lucky that nothing has happened to me before. In fact I've been embarrassingly healthy, the sort of lack of problems which seems to indicate you've taken excessive care of yourself, a sort of mark of physical cowardice. But when you're eighty, things do begin to fall off or you can't see or hear or lift weights or walk up a hill – that sort of thing. I thought I'd be sunken with misery, twist my hair round my finger, what's left of my hair, and wonder what was going to happen next. But I'm a fairly buoyant character. I suppose optimists are people who won't face facts, as a rule. And at first I wasn't facing the fact that this would be, for the rest of my life, a collection of physical handicaps. I didn't mind about most of it, but I do feel worried about my eyes because reading, writing and drawing are my greatest enjoyments. If they go, then the whole of my life's interests go. And the steroids are affecting my eyes.'

Despite the fact that he was making fewer drawings, the popularity of Hugh's work was slow to wane. Even now, when he was well into his eighties, there continued to be a steady market for prints of his water-colours and these can be seen in many a comfortable drawing room or well-furnished reception area. Never commercially adept, he did not capitalize on these assets, and sales were conducted in an amateurish manner from his home, with Hugh often answering the door himself to the surprise of putative customers expecting a rather more formal scene.

When he was eighty-two, Hugh talked at supper one night with fellow RA Norman Ackroyd, whose work as an etcher is renowned both in this country and in the USA. Fascinated as ever by the idea of exploring new techniques, he accepted Ackroyd's invitation to visit his studio and – under expert guidance – try his hand at etching. He worked on small plates, making pictures of buildings, but also of children, and the resulting print runs were extraordinarily successful. They went into the Royal Academy's exhibition for several years after that, years when he was increasingly unable to produce new drawings, and sold with the dispatch his work had always enjoyed.

Julian Trevelyan, the artist who had worked with Casson at the Festival of Britain and on the *Canberra* interior, was a good friend until his death in 1988. He once said that painters must be anarchists, ruthless egotists, pursuing only the truth of their unique vision which they must communicate at all costs. He added that if they came into conflict with society they should be prepared to defy it. Hugh very obviously could not ever have fulfilled any part of this manifesto. He wouldn't have wanted to. But he had an almost reverential admiration for those who did. And his life as an artist was rich, happy and effortful, none the less.

Continuing the habits of a lifetime into old age, he read a

newspaper only on Sundays – a waste of time, he thought, during the week – though the number of books he had managed to finish even when at his busiest was legendary. He had little interest in food and wine, which according to Ian Hessenberg he regarded as an interruption. But he definitely liked his position as *pater familias* and in his just perceptibly detached way would enjoy occasions when they were all around him, sailing dinghies at Needs Ore, or having Christmas together at Hereford Road. Reta's sister Freda was now living close by in the basement of Carola's house, and the Cassons would walk round to visit her on fine summer evenings.

Roger Zogolovitch always thought Hugh found it difficult to extend to family members the intimacy which was such an important currency throughout his life. 'It was definitely not easy. He couldn't separate his family from the world. They were sharing him with everybody. I suppose this is the curse of the public man.' And Hugh always was, always wanted to be a public man, who dreaded leaving the world stage.

It was at Hereford Road that his health, which had stood up well in all the arduous years before, finally began to become a perceptible problem, and troubles followed swiftly, one upon the other. He had had incipient diabetes for a long time, which had always been contained in such a way as to present no outward difficulty. Although the polymyalgia rheumatica was largely arrested and dealt with, he had pneumonia in 1992, and by 1993 the angina which had plagued him for some years began to get worse, causing him to have blackouts which were frightening to both himself and those around him. In June of that year he underwent a heart-bypass operation, a long eight-hour affair, from which, as sometimes happens with older patients, he emerged in a confused state which only slowly righted itself. From then on his behaviour fluctuated. There were times when he amused and delighted an audience as he had always done. But a series of minor strokes took their toll and though he struggled to maintain the hectic life he loved, eagerly responding to phone calls, continuing to employ a secretary to deal with his post, seeing a variety of people, it eventually became impossible. The last activity he relinquished was the one he had most dreaded giving up: drawing. Even as late as 1996, he gave an exhibition at the Boilerhouse Gallery in Battersea Park jointly with Reta, who had for several years been reviving and expanding her own exceptional abilities as a photographer. In this she had been helped and encouraged by friends like the architect Denys Lasdun and several professionals, but most of all by Ian Hessenberg, who was now head of the photography department at the Central School of Art.

It was a lovely summer's evening, the venue in its bucolic setting was an interesting one, and to all outward appearances this was a happy occasion, with a number of Hugh's more distinguished old friends loyally turning up to support him. The many absentees from amongst the great and the good would have had more important business than trekking out to Battersea for an elderly man's show. He greeted everyone with immense warmth, wide-flung arms and tight hugs, just as he had always done. But there was a difference. People who had known him for a long time noted a certain lack of concentration, a vagueness in his manner. And the more recent paintings lacked the old clarity and vigour. Some were bought, but not all. Reta's extraordinary photographs, pure and still, some of them employing esoteric printing techniques with which she had been experimenting over many months, were very beautiful. They were admired and bought, whilst she stood to one side, anxious that her husband's work should be seen and appreciated.

This was one of Hugh Casson's last public outings. The diabetes and the drugs he was taking to combat the effect of polymyalgia on his joints caused such a deterioration in his eyesight that by the end of 1996 he was no longer able to draw or paint. The frenetic rush to achieve was finally over. In his late eighties he sat, as he had never done before, looking out of the window, saying little, and with the old expression of amusement and pleasure only rarely lighting up his face. For a while, Neville Conder, retired by now, took him for drives once a fortnight, and to see old friends. The painter Mary Fedden, herself over eighty but as vital and warm as a woman in her fifties, welcomed them in her large room overlooking the Thames at Hammersmith, talking about her husband Julian Trevelyan who had been Hugh's friend, holding his hand, jollying him into response. Jo Pattrick, whose home was nearby, also overlooking the water, had them to lunch and listened to reminiscences from Neville, while Hugh said little but took obvious pleasure in the river view from the windows. Eventually, after Neville Conder had a slight stroke, the riverside outings ceased.

Hugh was no longer able to go to more formal social events, or to private views at the Royal Academy. His daughters called in on most days, protective of him and organizing life for him and their mother to an extent they could never have visualized in the eventful years. And gradually this enigmatic man, ostensibly so friendly and outgoing, but who had defied all attempts at closeness and real understanding, slipped further and further into a small closed world of his own. His gentleness and quiet good humour were never punctured despite the restrictions and tedium of his situation.

In the summer of 1999, he tripped in the flat at Hereford Road and broke a hip. He seemed to recover completely from the operation which followed, and his hip mended well. But inevitably he was perceptibly frailer after the accident, and as the time approached for him to be discharged from hospital, his daughters began to discuss the possibility of his now going to live in a comfortable nursing home, where he would be more easily cared for than at Hereford Road. That never happened. His condition gradually worsened and on Sunday, 15 August, surrounded by his family, he died peacefully in hospital.

Hugh's funeral was a warm and at times amusing ceremony. This was no tragic occasion, but a farewell from family and close friends to a man whose long life had been entirely successful and pleasurable, one in which he had almost unfailingly given enjoyment – and often help – to a huge variety of people. Carola had once asked him when they were leaving someone else's funeral how he would like his own. He'd had no particular suggestion or requests, except to say that he would like a blue coffin. On 24 August it was a blue-painted coffin which his grown-up grandchildren wheeled into the chapel where the service was held, and it was covered with the family's bunches of meadow and garden flowers. Few of the well-known people who would be at a later memorial service were there, but the place was crowded with those, young and old, who had been closest to him. Many of them wore cheerful red cotton handkerchiefs of the type which Hugh had often sported himself and there were few black ties. The young family friend Caroline Verney played Bach's Prelude in G major on the cello. His one-time partners Neville Conder and Michael Cain, Dinah's husband Alan Moses and Hugh's cousin John Casson, all gave readings, and so did Kitty Ockenden, director of the American Associates of the Royal Academy Trust, who had become a close friend of the Cassons, and who had come especially from New York for the service. Finally, there was an appreciation by fellow architect Michael Manser recalling Hugh at his most vigorous and successful – but also at his wittiest. It was then that waves of laughter began to ring round the room, to the surprise and perhaps the disapproval of the more conventional souls present, but it was exactly the atmosphere which Reta and her daughters had hoped for. Here was Hugh, to the very end, generating laughter and delight. The tears when two passages from C. Day Lewis's *A Time to Dance* were quoted were heartfelt:

> Let us sing then for my friend not a dirge, not a funeral anthem,
> But words to match his mirth, a theme with a happy end;
>
> His laughter was better than birds in the morning: his smile
> Turned the edge of the wind: his memory
> Disarms death and charms the surly grave.
>
> . . . we
> Saw his light put out: yet we could not grieve
> More than a little while,
> For he lives in the earth around us, laughs from the sky.

But they were brief tears. Leaving the chapel, his friends mused that the words might have been written for Hugh. Then everyone repaired to the Belvedere restaurant in Holland Park for a splendid and elegant afternoon tea. How he would have loved it.

With the reticence and stoicism which had always charac-
terized her conduct, Reta accepted Hugh's death calmly in the
early weeks. She was well supported by the two carers who
had helped during the long-drawn-out period of Hugh's illness
and continued to come to the flat. Her daughters were close.
Friends encouraged her to cope. Yet there was in her manner
the air of detachment which is sometimes apparent in a person
who has just been bereaved. In October, she fell ill with one of
the bladder infections to which she had been subject for some
years, and spent ten days in hospital. When she came home,
the actuality of Hugh's loss struck her with great force, the
depression against which she had struggled during the months
of his illness became overwhelming, and she worried at the
thought of the great memorial service to Hugh which was being
planned to take place in St Paul's Cathedral on 29 November.
Nevertheless, her health, if frail, gave no real cause for concern,
and on Friday 12 November 1999, Carola and Roger went away
to Wales for the weekend, certain that all was well. When they
telephoned her at eight p.m. everything seemed normal. At
midnight, though, Erica, the carer who came to stay in the
flat each night, became worried about Reta's breathing, and
telephoned Nicola and Dinah. They were with their mother
when she died, very quietly, shortly afterwards.

HRH Princess Margaret and the Duke and Duchess of

Gloucester were amongst the huge number of distinguished people who attended what was inevitably a grand memorial service in St Paul's Cathedral on 29 November. Both Reta and Hugh were honoured in addresses by the Dean of St Paul's, Viscount Norwich and Sir Philip Dowson, then President of the Royal Academy. As Sir Philip said, those whose lives Hugh and Reta had either touched, enriched or changed, had come to share in a celebration of an outstanding, memorable, moving and much-loved human and artistic partnership.

SELECT BIBLIOGRAPHY

In addition to consulting many papers and professional journals during my research for Hugh Casson's biography, I found the following of particular interest:

Hugh Casson's own writings:
New Sights of London (London Transport, 1937)
Rebuilding Britain (Lund Humphries, for the RIBA, 1943)
Houses: Permanence and Prefabrication (Pleiades Books, 1945)
Homes by the Million, written with Anthony Chitty and published under the pseudonym Hugh Anthony (Penguin Books, 1946)
Victorian Architecture (Art and Technics, 1948)
Red Lacquer Days (Lion and Unicorn Press, 1956)
Town Sense (the Farnham Society, 1961)
Nanny Says, written with Joyce Grenfell (Dobson Books, 1972)
Hugh Casson's Diary (Macmillan, 1981)
Hugh Casson's London (J. M. Dent & Sons, 1983)
Hugh Casson's Oxford (Phaidon Press Limited, 1988)
Hugh Casson's Cambridge (Phaidon Press Limited, 1992)

And:
The Byzantine Achievement: An historical perspective, AD 330–1453, by Robert Byron (Historical Perspective, 1929)
Lewis & Sybil, a Memoir, by John Casson (Collins, 1972)

A Tonic to the Nation, edited by Mary Banham and Bevis Hillier (Thames and Hudson, 1976)

A Speaking Part, Lewis Casson and the Theatre of his Time, by Diana Devlin (Hodder and Stoughton, 1982)

The Life of Sir Edwin Lutyens, by Christopher Hussey (Country Life Ltd, 1950)

The Royal Yacht Britannia, by Andrew Morton (Orbis, 1984)

The Villa Ariadne, by Dilys Powell (Michael Haag, 1985)

Young Betjeman, by Bevis Hillier (John Murray, 1988)

Edward James, by John Lowe (Collins, 1991)

The Authorised Biography of Orwell, by Michael Shelden (Harper Collins, 1991)

Christopher Nicholson, by Neil Bingham (Academy Editions, 1996)

Indigo Days: The Art and Memoirs of Julian Trevelyan, second edition (Scolar Press, 1996)

Canberra: In the Wake of a Legend, by Philip Dawson (Conway Maritime Press, 1997)

INDEX